THE MOUNTAINS OF ROMANIA

About the Author

Janneke Klop is a self-declared 'roamaniac' and has been exploring Romania since 2005. After studying English Language and Culture in the Netherlands and the UK she started working as a teacher, but the world on the other side of the window was so attractive that she decided to head outdoors. It was love at first sight between her and Romania and she has revisited almost every year. She writes about her Romanian adventures at www.roamaniac.com and also co-organises (self-) guided tours of the mountains of Romania. Born and bred in the Netherlands, Janneke now lives in Ghent, Belgium, where she works in Flanders' best-supplied travel bookshop, Atlas & Zanzibar. She is an active member of the Klimen Bergsportfederatie (Climbing and Mountaineering Belgium) and Grote Routepaden (Grandes Randonnées) associations.

THE MOUNTAINS OF ROMANIA

TREKKING AND WALKING
IN THE CARPATHIAN MOUNTAINS
by Janneke Klop

JUNIPER HOUSE, MURLEY MOSS,
OXENHOLME ROAD, KENDAL, CUMBRIA LA9 7RL
www.cicerone.co.uk

© Janneke Klop 2020
Second edition 2020
ISBN: 978 1 85284 948 1
This completely new guide replaces
The Mountains of Romania (ISBN: 978 1 85284 295 6) by James Roberts.

Printed in China on responsibly sourced paper on behalf of Latitude Press Ltd
A catalogue record for this book is available from the British Library.

Route mapping by Lovell Johns www.lovelljohns.com
Contains OpenStreetMap.org data © OpenStreetMap contributors, CC-BY-SA. NASA relief data courtesy of ESRI
All photographs are by the author unless otherwise stated.

Updates to this Guide

While every effort is made by our authors to ensure the accuracy of guidebooks as they go to print, changes can occur during the lifetime of an edition. Any updates that we know of for this guide will be on the Cicerone website (www.cicerone.co.uk/948/updates), so please check before planning your trip. We also advise that you check information about such things as transport, accommodation and shops locally. Even rights of way can be altered over time.

The route maps in this guide are derived from publicly available data, databases and crowd-sourced data. As such they have not been through the detailed checking procedures that would generally be applied to a published map from an official mapping agency, although naturally we have reviewed them closely in the light of local knowledge as part of the preparation of this guide.

We are always grateful for information about any discrepancies between a guidebook and the facts on the ground, sent by email to updates@cicerone.co.uk or by post to Cicerone, Juniper House, Murley Moss, Oxenholme Road, Kendal, LA9 7RL.

Register your book: To sign up to receive free updates, special offers and GPX files where available, register your book at www.cicerone.co.uk.

Front cover: The craggy limestone southern ridge of the Piatra Craiului in late May (Route 19)

CONTENTS

Mountain safety

Every mountain walk has its dangers, and those described in this guidebook are no exception. All who walk or climb in the mountains should recognise this and take responsibility for themselves and their companions along the way. The author and publisher have made every effort to ensure that the information contained in this guide was correct when it went to press, but, except for any liability that cannot be excluded by law, they cannot accept responsibility for any loss, injury or inconvenience sustained by any person using this book.

International distress signal *(emergency only)*
Six blasts on a whistle (and flashes with a torch after dark) spaced evenly for one minute, followed by a minute's pause. Repeat until an answer is received. The response is three signals per minute followed by a minute's pause.

Helicopter rescue
The following signals are used to communicate with a helicopter:

Help needed: raise both arms above head to form a 'Y'

Help not needed: raise one arm above head, extend other arm downward

Emergency telephone numbers
Emergency services: tel 112
Romanian mountain rescue (Salvamont): 0725 826 668

Weather reports
www.meteoblue.com

Mountain rescue can be very expensive – be adequately insured.

Symbols used on route maps

～	route		woodland
-`-	alternative route		urban areas
Ⓢ	start point	**10**	route start on overview map
Ⓕ	finish point	**17**	trek route on overview map
Ⓢ Ⓕ	start/finish point		(main stages, excluding excursions)
>	route direction		
	regional border		
	international border		
━■━	station/railway		
▲	peak		
⬆ ⬒	manned/unmanned refuge		
⛺ ⛺	official campsite/permitted camping spot		
■	building		
♦ ♦ †	church/monastery/cross		
ᛜ	castle		
)(	pass		
• ⌇	water feature/waterfall		
✳ ◖	viewpoint/cave		
≍	bridge		
•	other feature		
⬖⬖⬖	crag/outcrop/precipice		
○	sheepfold		
⸙	satellite tower		
P	car park		
≈	national road (DN)		
≈	county road (DJ)		
≈	communal road (DC – paved/unpaved/paths/tracks)		

Relief
in metres

	2600–2800
	2400–2600
	2200–2400
	2000–2200
	1800–2000
	1600–1800
	1400–1600
	1200–1400
	1000–1200
	800–1000
	600–800
	400–600
	200–400
	0–200

SCALE: 1:100,000

0 kilometres 1   2
0 miles   1

except where indicated

Contour lines are drawn at 50m intervals and highlighted at 200m intervals.

GPX files for all routes can be downloaded free at www.cicerone.co.uk/948/GPX.

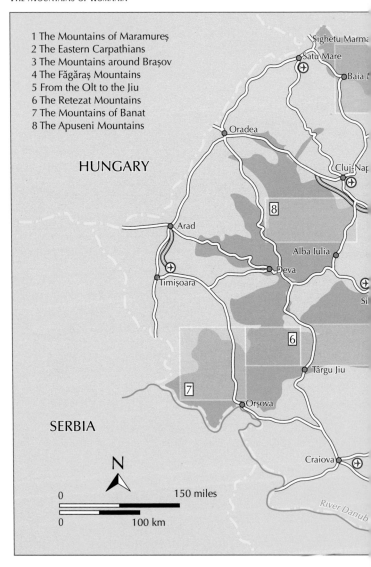

1 The Mountains of Maramureş
2 The Eastern Carpathians
3 The Mountains around Braşov
4 The Făgăraş Mountains
5 From the Olt to the Jiu
6 The Retezat Mountains
7 The Mountains of Banat
8 The Apuseni Mountains

Sighetu Marma
Satu Mare
Baia
Oradea
HUNGARY
Cluj Nap
8
Arad
Alba Iulia
Deva
Timişoara
Si
6
Târgu Jiu
7
Orşova
SERBIA
Craiova
N
0   150 miles
0   100 km
River Danub

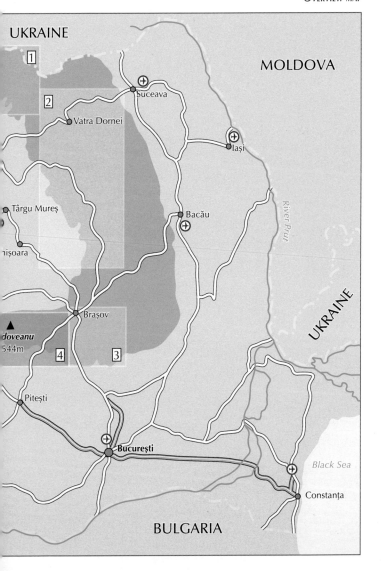

UKRAINE

MOLDOVA

1

2

Suceava

Vatra Dornei

Iași

Târgu Mureș

Bacău

River Prut

nișoara

Brașov

UKRAINE

doveanu
544m

4

3

Pitești

București

Black Sea

Constanța

BULGARIA

Publisher's acknowledgement and thanks

James Roberts was the pioneer of visiting Romania for walking and trekking and wrote Cicerone's first guide, published in 2005, to Romania's beautiful mountains and trails. After the revolution of 1989/90 he spent more than half of each year there and travelled throughout the country. James was an experienced backpacker, often travelling solo on trips in the Atlas and Himalaya as well as Romania. He married Elena, a Romanian, and developed an unrivalled knowledge of the country, its people and natural history, becoming an expert interpreter of the Romanian scene.

Sadly, James died very young, shortly before his guidebook was published, and Elena has shepherded the guidebook since then.

On behalf of Cicerone and all who have appreciated Romania and its mountains through his work, we give our heartfelt thanks to James and Elena.

The world doesn't stand still and I would like to take this opportunity to thank Janneke Klop who has also come to love Romania and was brave enough to take on the project of illuminating Romania's trails and mountains for a new generation of hikers and trekkers.

Jonathan Williams

Pastoral scenery after the Ricăjel Gorge (Route 9, Stage 3)

AUTHOR PREFACE

Here is a little tribute to Romania itself – the country that makes me feel sound and whole and happy like no other place I've been.

Home

The birds are big.
The sky is high.
The grass grows tall.
The apples fall.

The air is warm.
The wind sends wisps
of hay across
my bare tanned arms.

I lie face up
and I breathe in
until I burst.
Except I don't

because I'm whole:
There is no crack
this joy can't heal:
I am at home.

Janneke Klop

ACKNOWLEDGEMENTS

Writing a guidebook is a solitary business, and while I love solitude I am beyond grateful to everyone who supported me during the three years it took to complete this gargantuan project. First of all, I would like to thank Anamaria Cremers, who relentlessly searched until she had found someone to update the precursor to this guide – written by the late James Roberts, to whom I am hugely indebted. Anamaria, you truly are my guardian angel. I am so glad our paths crossed. Thanks also for going over the language appendix.

A heartfelt thanks to everyone in Romania who hosted me, fed me, hugged me, hiked with me, listened to me, gave me advice, became my friends: you have made my experience so much richer. Special thanks to the owners of the Babou Maramureş, De Oude Wilg, Ţară Nomadă and Zamolxe campsites: thank you for hosting me for extended periods of time and for your generosity and flexibility. You made me feel at home. Sorin Rusu – thank you for letting me stay at your beautiful apartment for next to nothing when I needed it the most, for driving me places (including the hospital) and for thinking along with me. Prof Dr Alexandru Diaconescu, archaeology professor at the Babeş-Bolyai University in Cluj, shared invaluable insights about Romania's history, without which it would have been considerably more difficult to write a sensible introduction to Romania's complex past.

I am very grateful for all the hard work the editorial team at Cicerone have put into making this book look the way it does: I am so glad I 'only' had to do the writing! Boatloads of gratitude go to Georgia Laval, my amazing copy editor. Thank you for making the book more readable.

Many thanks to my family and friends, old and new, for supporting me, and for reading my stories. Creating stories is so much more rewarding if you get to write them down – and people actually read them and respond to them.

I don't know why partners always come last in acknowledgements but they do – perhaps only so that one can say 'last but not least'. Thank you, Wilbert, for encouraging me and keeping me grounded – for being there for me, wherever I was. You are my anchor.

Janneke Klop

INTRODUCTION

'Romania is my refuge. The mix of people, the rugged, unkempt beauty of
Romania's nature that leaves me breathless. A country where nothing is taken for
granted, and everything is cherished for its true value.'
Lee Rammelt

'I breathe and sleep and do everything better here.'
Giulio da Sacco

*A glorious path to the Bucşoiu
ridge in the Bucegi on Route 16*

Romania is nothing short of breathtaking. It offers an almost bewildering array of options to the adventurous traveller. From the last inhabited medieval citadel in Europe, Sighişoara, to the robust fortified Saxon churches around Sibiu and Braşov; from the second largest underground glacier in Europe in the Apuseni Mountains to the best road in the world (according to *Top Gear*) – the Transfăgărăşan, which cuts through one of the wildest and highest mountain ranges of Romania; from the last primeval forests of Europe in which brown bears, wolves, chamois and lynxes still roam to the Danube Delta teeming with life – Romania has it all.

Approaching Curmătura Bucurei – a high pass in the Retezat Mountains – from the north (Route 27)

Travel to Maramureş and you will find yourself a hundred years back in time, surrounded by horse-drawn carts and haystacks and hospitable peasants in traditional attire, living in wooden houses. Crafts are very much alive here: you will meet woodcarvers, weavers and potters. Visit Braşov or Sibiu to find yourself surrounded by Saxon architecture and hear Hungarian and German on the streets besides Romanian. And wherever you decide to go, there will always be a mountain range or two, or three, or five, near you. One could spend a lifetime discovering all the riches of this country and still not be bored.

At the same time, Romania is a place where you can learn to breathe again if you have forgotten how to: in most of Romania, the pace of life is much slower than many of us living in throbbing cities are used to. Romania is also a very spacious country, and sparsely populated: although it is roughly the same size as the United Kingdom, it has only around 22 million inhabitants, compared to over 65 million in the UK. Over two million of these live in the country's capital, Bucharest. The second largest city and the unofficial capital of Transylvania, Cluj-Napoca, has only about 325,000 inhabitants and is a charming university town. The vast majority of the population still lives in the countryside, or in small towns. Agriculture plays an important part and many people in the villages are largely self-sufficient, although the promise of a

higher salary and dissatisfaction with the political climate has lured many away to Western and Southern Europe. About one-third of the country's surface is mountainous, with 14 mountain ranges reaching over 2000m, and 12 peaks reaching over 2500m. About another third is hill country, and the last third is taken up by endless plains, such as the Wallachian Plain between Bucharest and the natural border with Bulgaria, the Danube.

By now, most of the major mountain ranges are well mapped and well waymarked. There is a good network of huts, known as cabanas, that dates back to the communist era, when many sought their refuge in the mountains to escape from the daily wear and tear of harsh communist life. Of course, like anywhere, there are ranges and routes that are more frequented than others; however, there are plenty of places where you can experience true solitude. In mountains like the Rodna Mountains and the Munţii Maramureşului, both in the northwest of the country, you can walk for days without meeting many (or any) people, except for the odd shepherd. In the countryside and up in the more remote ranges you will find that most people do not speak a word of English; it is wise to glean a few Romanian words and phrases before you leave. The remoter the place, however, the more hospitable people seem to get: many a shepherd, farmer or villager will offer you food, drink (most likely the strong local brandy

17

Camping meadow at Cabana Diham in the Bucegi (Route 16, Stage 1)

known as *ţuică*, *horincă* or *pălincă*, often unceremoniously poured from a plastic bottle) or even shelter. And even if they do not speak English, they will do their utmost to help you out with whatever they think you need.

Romania really is a glorious country; many people find they have to visit over and over again after their first experience of it. Hopefully, you will see why with the help of this guide – which, comprehensive as it is, can only offer a glimpse of the versatile, vibrant and warm-hearted country that is Romania.

GEOGRAPHY

Look Romania up on a map and you will see it has the shape of a very fat fish. Its tail swims in the Black Sea, the Danube Delta making up the upper fin; its nose pokes into the Hungarian-Serbian border. Its dorsal fin forms the border with the Ukraine and Moldova; and its belly swims in the Danube, the natural border with Serbia and Bulgaria.

The Romanian Carpathians cover about one-third of Romania's territory and are shaped like a horseshoe, opening up to the west. They can be divided into three main areas: the Carpaţii Orientali, Meridionali, and Occidentali – respectively the Eastern, Southern and Western Carpathians.

The Eastern Carpathians consist of the mountains of Maramureş (which lie quite far to the west, in fact) and Bucovina, the Moldovan-Transylvanian mountains including the Călimani, Rarău-Giumalău, Ceahlău and Hăşmaş, as well as the Carpaţii de Curbură – the mountains of the Carpathians' Bend, near Braşov. These include the Piatra Mare, the Postăvaru, the Baiului-Grohotiş and the Ciucaş.

18

The Southern Carpathians comprise some of Romania's highest and best-known ranges, including the Bucegi, Piatra Craiului, Făgăraş and Retezat, as well as some smaller massifs. The Western Carpathians are among the lowest mountains in the country, consisting of the Apuseni and the Banat Mountains. The Western Carpathians are known for their great quantities of iron, silver and gold. Emperor Trajan took home tons of the latter after his conquest of Dacia in the second century AD. Scars of more recent mining activities can be seen in the village of Roşia Montană, originally a Roman settlement.

In a league of their own are the Măcin Mountains, in the extreme southeast of the country, near the Danube Delta. These are Romania's oldest mountains and have eroded to such an extent that they only reach a maximum altitude of 467m.

Bucharest (Bucureşti) lies in southeastern Oltenia, outside the Carpathian arc but less than three hours by train or car from Braşov, the base for many if not most of the hikes described in this book.

Romania is the most biogeographically diverse country in Europe: five of the 10 biogeographic regions officially recognised by the European Union can be found here. Venturing beyond the alpine areas (the focus of this book) brings you to the undulating, pastoral mountain hinterland, dotted with scattered houses and haystacks; descend from there and you often arrive in surprisingly large stretches of land as flat

Bee on a thistle in the foothills of the Rarău–Giumalău

as the Low Countries. Almost half of the country is covered by natural and semi-natural ecosystems. Deforestation is a major concern though: 366,000ha of forest was illegally chopped down in 1990–2011, according to Agent Green – one of the Romanian NGOs that try to combat deforestation. More worryingly still, old-growth forests within the bounds of national parks are being razed too. Timber export is a major source of income and employment for Romania. Many of its forests are in private hands due to (fairly random) land restitution after the end of the communist era, making it very challenging to control the situation. Other NGOs that combat illegal logging and organise reforestation projects include Foundation Conservation Carpathia, Plantează in România and Tăşuleasa Social.

Despite this brutal attack on Romania's ecosystems, Romania still has a forest cover of around 25%; some of Europe's last virgin forests can be found here. And thanks to the forests that have survived, the Romanian Carpathians are a haven for wildlife. Many of Europe's larger predators are found here: Romania is home to Europe's largest brown bear population (it is hard to say how many there are exactly because counts are often politically motivated) and has sizeable populations of wolves and lynx. Among the main non-predatory mammals are chamois, red deer and boar. All of these are under threat from hunters who exceed their quotas.

Marmot numbers are dwindling, but their shrill call can still be heard in many of the higher ranges such as the Făgăraş and Retezat.

Birds of prey are ubiquitous in Romania. Species you might be able to spot include the European honey buzzard (*Pernis apivorus*), the lesser and greater spotted eagle (*Clanga pomarina* and *Clanga clanga*) and perhaps even the golden eagle (*Aquila chrysaetos*), as well as several owl species. If you're lucky you'll spot the western capercaillie (*Tetrao urogallus*), endangered in much of Western Europe – in the Rodna or Călimani Mountains, for instance. The Danube Delta is an important refuge for many migratory birds; several species of pelican as well as cormorants and flamingos and many other species hibernate and/or breed here.

Romania's flora is incredibly rich. It is well worth visiting rural areas such as Maramureş and the wider Apuseni region in spring to see and smell the vast variety of flowers and herbs in unmown meadows, pollinated by an astonishing range of butterflies and bees that much of the rest of Europe has lost – the traditional agricultural methods of Romania's peasants certainly pay off. Romania has over 3700 plant species, many of them endemic to the region, such as the Garofiţa Pietrei Craiului (*Dianthus callizonus*), otherwise known as Piatra Craiului pink. Other endemic plants include *Thymus comosus*, a type of thyme that can be found virtually everywhere, and

Clockwise from top left: Dianthus spiculifolius; *oxlip; edelweiss; St John's wort; monkshood; arnica; orange hawkweed; Piatra Craiului pink*

the cornflowers *Centaurea pugioni-formis* and *Centaurea pinnatifida*. Purple crocuses (*branduşi*) open their petals at the foot of the mountains as soon as the snow melts away. Twice a year, in May and September, the alpine zones are adorned by *bujori de munte*, mountain jewels: the *Rhododendron myrtifolium*. Orchids can be found in all shapes and colours too, and, of course, *flori de colţ*: edelweiss. On your hikes you will most likely encounter mushroom pickers at some point. If you want to gather some yourself a useful guide to edible (and poisonous) mushrooms is *Ghidul culegătorului de ciuperci* by Locsmándi Csaba and Vasas Gizella (Casa, 2013; Romanian only but includes symbols). Be aware that picking them is illegal in national parks though.

HISTORY

Due to its important geopolitical location, Romania has always been at the crossroads of civilisations. The Romans, the Byzantine Greeks, the Bulgarians, the Ottomans, the Tartars, the Hungarians, the Poles, the Austrians and the Russians: they have all laid claim to parts of modern-day Romania at some point in time. Throughout history, Romanians have been governed by other powers – although no single power ever governed the whole territory. Romania has always been a buffer zone between Western and Eastern European cultures: Romanians speak a language of Latin origin but embraced the Greek-Orthodox confession.

The territories of present-day Romania were first inhabited by Palaeolithic (Old Stone Age) hunters and gatherers who wandered from Western Europe to the Siberian Plains. Starting in the sixth millennium, a warming climate caused some of them to retreat to the Balkans and into the Carpathians, leaving the lowlands to shepherds and farmers coming from Anatolia in the Neolithic (New Stone Age). According to recent genetic studies, more than half of present-day Romanians bear the genes of the prehistoric inhabitants of Romania's territories.

Towards the end of the third millennium BC (at the start of the Bronze Age) the first Indo-European populations arrived from the east, later known as Thracians, who during the Iron Age inhabited the Balkans and Carpathians. The northern branch of these people were called Getai by the Greeks and Daci by the Romans, which is why they are referred to as 'Geto-Dacians'. In the first century BC the Geto-Dacian tribes were united under King Burebista, a contemporary of Julius Caesar (in fact they were both assassinated in 44BC). They built an empire and started to dominate Central and Eastern Europe, conquering Budapest and Bratislava in the west and Tiraspol in the east, and frequently raiding territories south of the Danube, which were under Roman control. Their centre of power was

Rock formations in the Gaura Valley (Bucegi Mountains; Route 16)

Sarmizegetusa Regia. Its remains can still be admired today – that is, whatever the Romans left of it.

After the death of King Burebista, his empire fell apart into several smaller entities. Over a century later the Dacians were once again united under what would prove to be their last king, Decebalus. Their raids on the province of Moesia, south of the Danube, made Emperor Domitian determine to react to the Dacian threat. Initially the Romans were beaten by the Dacians in AD86, but later on a peace treaty was imposed which made Dacia a vassal state of Rome. It was the next emperor, Trajan, who decided to put an end to the Dacian threat. He launched his first campaign against the Dacians in AD101–102, after securing the Danube region to connect his fleet in Pannonia with the one in Moesia. Decebalus admitted defeat but rebelled again, which resulted in a second campaign in AD105–106. The Dacians were defeated and Decebalus was hunted down by the Romans, but he committed suicide, leaving his kingdom and its riches – gold and salt – to the Romans, as depicted on Trajan's Column in Rome.

Trajan decided to colonise Dacia (consisting of Transylvania, the eastern Banat and Oltenia) rather than administrate it. The Dacians were expelled from their lands and retreated into the mountains, or established small villages. Some 11,000 Dacians were taken to Rome to fight as gladiators in the Colosseum; another 2000 were enlisted as soldiers and sent to other parts of the Roman Empire. Trajan brought 55,000–60,000 soldiers into Dacia, all bringing their wives, mistresses and children with them. These came from various regions – many originated from Britain, others from Spain, Gaul, Batavia, Syria, Palmyra and North Africa. These soldiers would have spoken their own languages but needed Latin to communicate. On top of that came 10,000 legionnaires – Latin-speaking Roman citizens – as well as civilian colonists whose number is difficult to estimate.

Up to a thousand Roman-speaking families settled in Colonia Dacia Sarmizegetusa (Ulpia Traiana), the Romans' new capital of Dacia; 500 settled in Apulum (Alba Iulia) and another 500 in the rest of Dacia. They marginalised the Dacians and their language;

modern Romanian originates from these colonists. The legionnaires were mostly recruited from the poor north of present-day Italy; they wanted to try their luck in Dacia and besides that, it was considerably warmer in those days so moving north came with the added benefit of cooler temperatures and more rainfall. Recent linguistic studies show that the Romanian language has close ties to dialects found in northwest Italy. By the late eighth, early ninth century AD the population no longer spoke Latin but a rustic Roman language that would gradually develop into Romanian. It is difficult to follow the evolution of the Romanian language though, because there was never a literary tradition; not even in the Middle Ages.

Remains of a Roman column at Sarmizegetusa Ulpia Traiana, near Retezat

It is after the withdrawal of the Roman troops from Dacia in AD271–275 that things get a little muddled – it is virtually impossible to present a neat timeline from this point onwards since there is little in the way of archaeological or literary evidence (although there is a plethora of theories). The era of the great migrations followed, partially fuelled by climate change; after the Romans retreated from Dacia under pressure from barbarians invading Pannonia and Moesia from the north and reaching as far as Greece, the Goths arrived in the Balkans in the fourth century and the Huns conquered the Pannonian Plain at the beginning of the fifth – in other words, they conquered territories east, west and south of the Carpathian arc, but it seems they didn't massively settle in present-day Transylvania, well protected by its natural mountainous border as it is. They contented themselves with controlling and further exploiting the salt mines, essential for cattle breeding.

In the meantime, those who did not retreat with the Roman troops – the Daco-Roman ancestors of the Romanians – moved progressively towards rural areas. That is, according to the continuity theory, which alleges that in fact the majority of the population stayed behind. Some scholars argue that the later Romanians were not the offspring of the Daco-Romans but migrated into Romanian territory from south of the Danube much later on, and that few stayed behind when the Romans left the province. Most of these scholars are likely to be Hungarian, whereas the majority of those in favour of the continuity theory are Romanian. This is very much a political debate about the rights of the first-born: who got to Transylvania first and can historically lay claim to its coveted lands? It is not possible to go into the details of this thorny question here, but for various reasons – the Romanian language being one of them – it seems unlikely that almost the entire Roman and Romanised population left in AD271–275. In addition, the Romans never intensively colonised the Balkans (of which the Albanians are vivid proof), which goes some way to explaining why no Romance languages survive south of the Danube.

The Roman settlements crumbled and were vandalised, pagan temples destroyed; in some cases the stones of their ruins were used to erect churches. An interesting example of this is the architecturally eclectic church in the village of Densuş, built (in its current form) in the 13th century using materials from nearby Sarmizegetusa. Colonia Dacica Sarmizegetusa was transformed rather than entirely abandoned; in the fourth century the amphitheatre was turned into a fortification. The last artefact found in the former Roman capital is a brooch, dated at the beginning of the seventh century. Several Christian artefacts imported from the late Roman–early Byzantine Empire were found elsewhere in Transylvania, but

THE MOUNTAINS OF ROMANIA

not outside the boundaries of the former Roman province – indicating the presence of the later Roman people in the heart of Transylvania but not beyond its borders.

More migration waves followed – the Gepids, the Avars – then Slavic tribes settled in the western plains (Banat, Crişana, Sătmar and Maramureş) and in the eastern lowlands (Moldavia and Wallachia) from the sixth century onwards, and in Transylvania later on – but they assimilated to the more numerous ancestors of Romanians, known as Vlachs at the time. The Vlachs lived in the hills, whereas the Slavs settled in the lowlands – hence many place names in the plains today have Slavic origins. In the ninth century Bulgarians gained control over the region, leading to the establishment of the Orthodox Church and the introduction of Old Church Slavonic with its Cyrillic script.

At the close of the ninth century the Hungarians (Magyars) arrived on the scene. This nation of horsemen settled in the Pannonian Plain and established a kingdom. When their westwards expansion was halted – they frequently raided modern France and Germany – they sought to expand eastwards. After defeating the Bulgarian dukes from Banat and Crişana, they slowly but surely conquered Transylvania (also known as Ardeal, from Hungarian Erdély) – the land beyond the forests, defeating the Slavic-Romanian voivodes (dukes). To defend their new territory against other migratory tribes

such as the Pechenegs and Cumans, they commissioned first the Székely people to defend the eastern frontier, at the foot of the Carpathians; then in the 12th and 13th centuries Hungarian kings invited Saxons, from modern-day Germany, but also Luxembourg and Flanders, to colonise Transylvania. At the same time, the Teutonic Knights were invited for defence purposes, but they were expelled after 25 years or so because they gained too much power.

The Saxon settlers prospered and received privileges from the Hungarian kings: autonomy, cities and exemption from military duty – but they had to pay hefty taxes to the king and the church. They were skilled craftsmen and brought trade to Transylvania, whereas the Romanians were peasants and hunters. In terms of governance, the Saxons had more influence than the Romanians, whose social institutions were never very strong due to the way they were organised – they lived in the hills for a long time, only cooperating whenever necessary, and only started descending to the plains again in the 10th and 11th centuries.

In the 14th century two other principalities emerged alongside Transylvania, now part of the Hungarian kingdom: Moldova and Wallachia. After the devastating Mongolian raid mid 13th century, the Romanian voivodes from terrae such as Maramureş and Făgăraş were encouraged to cross the mountains and become vassal states to Hungary. By the middle of the 14th century

1
26

they obtained independence – until the Ottomans arrived.

Mid 15th century the Ottoman advance was stopped at Belgrade thanks to the victory of Iancu de Hunedoara (Hunyadi Janos), voivode of Transylvania and regent of Hungary. His well-preserved castle can still be visited in Hunedoara. A century later, the Ottomans occupied Wallachia and Moldavia, but they let local voivodes administrate the territories. The economic burden of Ottoman suzerainty was considerable: the Ottomans' demand for wheat and other goods was insatiable. Only Transylvania valiantly resisted and became an independent principality. It became one of the most liberal states of Europe, with Lutherans, Calvinists and Unitarians being acknowledged alongside Catholicism, and Orthodox religion being tolerated.

At the close of the 17th century Hungary, Crişana, Banat and Transylvania came under Austrian rule. Meanwhile, the Russians made their appearance in Moldavia. The Ottomans reacted by replacing the local rulers of Wallachia and Moldavia with Greek officials, under whose rule the population was bitterly exploited. The 18th and 19th centuries saw the three empires – Austrian, Russian and Ottoman – continually disputing the territories inhabited by the Romanians. Transylvania would remain under Austrian and/or Hungarian rule until the disintegration of the dual monarchy following its defeat in World War 1.

The Peleş Palace in Sinaia

In 1859 Moldova and Wallachia united under Prince Alexandru Ioan Cuza, and formally became the Romanian United Principalities in 1862 – the core of the Romanian nation state. In 1866 Cuza lost favour and was replaced by the German prince Carol von Hohenzollern, and Romania got its first constitution. Romania proclaimed itself fully independent in 1877 and became the Kingdom of Romania in 1881, with Carol I as its first king. Romania would remain a kingdom until 1947, when King Michael I was forced to abdicate by the communist leadership. Towards the end of World War 1, on 1 December 1918, Transylvania was assigned to Romania, uniting the three Romanian principalities and marking a great loss for Hungary. To this day, the Great Union is celebrated on 1 December. Hungary temporarily regained northern Transylvania during World War 2, but it got reassigned to Romania in 1947, in accordance with the 1920 Treaty of Trianon.

From 1949 until 1989, Romania fell under a communist regime, after fraudulent elections in 1946, and became a Soviet satellite state. Private firms were nationalised, agriculture collectivised; a rigorous planning economy was installed. The Securitate (the Romanian secret police) sowed terror by rounding up numerous 'enemies of the state'. The Memorial of the Victims of Communism and of the Resistance museum, housed in a former prison in Sighetu Marmaţiei,

Maramureş County, is a living monument to this age of terror (see www.memorialsighet.ro/memorial-en for further information). The situation deteriorated when the megalomaniac Nicolae Ceauşescu came to power in 1965 – probably the most brutal of Eastern Europe's communist dictators, leading his country to the brink of the abyss. He disastrously mismanaged the economy and by the 1980s living conditions were unbearably austere. At the same time he fostered a personality cult based on the North Korean model. He bulldozed much of the old city centre in Bucharest to erect the colossal Casa Republicii (House of the Republic), later known as the Casa Poporului (House of the People), which now houses the two houses of parliament. The Romanian Revolution of 1989 – part spontaneous uprising, part conspiracy – brought an end to his totalitarian reign. After the crowds started to protest during his final speech on 21 December, Ceauşescu and his wife Elena fled the scene by helicopter, but they were captured hours later and were executed after a mock trial on 25 December 1989.

The power gap was quickly filled by the FSN (National Salvation Front), led by Ion Iliescu – its members mostly consisting of former communists. After the FSN fell apart, the PSD (Social Democratic Party) filled its shoes – it is still the most powerful left-wing party in Romania. The social democrats benefit from a disciplined mass of voters, mostly consisting of older people living in the countryside. Interestingly, with one exception in the 1990s (Ion Iliescu), the presidency has been in right-wing hands, counterbalancing the influence of the left.

Romania formally became a democracy with a market economy and joined NATO and the EU in 2004 and 2007 respectively. Freedom of movement became a reality and intellectual liberty is now guaranteed, as well as all civic rights. On the other hand, frustration is growing in many circles: the most successful businessmen and many public officers are ex-communist leaders and former members of the Securitate. The new ruling class gained wealth by selling out important industrial sectors to foreign investors, including mines and huge swathes of forest, thus impoverishing Romania once again.

Corruption within the government is a major challenge, and Romania's citizens increasingly stand up against it. The Corupția Ucide ('corruption kills') movement has repeatedly brought vast numbers of people out into the streets to demonstrate against the PSD-led government, and the DNA (the anti-corruption directorate) continues to round up compromised politicians. In 2019, Ion Iliescu and two other high-ranking officials were indicted for crimes against humanity during the 1989 Revolution – they were accused of deliberately using the security agencies and the army to sow terror and create organised chaos, resulting in

862 deaths and 2150 wounded. A very thorough English-language study of the 1989 Revolution can be found at www.romanianrevolutionofdecember1989.com. Visiting the Memorialul Revoluției in Timișoara is also worthwhile; see www.memorialulrevolutiei.ro/sitenou/en.

To sum it up, politically and socio-economically Romania is very much in a state of flux. Both Romania's distant past and its more recent history have been turbulent; considering all the troops and tribes that have fought over and marched through its territories it is somewhat miraculous that such a beautiful, vibrant country has emerged – a country that has enticed many visitors with its rugged beauty, mysterious past and warm-hearted inhabitants.

LANGUAGE

Romanian, or *limba română*, is a Romance language, as the name suggests. What sets it apart from its linguistic relatives is that it is surrounded by Slavic languages and Hungarian: in none of the surrounding countries did a Romance language survive. There are several hypotheses as to the origins of the language; commonly it is thought that it is a descendant of Vulgar Latin, adopted by the local population during the Roman occupation of Dacia in the second and third centuries AD. Not much is known about the original language spoken in Dacia prior to Roman occupation.

A wedding party in the traditional village of Breb in Maramureş (Route 2)

Ever since the departure of the Romans, Romanian (also known as Daco-Romanian to distinguish it from other branches) has led a life of its own. It has preserved three of the cases found in Latin and the majority of its vocabulary has Latin roots. However, it has also clearly been influenced by the surrounding languages; about 20% of modern Romanian vocabulary can be traced back to Slavic languages. The most obvious Slavic influence is the word for yes, *da*.

French became a major influence in the 19th and 20th centuries. Other languages that influenced Romanian are Hungarian (*oraş*, city, from *város*), German (*cartof*, potato, from *Kartoffel*) and Turkish (*ciorbă*, soup, from *çorba*). It is closely related to other Romance languages such as Italian, Spanish, French and Portuguese, but in practice these

languages are far from mutually intelligible. Romanian has many unique words that do not have an equivalent in any of these other languages, such as *prieten* (friend), *a vorbi* (to speak), *fără* (without), and *bărbat* (man).

Pronunciation is vastly different from any of the other Romance languages as well. Spelling is largely phonetic, which makes pronunciation a little easier. Intonation is fairly flat, at least compared to French or Italian. However, you will often hear Romanians pronounce the first part of a sentence in a very high-pitched voice, with a sudden steep drop towards the end – especially in situations when they want to express irony or indifference, it seems.

Up to the 19th century Romanian was written in Cyrillic script (still used in Transnistria to this day). Thankfully, scholars adapted the Latin alphabet for Romanian use in the late 18th century; the use of the Cyrillic alphabet gradually declined and then disappeared towards the 1860s.

Hungarian is still an important minority language. In some cities, such as Târgu Mureş, up to or over 50% of the population is Hungarian. Hungarian enclaves can be found in Rimetea (Torockó) south of Cluj and around the city of Miercurea Ciuc (Csíkszereda), where the population is almost 100% Hungarian (or Szekler) and may not be very fluent in Romanian. Although the Saxon population has dwindled dramatically after the exodus following the demise of the communist regime in 1989, German is still spoken in the Saxon land, roughly around and in between the cities of Sibiu and Braşov. Romania also has a sizeable Roma population which speaks Romani.

A list of useful words and phrases in Romanian and a short guide to Romanian pronunciation and grammar can be found in Appendix D.

CULTURE

It will be immediately apparent to the first-time visitor to Romania that Romanians cherish their cultural heritage. Wherever you go, you will encounter expressions of folklore, celebrating the country's colourful past and keeping traditions alive. Every region has its own lavishly decorated and costly traditional costumes, lovingly created by *bunicii* (grandmothers) – and they are used often. Romanians grab every chance to celebrate a religious holiday, and if this does not require fasting, it will involve feasting: dancing to live folk music and eating while wearing the aforementioned traditional dress.

Religion plays an important role in the life of Romanians, especially those living in the countryside; the overwhelming majority (81% according to the 2011 census) identifies as Romanian Orthodox. Small minorities are Roman Catholic, Reformed or Greek Catholic. Very few people identify as not religious at all. The prominent role of religion can also be seen in architecture: new Orthodox churches are being constructed continually (to the dismay of many who would rather see the funds go to hospitals and schools), and many ancient and lavishly decorated monasteries can be found all over the country.

There are too many public holidays (religious or otherwise) to mention here, but you might want to look up a list online to avoid getting stuck – buses might not operate and shops might be closed. In fact, hardly a month goes by without a major public holiday. The most important national holidays are 1 May (Labour Day) and 1 December (Unification Day); the most important religious holiday is Orthodox Easter (dates vary). For someone living in the countryside, observing a religious holiday means not doing any work – so this is something to bear in mind while travelling.

The Cistercian monastery at Cârţa in southern Transylvania

Romania features prominently on the UNESCO World Heritage List – sites include the painted churches of Bucovina, the wooden churches of Maramureş, the fortified churches of Transylvania and the unbelievably well-preserved medieval citadel of Sighişoara, thought to be the birthplace of Vlad the Impaler, the 15th-century voivode of Wallachia who gave rise to the Dracula myth. Bran Castle near Braşov has also been linked to Dracula; there is not much of a historical connection but it has led to an enormous increase in visitor numbers. Other castles worth visiting include Peleş Palace in Sinaia, Bánffy Castle near Cluj (scene of the Electric Castle Festival) and Corvin Castle in Hunedoara. Transylvania's medieval city centres are often dominated by a citadel, as is the case in Braşov, Alba Iulia, Deva, Râşnov, Sighişoara and Rupea. Many of these cities have Saxon origins. Other cities very much worth visiting are Cluj-Napoca and Sibiu. Transylvania is also often called Siebenbürgen, after the original seven Saxon cities. Many cities have a nearby open-air village museum, such as the Astra Museum near Sibiu, the Dimitri Gusti National Village Museum near Bucharest, the Muzeul Etnografic al Transilvaniei near Cluj, the Muzeul Satului Maramureşan near Sighetu Marmaţiei and the Muzeul Satului Vâlcean din Bujoreni near Râmnicu Vâlcea.

The Paris-based sculptor Constantin Brâncuşi was Romanian; his Endless Column (1938) can be found in Târgu Jiu, a tribute to the Romanian heroes of World War 1. Romania's most famous composer is George Enescu (1881–1955), who also studied and worked in Paris. More recently and in a different department, the Romanian New Wave has emerged – a genre of minimalist and realist cinema that has resulted in numerous award-winning films, such as The Death of Mr Lăzărescu (Cristi Puiu) and 4 Months, 3 Weeks and 2 Days (Cristian Mungiu). Many of these gems can be watched for free at http://en.cinepub.ro – quite a few come with English subtitles. It is an excellent way to get acquainted with Romanian culture, and the Romanians' black sense of humour, born out of the austere circumstances many of them grew up in.

encounter snow patches until well into July, or perhaps even in August. In winter temperatures can dip below -20°C in the higher mountain ranges but don't usually fall below -10°C in the lowlands. Precipitation naturally is highest in the mountains, with the forbidding 70km east-to-west Făgăraş range, and the region north of it, receiving the most. Do not be deceived by the high temperatures down below; it can get very chilly up in the mountains during the nights, although you probably needn't fear frost if hiking in June, July or August. Meteoblue (www.meteoblue.com) gives fairly reliable forecasts and has good weather maps, although of course in the mountains the weather changes from valley to valley and peak to peak – but many meteo stations are located in the mountains so look for info from these.

CLIMATE

Romania has a temperate continental climate with harsh winters and hot summers and very distinct seasons. Temperatures can rise to above 35°C in the lowlands during summer, but usually do not exceed 25–30°C. Bucharest in southeastern Oltenia tends to get very hot during the summer months so that many people flee it whenever they can. Winter sees a lot of snow, which starts to fall from early October or even late September. Most of it will have gone by June, although above 2000m you may

WHEN TO GO

The best months to visit are May to September. It is a delight to explore Romania in spring, which is absolutely exuberant. Especially if heading to the Apuseni region or Maramureş, you will find yourself surrounded by an incredible wealth and diversity of floral beauty: fragrant elderflower, the basis for the popular socată (elderflower syrup), lines the roads; rhododendrons and irises spring up in the mountains. Purple crocuses adorn the valleys north of the Făgăraş as early as late March. The grass

The rugged summit of Piatra Mică in winter (Route 18)

of the sweet-scented meadows of Maramureş and Bucovina is allowed to grow very tall before it gets scythed, resulting in great floral variety and healthy bee and butterfly populations. June sees the highest precipitation, so if you want summer weather and temperatures July and August are the safer months. August is the busiest month too, since that is when most Romanians will take their holidays. September may be the best month for hiking in terms of weather: it is the driest month and you will be surrounded by spectacular autumn colours – and encounter far fewer other hikers on the trail.

Winter walking in Romania is a different game altogether. Romania gets boatloads of snow during the winter months (January and February seeing the most); even the lower mountain ranges such as the Cozia and Buila-Vânturariţa receive plenty. And although this can make for truly magical hiking, winter hiking is not recommended unless you have the relevant experience and equipment (ice axe and crampons are the bare minimum). You are advised to book a guide if you are not an experienced winter walker.

WHAT TO TAKE

Excellent trekking packlists can be found all over the internet – what follows is a short list of items you should definitely bring. Also see www.cicerone.co.uk/top-tips-for-european-trek-packing for general recommendations of what to bring on a trek.

- Hiking boots with Vibram sole, B or B-C category
- Sturdy sandals such as Tevas (useful for traversing streams and when resting)
- Raingear
- Plastic bags or other waterproof bags to keep your gear dry (your backpack cover isn't going to save you during a day of pouring rain)
- Warm mid-layer (such as a fleece or down jacket)
- Thermal base layer
- Shorts and long (zip-off) trousers; bring a warmer pair for spring or early autumn
- Good-quality (woollen) walking socks
- Gloves
- Buff or hat
- Sunglasses, category 3 or 4
- Sunblock
- Mosquito repellent
- Lightweight tent
- Sleeping bag (three-season) plus liner
- Sleeping mat
- Water bottles (2–3L)
- Water filter (the Sawyer Mini does an excellent job)
- Stove compatible with multiple types of fuel (such as the MSR PocketRocket; Campinggaz is hard to find but other types of gas such as Primus are widely available)
- Headlight
- First aid kit including an emergency blanket and tick remover
- Powerbank
- Walking poles (to keep dogs at bay)
- Consider bringing an ultrasonic device (also to keep dogs at bay)

Approaching Ascuțit Peak (Route 18, Stage 3)

GETTING THERE

By air

Romania is well provided with airports. The international airports that are most important to the mountain-bound traveller are Bucharest Henri Coandă, Cluj, Sibiu and Timişoara airports; Suceava and Bacău airports are useful if travelling specifically to northeast Romania.

Direct flights from the UK and Western Europe are operated by low-cost airlines Blue Air, WizzAir, Ryanair, as well as Tarom (Romania's national airline), KLM, Air France and many others. See www.uncover-romania.com for a complete overview of flight options (from the menu, select 'Resources' and then 'Flights to Romania'). All airports and their websites are listed in Appendix C.

By train

A train journey to Romania from Western Europe is going to take two days but doesn't have to be difficult, and allows you to make stops in Vienna and Budapest. If travelling from the UK, take the Eurostar from London St Pancras to Brussels. From there, there is an excellent connection via Frankfurt to Vienna and onwards to Budapest, from where you can take a train towards Oradea and then Cluj. Travelling to the east of Romania will add another day to your journey. Until Budapest, trains are luxurious and first-class travel hardly costs more than second class; there is onboard

wi-fi and a dining car and plenty of leg space. Trains from Budapest to Romania are slightly more rustic. A train journey does not have to be expensive either; simply pick your dates wisely and you may find surprisingly good offers. See www.bahn.de for an international train schedule (fill in sections of your journey, such as Frankfurt–Vienna and Vienna–Budapest to see prices) and www.seat61.com for a wealth of information on international train travel in general.

By bus

Flixbus and Eurolines operate several buses to Cluj, Bucharest, Oradea and many other cities in Romania, as does the Romanian company Atlassib. A journey is going to take up two days. Buses take longer and are not necessarily cheaper than flights or trains; trains are definitely the more convenient option. However, international buses can be a good option when covering shorter distances, such as Sibiu–Budapest.

By car

If travelling by car, please be aware that you have to buy a 'Rovinieta' – an electronic vignette through which you pay the toll for using Romania's national road network. See www.roviniete.ro/en for more information. You can also purchase the vignette there. Romania only has one motorway (a much-lamented fact) and many of its local roads are in a deplorable state, although matters are slowly improving. National roads can be recognised by the prefix DN (*drum national*); county roads are called DJ (*drum judeţean*); communal roads (often unpaved) are called DC (*drum comunal*). Sadly, Romania also has one of the highest rates of road traffic deaths in the EU: almost double the EU average with 96 deaths per million inhabitants in 2018.

Cars can be rented at major airports and in most cities. Renting a car for three days costs as little as €50–€100 (excluding insurance and one-way charge if dropping the car off at a different location). Popular companies include Hertz, KlassWagen and EuroCars, and www.rentalcars.com is a useful online comparison and booking site.

LOCAL TRANSPORT

It is very feasible to get around in Romania without a car, as long as you are willing to be creative and have enough time on your hands. Using public transport is an excellent way to get to know the local population and see the country from a different perspective. Bus or train rides without a local trying to strike up a conversation are rare – and don't be surprised if people offer to share their food and drink with you. Details of how to access the routes in this guide by all available modes of transport are provided in the overview for each route.

Trains

Romania has the 15th most extensive railway network in the world, while it is only the 81st largest country. Train travel is cheap and trains stop at many minor stations (these are called *haltă* as opposed to *gară*). There are several types of trains; the interregional (IR) trains are much faster than the regional (R) trains. Most trains are operated by Romania's state railway carrier, CFR, but there are several other rail operators, often competing with CFR at lower prices (but with slower trains); see Appendix C for web addresses.

Trains are usually slower than buses and are often delayed; if you have to change trains somewhere, make sure you have plenty of time in between. There are a few night trains as well, such as the train from Sighetu Marmaţiei in the northwest to Bucharest – these are definitely worth a try. Train stations are never announced, so you will have to keep your eyes peeled.

Tickets for CFR trains can be bought ahead online at a discount, or at the station; you will need to create an account at www.cfrcalatori.ro/en for the former. Tickets can only be bought at larger stations, not at the smaller *halte* (stops; singular *haltă*). If you board at a *haltă* buy your ticket on the train. Likewise, Regio Călători tickets can be bought at a desk at the station or on the train when boarding at a *haltă*. TFC and Interregional let you buy tickets online too, as well as on the train. International tickets can

A typical scene at a Romanian railway station

be bought from international desks at larger stations such as Cluj and Bucharest (Bucureşti Nord).

Buses

Travelling by bus or minibus (*maxitaxi*) is a good alternative to the train, especially if travelling to the mountains – buses usually take you a bit closer to your destination. All buses are (or should be) listed on https://autogari.ro. However, this website is not always up to date – announcements about changes to the schedule are sometimes made at bus stations only. Again, as with the trains, flexibility is key – make sure you have plenty of leeway in your schedule so that you can take a later bus if necessary. If you want to ensure you have a seat it is wise to make a reservation; however,

this will probably have to be done in Romanian, over the phone. In most cases this is not necessary though.

Larger cities have excellent bus networks; see Appendix C for websites. Tickets can be bought from kiosks on the street near main hubs or from ticket machines, and usually come in pairs. Tickets need to be stamped or punched on the bus; if you fail to do so you might incur a hefty fine.

Taxis

Taxis come cheap and are ubiquitous in cities like Bucharest, Cluj, Braşov, Sibiu and Timişoara. Especially in Bucharest, do make sure that the meter is on. Do not attempt to strike a bargain; if you do you will almost certainly get charged too much.

Hitchhiking

If all else fails you can always try hitch-hiking, which is a popular method of transportation in Romania among locals and tourists alike. Indeed, in a few cases it may be the best if not the only way to get to or from a route or stage; where this is the case it is made clear in the route or stage introduction. Locals usually pay the driver a few RON per kilometre; if you're a tourist your money probably won't be accepted, but it doesn't do any harm to offer it – people can often do with the extra income. The carpooling service BlaBlaCar (www.blablacar.com) also functions well in Romania.

There are two words you should keep your eyes peeled for when looking for accommodation: *cazare* (rooms for rent) and *pensiune* (pension). There is no shortage of these in Romania; most of the time it is much more pleasant to stay in an often privately owned *pensiune* than in a hotel, most of which are cheerless grey buildings which seem to have been built during the communist era.

Mountain huts, *cabane* (singular *cabana*), are a little less luxurious then their counterparts in the Alps, but they offer the chance to mingle with Romanians and experience the Romanian mountain culture. The best way to book a bed in a cabana is by phoning them (see Appendix B for contact details); however, many *cabaniers*

(hut wardens) do not speak English, so you may want to find a local to make the reservation for you. At some huts reception is poor and you may have to send a text instead; if this is the case it is indicated in Appendix B. See Appendix D for a language glossary. Book well in advance (at least two weeks) if you're planning to stay at a cabana in a popular area, such as Cabana Curmatura in the Piatra Craiului or Cabana Pietrele in the Retezat. Phone numbers are, of course, subject to change. If you can't reach a cabana you may want to ask around in the 'Nu sunt singur pe munte' Facebook group, which is an excellent place for queries of all kinds.

Cabanas usually offer a choice between a bed in a dorm, either with bunk beds or single beds, or a private room (sizes vary from two to four beds). One thin blanket is usually provided; huts are heated with wooden stoves. It is never a bad idea to bring your own sleeping bag or at least a liner. Food is served at all cabanas unless otherwise specified in Appendix B; sanitary provisions are often very basic. More often than not there is no bathroom and just an outdoor toilet.

There are also quite a few unstaffed basic refuges (*refugiu*, pl. *refugii*) in the Romanian mountains. These come in all shapes and sizes, but the dome-shaped red and white variety is most common, especially in the Southern Carpathians. They have sleeping platforms and little else; there may be a table and there's usually a spring nearby. Technically speaking,

Cabana Giumalău (Route 6) has its own windmill

refuges are only meant to be used in case of emergency, although in practice many Romanians count on finding a place there and leave their tent at home; and blueberry pickers also use them to spend the night in. They usually have no more than six to eight berths and tend to fill up quickly during summer. For these reasons, do not count on finding a place at a refuge – always take your tent on a multi-stage trek with no cabanas.

Romania is well provided with campsites – the majority of them owned by non-Romanians (mostly Dutch, Belgians and Germans). The campsites that are owned by Romanians often have *casutas* for rent: little tent-shaped wooden cabins with two or three beds. See Appendix B and https://takethelongwayhome.eu for an overview of campsites; the website differentiates between campsites and camping spots – places where you can pitch your tent and access a bathroom and a tap but without all the facilities

of a campsite. It is usually possible to camp on the grounds of a cabana for a small charge. Officially, wild camping is not allowed in Romania but in practice authorities turn a blind eye and many hikers camp wild. This makes Romania an ideal country for a purely tent-based trip: as long as you abide by the 'leave no trace' principle you can bivouac practically anywhere. National parks form an important exception: camping outside the designated camping spots can result in a hefty fine and rangers do patrol the parks.

Accommodation options are provided at the beginning of each route description in this guide, while Appendix B offers an overview of accommodation on the routes and in the most important bases. Airbnb (www.airbnb.com) and Booking.com (www.booking.com) are widely used in Romania. Bigger cities such as Bucharest and Cluj have a wide range of affordable hostels as well.

FOOD AND DRINK

Romanian cuisine features versions of dishes found elsewhere across Eastern Europe, such as *sarmale* (cabbage rolls stuffed with rice and minced meat). A meal is not complete without a soup or *ciorbă* (clear, sour soup) as a starter. Traditional Romanian food features a lot of meat, cabbage (*vârza*), aubergines (*vinete*) and sour cream (*smântână*). Generally, it can be described as rustic and full of flavour; Romanian vegetables are incredibly tasty. See Appendix D for a list of traditional Romanian dishes. If you're vegan and don't want to receive quizzical looks when trying to explain this, ask for *mâncare de post* – food for fasting – which is free of animal products. Finding vegetarian or even vegan restaurants should not pose a problem in bigger cities like Bucharest, Cluj, Sibiu and Brașov. Unbeknown to many, Romania is the world's 12th biggest wine exporter, and the fifth biggest in Europe. Perhaps the best-known grape varieties native to Romania are the *Feteasca neagră*, *albă* and *regală*. If you are a wine lover you might be in for a pleasant surprise.

HEALTH AND SAFETY

Overall, Romania is a very safe country to travel in. Take basic precautions – carry your valuables and documents on you and do not wave large wads of cash around. Do not bargain with taxi drivers or they might take advantage of you – just make sure they have

their meter on. Taxi rides that take you out of town and into the mountains over unpaved roads form an exception; for these drivers usually charge a fixed fee. You will probably encounter some (or many) Roma beggars – they make a living out of begging. It's best to ignore them since they might pester you for more once you start giving.

Bring your EU health card if you have one and make sure you have good travel insurance that covers air medical services and repatriation. You may want to get vaccinated against tick-borne encephalitis and, while you're at it, get rabies and tetanus injections as well (see 'A note on dogs', below).

Solo female travellers

While overall Romania is a very safe country, solo female travellers should be aware that they might be at risk when hitchhiking with male drivers. The author experienced harassment a couple of times. Some precautions you could consider include installing a tracker app on your phone (such as FollowMee) to inform a close friend or relative of your whereabouts during the ride, noting down the number plate and texting it to a friend or phoning someone. Always ask the driver to drop you off the moment you feel unsafe.

Emergencies and mountain rescue

Like elsewhere in the EU, call 112 in case of an emergency. The Romanian mountain rescue brigade is called Salvamont; save their

Viper in the Piatra Craiului Mountains

number in your phone: +40 725 826 668 (+40-SALVAMONT). Their website is www.salvamontromania.ro (Romanian-language only). Always take the necessary precautions when heading into the mountains; not doing so means putting your own life in danger, and others may have to risk their life for you if you fail to prepare well. Always observe the following basic precautions:

- Leave your itinerary with someone at home
- Carry a list of useful phone numbers (emergency numbers, huts, contact at home)
- Dress adequately (wear the right footwear, bring clothes for cold and wet weather)
- Pay heed to the weather: do not set off if conditions are unfavourable
- Carry an adequate amount of water and food
- Bring an emergency kit
- Carry the relevant map(s) and preferably a compass as well

A note on dogs

If you go trekking in the Romanian mountains you are likely to encounter a sheepfold (*stâna*) at some point or other. Although many Romanians will warn you about bears (see 'A note on bears', below), the bigger danger is sheepdogs – or, more accurately, livestock guardian dogs. It is important to be aware of the risks and to know how to be prepared.

A flock of sheep is usually herded by a Hungarian Pumi, Puli or Mudi dog. These are small and are unlikely to be the ones to attack you. The dogs to watch out for are the much bigger and

A sheepdog protecting its flock

fiercer guardian dogs. The most common breeds are the Carpathian shepherd (*Ciobănesc Românesc Carpatin*), the Caucasian shepherd (*Ciobănesc Caucazian*) and the Mioritic shepherd (*Ciobănesc Românesc Mioritic*). To give you some idea of their size, they can reach a height of 75cm. Their job is to protect the flock against bear and wolf attacks, but if you are in their territory they might feel provoked and attack you. These dogs are trained to kill if they need to; a dog bite can be very serious.

Although they are not supposed to attack you and normally won't, it is necessary to be well prepared: not all dogs are well trained and sadly these days many shepherds are hired hands who are not in control of their dogs. As soon as you see you are approaching a flock, get your walking poles out.

Never provoke dogs with these; just keep them close to your legs for protection. If you can circumvent a flock, do so. Otherwise, wait until they have crossed your path. Often, however, you will find that you can do neither, for the simple reason that the flock has spread out over a large area. In all cases, make contact with the shepherd so that he can keep his dogs at bay and, if necessary, safely guide you through the flock. Don't provoke the dogs: only defend yourself with sticks and stones after it's clear they are going to attack you. Never run. You can try to fend off dogs with an ultrasonic device; however, many of the larger dogs simply do not seem to care. If you do sustain a dog bite, you will have to go through a course of rabies and tetanus injections. You may want to consider getting these before you leave, especially if you plan

43

to spend a lot of time in the Romanian mountains. It will save you a lot of time and hassle in Romanian hospitals.

That said, most livestock guardian dogs are well trained and encounters with shepherds and their flocks are usually pleasant. Shepherds know the mountains like no-one else and can be a great help if you're lost. In the north (Maramureş and the Eastern Carpathians) dogs tend to be wilder and less accustomed to tourists than in the south. Shepherding is an ancient part of Romanian culture. Tourists have to negotiate space with the flocks; it is important to be aware you are entering their territory and act accordingly.

A note on bears

Although you are much more likely to encounter livestock guardian dogs, Romania has a sizeable population of brown bears (estimates range from 2000 to 6000 individuals), so they do deserve a mention. Bears are very shy of humans and will most likely stay off your path, but it's important to know how to avoid an encounter and what to do if it does happen.

Firstly, make sure you stay on the trail at all times – don't delve into the woods. Make some noise now and again to make your presence known – talk, sing, or use a bear bell to make a constant tinkling noise (although some argue this makes hikers sound like sheep!). If you do meet with a bear and it sees you, the most important thing is to stay calm. Do not look the bear in the eye but keep facing it as you retreat into the direction you came from (but make sure you are not between a mother and her cub). Do not run. Consider changing your itinerary after

Bears can often be seen at Sfânta Ana Lake (Eastern Carpathians) and at the nearby spa town of Baile Tuşnad (photo: Kinga Mihaly)

you've retreated beyond the bear's line of sight – although the bear will most likely run away from you.

If a bear does approach you, hold your arms up to make yourself look more imposing; talk to help the bear recognise you as a human being. Do not panic if the bear stands up on its hind legs; this just means it's gauging the situation. Attacks are very rare, but if it does look like it's going to attack you, crouch down, clasp your hands behind your neck and bring your chin and knees to your chest. If you feel more comfortable carrying bear spray, you can buy a canister at arms shops such as Ultra Armory in Braşov. That said, it's highly unlikely you'll meet with a bear at all.

MONEY

Romania's currency is the *leu* ('lion', plural *lei*) – its code is RON. One *leu* is subdivided into 100 *bani* – also the word for money in Romanian. Banknotes come in 1, 5, 10, 50, 100, 200 and 500 RON (the latter is rarely used). Coins are either 50, 10, 5, 2 or 1 *bani* – you will find that people often leave the 5, 2 and 1 *bani* coins behind at checkouts because their value is negligible. After the downfall of communism inflation ran so high that it resulted in a revaluation of the *leu* in 2005; basically, four zeroes were dropped so that 10,000 old *lei* became one new *leu*.

Romania is a very affordable country to travel in for Western visitors, although life is expensive for Romanians themselves because salaries are, say, about four times lower than in Western Europe whereas food prices are only half. However, prices of food and drink vary widely across the country – a beer could cost as much as 15 RON in Bucharest but less than 10 RON in Braşov, and perhaps just 7 RON in a village. In most places it's possible to have a good dinner for two for as little as €30. The *leu* isn't very stable, but the exchange rate has been between 4.5 and 5 RON for €1 for a number of years.

ATMs (*bancomat*) are widely available in Romania although you should not expect to find them in smaller villages. Credit cards and Mastercards are usually accepted in supermarkets and hotels; in smaller shops or private accommodation you may have to pay cash. Payment in cabanas is cash only. You may want to bring a separate wallet for your Romanian money – you'll find that all those 1, 5 and 10 RON notes soon result in an impressive wad of cash.

STAYING IN TOUCH

If you're staying in Romania for an extended period of time, or even if you're just going for two weeks, you may want to consider buying a local prepaid unlocked SIM card. For as little as €5–7 you can get a ridiculously good deal: near endless calling credit within Romania, international calling credit to countries where many

Romanian expats reside (including the UK) and, most importantly, an amount of data you'll find it hard to burn through in one month. The main providers are Vodafone, Orange, Telekom and Digi. Vodafone is the only one that lets you top up online with an international credit card, but you can also buy top-up vouchers from kiosks and supermarkets. Romania has one of the fastest downloading speeds in the world (competing with Sweden and Singapore), so you might as well benefit from that while you're there.

NATIONAL PARKS

Romania has 14 national parks and 17 natural parks; what distinguishes the two isn't entirely clear. Fourteen of this combined total make their appearance in this book. All are protected areas that come with their own rules and regulations. These are usually announced on info panels at the main entrances to the park, but it doesn't do harm to have a look at the website of the park you plan to visit first. See Appendix C for a list of websites. In all parks, camping is restricted to designated camping areas, and picking flowers is not allowed. If you abide by the rule 'Leave nothing but footprints, take nothing but pictures' you are probably doing it right.

RULES AND REGULATIONS

Although there is a lot of red tape in Romania, in everyday life Romanians

tend to be very creative with the rules. Perhaps the main thing to remember as a visitor is to be very sure you have scanned, stamped or punched your bus ticket adequately. Especially in Bucharest, ticket inspectors are rather keen on handing out hefty fines to unsuspecting tourists. If you're in a national park, make sure you do not camp outside designated areas. And, like everywhere, dress respectfully when entering a religious building. Generally speaking, Romania is an easy-going country and you don't have to worry too much about codes of behaviour.

MAPS

Since the publication of the precursor of this guide in 2005, much has changed in Romania. For one thing, the mapping situation has drastically improved. Virtually every mountainous area is now covered by at least one good map. Schubert & Franzke, publisher of the Munții Noștri collection, rapidly releases map after map. The other main publishers are Dimap, Eco-Romania and Bel Alpin. Maps are easy to obtain; they can be ordered from webshops such as www.stanfords.co.uk and www.manymaps.com. If you need to buy maps locally, go to a bookshop or outdoor store; see Appendix C for a list of those. Online, maps can be downloaded from www.carpati.org; click 'Hărți' under the 'Ghid' tab. (These are mostly older maps but in

A mountain biker heads up the smooth slopes towards Vinderel Lake, Maramureş (Route 4)

some cases it's all there is.) There are also mapping apps available – see https://muntii-nostri.ro and www.eco-romania.ro.

WAYMARKING

Trails are usually maintained by volunteers and the quality of waymarking depends on the volunteer network and the funds available. Generally speaking, you will find that waymarking in the south is better than in the north. The waymarking system used is that of red, yellow and blue stripes, circles and triangles. Stripes usually denote a ridge trail; triangles are usually alternative routes (to the ridge trail); circles are often circular trails or extensions of a stripe or triangle trail. Sometimes dartboard-type marks are used for circuits off the main trails. Foresters often spray vertical red stripes on trees; do not confuse these with the red stripe waymarks, which always have a white background. On quite a few of the routes described in this guide, trail

maintenance has been neglected, as a result of which the descriptions have become rather lengthy.

WATER, FOOD AND OTHER SUPPLIES

Most of Romania's mountains are well supplied with a network of springs and streams, excepting porous limestone ridges like the Piatra Craiului and the Buila-Vânturariţa. Although spring water is usually very clean, you should avoid drinking from a spring that can clearly be accessed by cattle – or filter the water. If a spring is in a grazed area but covered or the water comes from a pipe you can safely drink it. Water from streams, rivers and lakes should always be filtered.

Since summers can be hot and dry in Romania, make sure you carry enough water – two to three litres per day per person is recommended. Springs are marked on the maps and mentioned in the information boxes preceding the route descriptions. Tap water is normally drinkable in Romania although the quality varies greatly per area; water in towns at the foot of the mountains will naturally be much better than in Bucharest, for example. Water in cabanas and meteo stations at higher altitudes may come from a tank and hence not be drinkable (*apă nepotabilă*); check before using.

In larger towns food is easy to obtain from supermarkets and hypermarkets such as Kaufland, Carrefour and Lidl. Kaufland and other bigger supermarkets (Carrefour, Mega Image) sell powdered milk (*lapte praf*) and oatmeal (*fulgi de ovaz*). These products cannot usually be found at smaller shops. Every village will have at least one Magazin Mixt, Magazin ABC or Magazin Alimentar; small corner shops where you should be able to buy the

basics – some fruit and vegetables, pasta, rice, oil, salami, canned foods, snacks (you'll see huge bags of *pufuleţi*, corn puffs, everywhere), chocolate and drinks. Many of these shops double as a bar. In small villages you may be able to buy eggs, milk, honey and cheese from the locals – just ask around. Instant meals and gas canisters can be bought at most outdoor stores; see Appendix C. DIY stores such as Praktiker and Dedeman often sell gas as well. Cabanas usually serve meals (unless otherwise specified in the route description) and sell water, alcoholic beverages, chocolate and other snacks.

USING THIS GUIDE

The routes
The 37 routes in this guide follow the Carpathian arc clockwise, starting in

A towering limestone wall of the Zănoaga Gorge in Bucegi Natural Park (Route 17)

the northwest. In many cases, connecting walks from one range to another are offered. Routes vary widely in length and difficulty; from easy day walks in the Piatra Mare to a challenging five-day, 90km traverse of the Făgăraş Chain. Most routes follow waymarked trails, but the quality of the waymarking varies widely across the country; you may want to bring a GPS device to use alongside your map and compass on less well-maintained trails. If this is the case it will be pointed out in the route description.

Most routes are linear, taking you from A to B, but there are a few exceptions, most notably in the Piatra Craiului (Route 18) and the Apuseni (Routes 36 and 37). In the case of the Piatra Craiului, all walks depart from a single base, Cabana Curmatura, except for the Southern Ridge (Route 19). In the Apuseni, the most interesting bits – the karstic areas – lie off the main trail; these are called 'excursions' and can always be tackled on the same day as the preceding stage. In quite a few cases you can pick and mix, combining stages from different routes – this includes the Bucegi (Routes 16 and 17), the aforementioned Apuseni and the Retezat (Routes 26 and 27).

Timings

The walking times indicated in the route descriptions are based on the author's own times and are 'flat time' only, which means they do not include breaks, time needed for orienting, taking photographs, etc. Everyone is different; some people will be faster and others slower, and of course pack weight makes a difference – but the timings mentioned should give a rough indication of how long you should reserve for a walk. As a rule of thumb, add an extra 10min to every hour of walking time to allow for breaks, or more if you want to go at a leisurely pace and/or are an inexperienced walker. You will probably find that you are consistently faster or slower than the stated times and will quickly learn to adjust your estimates accordingly.

Many if not most of the stages or walks in this book will take an entire day or the better part of a day; in all cases you are advised to leave early, especially in July and August when temperatures can soar into the high 30s in the lowlands; and although of course they will be much lower once you're up in the mountains the sun can still be particularly unforgiving.

Grading

Every stage has been graded easy, moderate or difficult. Although this is partly subjective and based on the author's experience of the trail, you can roughly expect these grades to mean the following:

Easy: Total ascent of no more than 1000m but usually a lot less than that – most likely no more than 500m; well-marked trails over cart tracks or grassy trails. Many of these are suitable for families with young children. Navigation is easy most of the time.

Moderate: Total ascent can amount to 1500m but usually no more than 1000m. May involve some scrambling, cables, crossing boulder fields and a moderately steep ascent or two, but nothing major. Some of these are still suitable for families with young children, such as the walks in the Piatra Mare. Navigation may be a little difficult at times.

Difficult: Total ascent can amount to 1500m or more but usually no more than 1000m. The difficulty usually lies in very steep ascents that involve chains and/or cables and other technical passages; expect to spend a considerable amount of time on all fours. You will never need climbing or via ferrata gear though – it still falls into the walking bracket. Navigation may present some challenges at times.

The grading doesn't say very much about the distance of a trail – an easy trail may be 5km or 20km long; the same goes for a difficult trail although these tend to cover shorter distances because of their difficulty. Of course, there is a whole range of factors that influences how difficult a trail is in practice, such as fitness level, pack weight, experience and weather conditions. Don't embark on a trail that is likely to be beyond your experience; if something happens (dehydration, hypothermia, injuries) and you need help it may take a long time for the mountain rescue service (Salvamont) to reach you, if you can contact them at all – you will not have reception everywhere.

Altitude readings

The total ascent and total descent values in the information boxes are based on GPS and barometric readings and are not going to be 100% accurate, but should nevertheless give you a good idea of what to expect in terms of effort.

Names of geographical features

Names of geographical features have been translated into English in the route descriptions; eg Şetref Pass instead of Pasul Şetref. Names of mountain ranges have undergone the same treatment; eg Munţii Rodnei is written as the Rodna Mountains. The only exception to this are the Munţii Maramureşului, which have kept their name in the chapter title and the route description to avoid confusion with the part title, The Mountains of Maramureş, which covers a wider area.

If in doubt about something when reading the map, the original Romanian name of a feature can be looked up in Appendix D.

GPX tracks

GPX tracks for the routes in this guidebook are available to download free at www.cicerone.co.uk/948/GPX. A GPS device is an excellent aid to navigation, but you should also carry a map and compass and know how to use them.

THE MOUNTAINS OF MARAMUREŞ

Window onto the Munţii Maramureşului ridge (Route 4, Stage 2)

Maramureş fully deserves its first place in this book: it is breathtakingly gorgeous and offers the greatest possible variety in scenery. Hemmed in by the Munţii Maramureşului in the north, the Rodna Mountains to the east and the Lăpuş and Ţibleş Mountains to the south, Maramureş is one of the most isolated counties in Romania. It was never part of the Roman imperial province of Dacia, and most subsequent invasions have passed it by as well. And it shows: the valleys, mountains, villages and traditions of Maramureş have survived the ages like nowhere else in Romania. Visiting Maramureş is like going back in time a hundred years. Here, you can combine walking in the unspoilt Rodna Mountains with exploring the wonderfully preserved villages of the Iza and Mara Valleys; or, if you want complete solitude, travel up the Vaşer Valley by the narrow-gauge railway and hike in the Munţii Maramureşului, the northernmost mountain range of Romania that marks the border with the Ukraine. The inhabitants of Maramureş must be among the most hospitable people in the world: in the mountains you may meet shepherds who offer you fresh cheese; in the villages, farmers who pour you

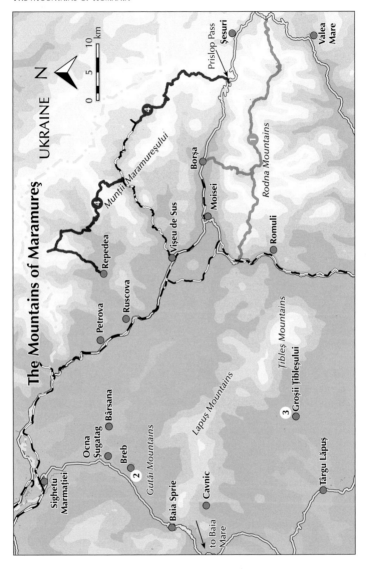

The Mountains of Maramureş

UKRAINE

Prislop Pass

Şesuri

Valea Mare

Borşa

Moisei

Rodna Mountains

Romuli

Munţii Maramuresului

Vişeu de Sus

Repedea

Petrova

Ruscova

Ţibleş Mountains

Lapuş Mountains

Groşii Ţibleşului

Bârsana

Ocna Şugatag

Breb

Gutâi Mountains

Sighetu Marmaţiei

Baia Sprie

Cavnic

Târgu Lapuş

to Baia Mare

km

glasses of ţuică (homemade plum or apple brandy). And don't be surprised if you are offered a traditional meal made of home-grown ingredients, or even a bed. Here, people still know what hospitality means – and how to love the land.

Baia Mare is the county capital of Maramureş and is an excellent base to start from. It is only a 3hr bus ride away from the nearest airport, Cluj-Napoca. Maramureş is thinly populated – the only other town of some size is Sighetu Marmaţiei, on the border with the Ukraine, reached by local bus in about 1hr 30min from Baia Mare. It is possible to take a train from Cluj to Baia Mare or Sighetu Marmaţiei, but it will take longer than the bus (4hr 15min to Baia Mare; 7hr to Sighetu Marmaţiei). In Sighet (this is how the locals refer to it) you can visit the Elie Wiesel House where the history and fate of the Jewish community of Maramureş are told; and the Memorial of the Victims of Communism and of the Resistance museum, housed in Sighet's former communist prison. The open-air village museum (Muzeul Satului Maramureşean, Strada Muzeului 1) is nearby, on the road to Baia Mare.

PLACES TO VISIT IN SIGHETU MARMAŢIEI

- Elie Wiesel House: www.muzeulmaramuresului.ro (Romanian website)
- Village museum (website as above)
- Memorial of the Victims of Communism and of the Resistance museum: www.memorialsighet.ro/memorial-en

See also www.visitmaramures.ro for English-language info on these museums and other cultural attractions in the area.

Maramureş is famous for its wooden churches – feats of excellent craftsmanship. Some 100 tall wooden spires reach towards the heavens. Perhaps the best-known examples can be found within the perimeter of Bârsana Monastery, in the Iza Valley south of the Rodna Mountains – an old church dating back to the 18th century, and a recent construction that was built upon the same principles. There is a museum dedicated to the history and traditions of Maramureş on the grounds as well.

Also worth visiting is the Merry Cemetery (Cimitirul Vesel) in Săpânţa, famous for its colourful tombstones, on which the lives of the deceased are described in humorous verse. If you want to rest your legs for a day, take the narrow-gauge train up the Vaşer Valley. It departs from the town of Vişeu de Sus; tickets are best bought early in the morning or the day before. See www.cffviseu.com/en for a timetable. But perhaps the best way to get a feel for Maramureş is by wandering from one charming village to another through flowery meadows – such as Breb, Budeşti and Deseşti, admiring unique craftsmanship and enjoying home-grown

Looking towards the Munţii Maramureşului (Route 1, Stage 1)

and homemade food at a local's dinner table afterwards – more and more people open up their backyards or dining rooms to welcome tourists.

The **Rodna Mountains** are a beautifully pristine mountain range in the northeast of Maramureş. Only the Munţii Maramureşului range is further north. With a length of 57km, the Rodna represents one of the longest continuous ridges in Romania. The terrain varies throughout: from long grassy stretches where sheep, cows and horses graze to a challenging serrated section in the east that requires some bravery and skill to conquer. There is a good chance of seeing marmots and chamois; the Rodna is also home to a sizeable bear population. There are no cabanas in the Rodna except for an inn at the Şetref Pass, and two huts at the other end of the ridge, Rotunda Pass. This means you will have to be self-sufficient in order to explore this area. The Rodna Mountains are a national park; camping is only permitted in designated areas. Although the highest point of the massif, Pietrosul Peak (2303m) is a popular destination for day hikes from the town of Borşa, chances are you will meet very few people when you traverse the entire ridge from west to east (Route 1).

The **Gutâi Mountains** lie just north of Baia Mare. These are volcanic mountains; their most characteristic feature is the Creasta Cocoşului ('the Cock's Comb'), which can be seen from afar if approaching from the north (Sighetu Marmaţiei). Traversing the main ridge, over Gutâiul Mare Peak (1443m) offers beautiful views over the western Maramureş Depression. Two approaches are offered to the Gutâi Mountains (Route 2); the first from the beautiful village of Breb and the second from Baia Sprie. Alternatively it is possible to walk from Baia Sprie to Breb by combining these routes.

The volcanic **Ţibleş Mountains** (Route 3) can be reached from Baia Mare as well, but are so remote that few tourists find their way to them. Their most faithful visitors are the villagers of Groşii Ţibleşului, who dance and sing in traditional attire on Ţibleş Peak every July to celebrate these mountains. During the

communist era several armed resistance groups hid in the Țibleș Mountains, supported by the population from the surrounding villages.

Munții Maramureșului simply means 'The Mountains of Maramureș' (they are called by their Romanian name in this book to avoid confusion with the 'Mountains of Maramureș' of the title above, which also cover the Rodna, Gutâi and Țibleș Mountains). The Munții

Maramureșului (Route 4) are the northernmost mountain range in Romania and have a Ukrainian counterpart on the other side of the border. These are among the remotest mountains of Romania and were the scene of heavy fighting in both world wars. Although in recent years the national park staff has re-marked the red stripe route and published a very accurate map, few tourists decide to come here. It isn't an easy range to access – which, thankfully, also means the ecosystems have been well preserved and wildlife flourishes. Finding your way can be a bit of a challenge due to the wildness of the area – waymarks are few and far between and trails are sometimes overgrown – so a GPS is no luxury.

The monastery at Prislop Pass (Route 4, Stage 4)

THE RODNA MOUNTAINS

ROUTE 1
Şetref Pass to Rotunda Pass

Start	Şetref Pass or Borşa
Finish	Rotunda Pass
Distance	60km or 49.6km from Borşa
Total ascent	4220m or 4240m from Borşa
Total descent	3770m or 3660m from Borşa
Grade	Moderate-difficult
Time	4 days
Maximum altitude	2279m (Ineu Peak, Stage 3) or 2303m (Pietrosu Peak, Stage 2)
Maps	Preferably Munţii Rodnei, 1:55,000, Munţii Noştri; or Rodnei Mountains, 1:50,000, Dimap

This trek enables a traverse of the 57km main ridge of the pristine Rodna Mountains in four days. The landscape is pastoral; most of the ridge is grassy and doesn't pose any major challenges, and you will see lots of sheep, cows and horses grazing (and therefore quite possibly livestock guardian dogs too; see 'A note on dogs' in the book's main introduction). However, there is a lot of ascending and descending to be done and there is a challenging serrated section on Stage 3 that involves some scrambling. You might encounter wildlife too – the Rodna is home to a sizeable bear population. Bears being shy of humans, you are more likely to see chamois and marmots though. If you want to climb the massif's highest peak, Pietrosu (2303m), which is off the main ridge, consider adding an extra day – although it can be included at the beginning of Stage 2. Every stage except the last one ends at a lake or tarn. The lack of cabanas in the Rodna demands a high level of self-sufficiency, and the range's national park status means camping is only allowed in designated areas (see 'Accommodation and food', below). If strapped for time it is possible to start from the town of Borşa, which offers a worthy alternative to the lengthy Stage 1 from Şetref Pass. See below.

Access

To get to the Şetref Pass (at the border between the counties of Maramureş and Bistriţa-Năsăud), take a bus or train to Săcel or Dealu Ştefăniţei from Sighetu Marmaţiei. The bus to Săcel takes around 1hr 15min; ask the driver to drop you off at the Şetref Pass. There's also a direct train from Cluj-Napoca to Săcel or Dealu Ştefăniţei but this takes a long time and departs at inconvenient hours (4hr 30min, 12.45am or 5.15pm). From the railway station in Săcel or Dealu Ştefăniţei, walk or hitchhike your way up to the Şetref Pass (7.5km or 3km, respectively).

If starting from Borşa: several buses a day reach Borşa from Sighetu Marmaţiei (2hr 15min) and Baia Mare (4hr). Most of these are run by Dracard; in Sighet they leave from the bus station opposite the train station; in Baia Mare the bus station is right next to the train station.

From the Rotunda Pass you can walk or hitchhike the 4.5km down to the DN18 road. This brings you to the hamlet of Fluturica, from where you can hitchhike or take a bus west towards Borşa (less than 1hr). It's also possible to continue into the Suhard Mountains; see Route 5.

Accommodation and food

There is a good pension at the Şetref Pass called Hanul Tentea. Other than this and the cabanas at Rotunda Pass, at the eastern end of the main ridge, there are no cabanas. You can camp at the Şetref Pass though (ask for water at the pension). Camping is also allowed at La Jgheaburi (the cowboy who lives there will happily offer you shelter from the rain), Pietrii Pass and the meteo station, as well as at the stage ends. In Borşa, your best option is the Borşa Turism campsite and pension; otherwise, try Camping Laura Borşa, Str. Independenţei, nr. 139. In 2017 a refuge was built just south of Între Izvoare Saddle (Stage 2).

Hanul Tentea serves decent meals; the cabanas at the eastern end are self-catering. There are plenty of restaurants and bars in Borşa, as well as several supermarkets such as Profi and Penny that sell supplies for a hike.

Looking towards Pietrosu Peak (Stage 1)

STAGE 1
Şetref Pass–Rebra Lake

Start	Şetref Pass
Finish	Rebra Lake
Distance	23km
Total ascent	1740m
Total descent	630m
Grade	Moderate
Time	7hr
Maximum altitude	1985m (Tarniţa La Cruce Saddle)
Water	At the pension at Şetref Pass; at La Jgheaburi meadow, as well as 1km further along the route from La Jgheaburi. Plenty of springs around Tarniţa Bătrânei; spring at Rebra Lake.

This is a long stage; if you want you can split it up and camp at La Jgheaburi or Pietrii Pass. There is no water at the latter though, unless you are willing to descend north towards Moisei for 30–45min: there is a spring called 'Izbucul Izei' to the right of the watermill.

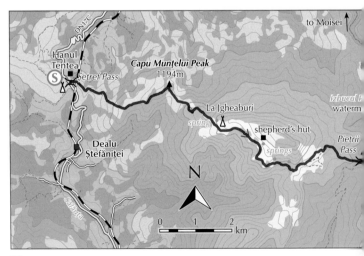

Two paths depart east from **Şetref Pass**; take the upper one that departs from behind the Hanul Tentea pension. (Deceptively, the lower cart track is marked with a signpost that suggests you go down this path. However, this will only lead you down into the valley.) After 500 metres or so you will see the first red stripe waymark on a tree. After 1km the path forks at a sheepfold; keep right – the trail goes through a ditch. Waymarks are far apart. You can see the Ţibleş to the south-west and the Munţii Maramureşului to the north.

When the track bends to the right after 2km, continue straight ahead (east) on a narrow trail; there is a waymark on a tree. At **Capu Muntelui Peak** (1194m) the trail sharply bends to the right (southeast). When it forks after 1km keep right, then turn left (northeast), off the track and onto a grassy trail after 200 metres. Climb for 500 metres to reach a picnic table (with roof). You will encounter several of these today. Continuing, there is a spring 200 metres further up, just before the signpost at **La Jgheaburi meadow** (1532m) where you may well find a herd of cows and horses.

Continue climbing eastwards for 1.5km until you reach a fork; keep right here. If you need shelter, there is a small abandoned **shepherd's hut** up to the left, and a spring in between the two paths. Fill your water bottles at the springs after a further 1km if you plan to camp at Pietrii Pass; there is no water there. After 400 metres a track comes in from the right – keep going straight ahead and up. When the path forks after a further 600 metres keep left, even though the waymarks point to the right – they indicate an unnecessary detour. Gently descend through the forest to **Pietrii Pass** (1196m) – you might well see bear prints on this section.

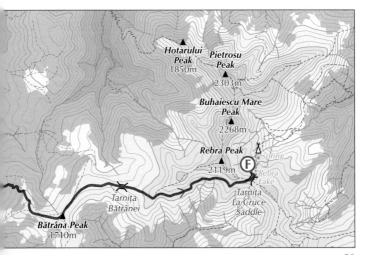

Rocky outcrops after La Jgheaburi

From the pass, steadily climb for 4km to **Bătrâna Peak** (1710m), then continue climbing for 2.7km to **Tarniţa Bătrânei**. There are several springs here. About 700 metres later the path forks; if you go left the trail will take you over Rebra Peak (2119m). The easier option is to keep right and head straight for Rebra Lake. Continue for 3km until you arrive at **Tarniţa La Cruce Saddle** (1985m). From here, descend north to **Rebra Lake**.

ALTERNATIVE STAGE 1
Borşa–Rebra Lake

Start	Bridge over Vişeu River, Borşa
Finish	Rebra Lake
Distance	12.6km
Total ascent	1760m
Total descent	520m
Grade	Moderate
Time	5hr 45min
Maximum altitude	2303m (Pietrosu Peak)
Water	Spring after about 6km; spring in between the meteo station and Iezer Lake; spring at Rebra Lake

Starting in Borşa comes with several advantages: it's easier to access than the Şetref Pass; the trail goes over the Pietrosu Peak, the massif's highest point; and if you're strapped for time this is the shorter route.

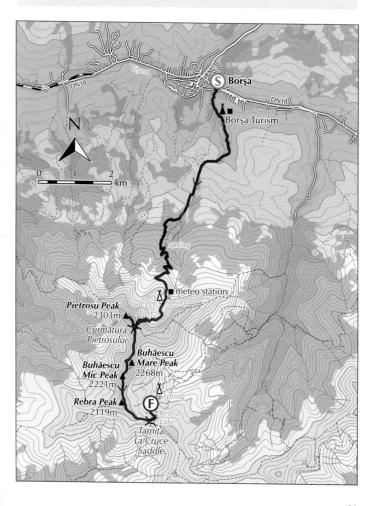

Cross the bridge over the Vişeu River in the centre of **Borşa**, just east of the hospital, to the south. You should start seeing blue stripe marks from here. Walk up Strada Avram Iancu, then keep left to stay on Strada Pietroasa. When the path splits, keep left for the Munţii Rodnei National Park; the path to the right will take you to Pietroasa Monastery.

After about 7km and a 1000m climb you'll arrive at the **meteo station**; there is a camping spot here. The path takes you on to **Iezer Lake**, which happens to have exactly the same shape as Romania. From the lake, ascend another 500m to **Curmătura Pietrosului**. Turn right and head northwest for the very short climb to **Pietrosu Peak** (2303m); you can leave your pack at the saddle as you'll have to return here to continue to Rebra Lake.

Back at the saddle, the path takes you down towards **Buhăescu Mare Peak** (2268m). The path swings round the summit, then take the left path that hugs the southeastern side of **Buhaescu Mic Peak**. You will see Rebra Lake (very tiny and swampy) on your left. Either take a shortcut from the side of Buhaescu Mic Peak or continue to **Tarniţa La Cruce Saddle** and walk down to **Rebra Lake** from there.

STAGE 2
Rebra Lake–Cailor Lake

Start	Rebra Lake
Finish	Camping spot 650 metres beyond Cailor Lake
Distance	13km, or 21km including Pietrosu Peak
Total ascent	690m, or 1450m including Pietrosu Peak
Total descent	740m, or 1500m including Pietrosu Peak
Grade	Moderate
Time	4hr, or 7hr including Pietrosu Peak
Maximum altitude	2074m (Repede Peak) or 2303m (Pietrosu Peak)
Water	At Rebra Lake, Între Izvoare Saddle, and at the camping spot beyond Cailor Lake

To climb Pietrosu Peak
If you want to climb Pietrosu Peak (2303m), leave your gear at the lake and walk back up to **Tarniţa La Cruce Saddle**. From here, head north up the blue stripe trail (not the red stripe trail as the Dimap map suggests) to **Buhăescu Mic Peak** (2221m) and then **Buhăescu Mare Peak** (2268m). Descend slightly, then ascend to **Curmătura Pietrosului**; from there bear left (northwest) for the short

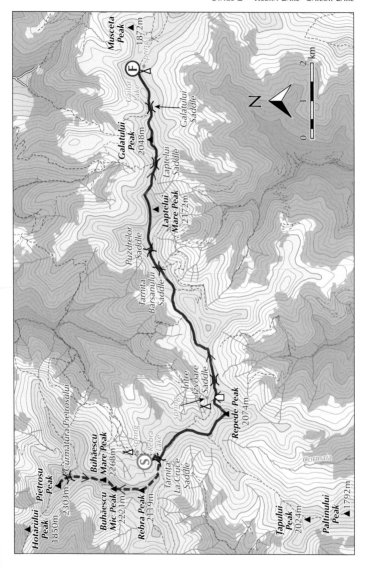

Horses near Cailor Lake

climb to **Pietrosu Peak**. From the summit, retrace your steps back to **Rebra Lake**. Alternatively, from Curmătura Pietrosului you can descend to Borşa in about 4hr, following 'Alternative Stage 1' (above) in reverse. Please note there is no cabana at Pietrosu Peak, which the Dimap map suggests; just a small derelict shelter.

From **Rebra Lake**, walk back up to **Tarniţa La Cruce Saddle**. From the saddle, take the grassy trail that leads southeast up the ridge – not the cart track down south, even though the signpost suggests you should, as it will only take you down into the valley. After 3km of alternate ascending and descending you will reach **Repede Peak** (2074m). From here, take the (initially unmarked) path that swings sharply to the north. This takes you down to **Între Izvoare Saddle**, which is a camping spot as well. There is a refuge just south from here.

Continue down the red stripe trail. From **Tarnita Bârsanului Saddle** the path leads up towards Laptelui Mare Peak through juniper trees; at times the path is barely visible and you will have to climb over the trees. It is also quite poorly marked here, but just keep making your way up. At **Puzdrelor Saddle** just before **Laptelui Mare Peak** (2172m), take the path just to the right of the ridge. This leads to **Laptelui Saddle**. If you squint you'll see a red stripe on a rock at the saddle; from here the path is well-marked again.

After going over **Galatului Peak** and **Galatului Saddle**, the path goes north-east. The camping spot is about 650 metres beyond **Cailor Lake** ('Horse's Lake'; presumably named after the wild horses that live here). Take a grassy trail to the right of the main path to reach it.

Exit route: Cailor Lake–Prislop Pass

From the camping spot just beyond Cailor Lake there's an easy exit route to the monastery at the Prislop Pass. Follow the red stripe trail to **Gărgalău Saddle**, 1km from the camping spot. From here the blue stripe trail takes you northeast to the **Prislop Pass** in about 3hr (8km). (After about 3km there's an option to turn left to visit Cascada Cailor – 'Horse's Waterfall'.) From the monastery at the Prislop Pass you can take a bus or hitchhike back in the direction of Borşa and Sighetu Marmaţiei, or east towards Vatra Dornei and Suceava.

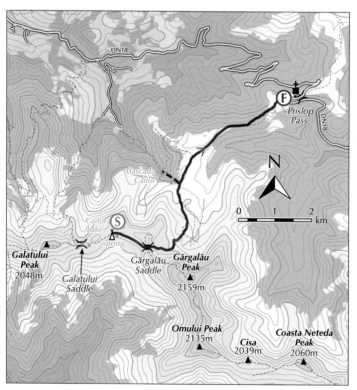

STAGE 3

Cailor Lake–Lala Mica Lake

Start	Camping spot 650 metres beyond Cailor Lake
Finish	Lala Mica Lake
Distance	11.6km
Total ascent	1240m
Total descent	1190m
Grade	Difficult
Time	4hr 30min
Maximum altitude	2279m (Ineu Peak)
Water	Spring at start point; another one at Lala Mica Lake (nothing in between)
Note	Râpa Coasta Netedă is a difficult and potentially dangerous craggy section that involves some scrambling. In bad weather it may be safest to head down into the valley to the right of the trail. This can be done by descending south to reach a path that continues east, parallel to the main route. From there you can walk up to Ineu Peak.

From the camping spot, walk east on the red stripe trail until you reach **Gărgalău Saddle** after almost 2km. From the saddle, take the red stripe trail back up the ridge, south-southeast, and climb steeply to **Gărgalău Peak** (2159m). From here the trail goes south, not east (ie right, not straight ahead). The waymarks have faded on this section, so keep your eyes peeled. After **Omului Peak** (2135m) the ridge swings east again.

Descend over a grassy trail to **Coasta Netedă Peak** (2060m), and then carefully negotiate the craggy **Râpa Coasta Netedă**, using your hands where necessary. It is well marked and about 1.5km long. When you reach **Ineului Saddle** at the end of it, you have two options: you can either leave your pack behind and climb **Ineu Peak** (2279m) then retrace your steps and continue on the trail, or you can climb the peak and then walk down its southern slope to rejoin the trail a little further on. Either way you will reach **Ineuţului Saddle**, where you turn northeast as indicated by a rock marked 'Lala'. Walk down the blue dot trail for about 750 metres to reach the camping spot at **Lala Mica Lake** (1920m).

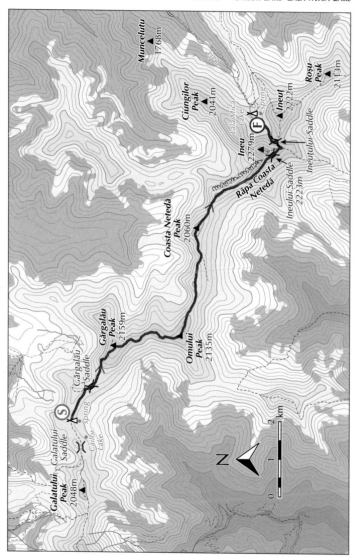

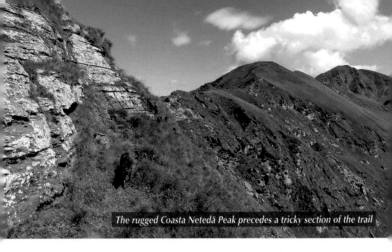

The rugged Coasta Netedă Peak precedes a tricky section of the trail

STAGE 4

Lala Mica Lake–Rotunda Pass

Start	Lala Mica Lake
Finish	Rotunda Pass
Distance	12km
Total ascent	550m
Total descent	1210m
Grade	Moderate-easy
Time	3hr 30min
Maximum altitude	2222m (Ineuţ Peak)
Water	At Lala Mica Lake; several springs after Gajei Saddle

From **Lala Mica Lake** (1920m), walk back up the blue dot trail to reach **Ineuţului Saddle** and the red stripe trail. Turn left (east) to get back up on the ridge. From **Ineuţ Peak** (2222m), make a sharp left (northeast) and descend a rather steep and rocky mountainside. After about 1.5km you will reach Gajei Saddle (1721m); continue on a cart track. From here, the going is easy: just walk down the track until you reach **Rotunda Pass**. There are two cabanas and a camping spot at the pass, but if you want to move on straight away, either walk or hitchhike the 4.5km down to the DN18 road. It's also possible to continue into the Suhard Mountains from here; see Route 5.

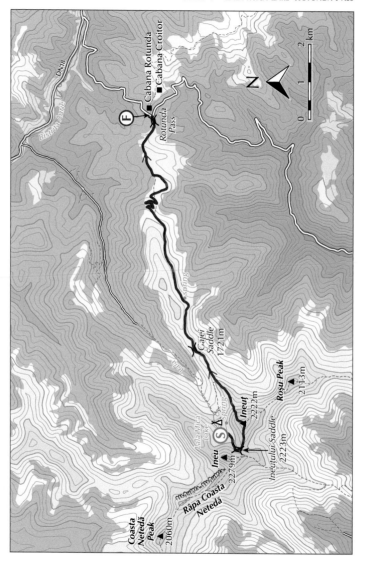

THE GUTÂI AND ŢIBLEŞ MOUNTAINS

ROUTE 2
Breb–Creasta Cocoşului–Neteda Pass

Start	Breb or Bodi Lake
Finish	Neteda Pass
Distance	16km from Breb; 18km from Bodi Lake
Total ascent	1000m from Breb; 865m from Bodi Lake
Total descent	500m from Breb; 225m from Bodi Lake
Grade	Moderate
Time	6hr from Breb; 4hr 30min from Bodi Lake
Maximum altitude	1450m (Creasta Cocoşului)
Maps	Igniş, Pietrii and Gutâi Mountains, 1:50,000, Erfatur-Dimap
Access	For Breb: take a bus from Sighetu Marmaţiei in the direction of Ocna Şugatag. Breb is about 8km south of Ocna. You will be dropped off at the top of the road that leads down into the village; walk past the big white church and follow the wooden signs to the Babou Maramureş campsite. For Bodi Lake: take the no. 8 bus from Baia Mare to Baia Sprie (about 30min); from there it is possible to hitchhike or walk to Bodi Lake. From the Neteda Pass at the end of the walk you can hitchhike the final 8km to the skiing town of Cavnic, from where there are buses to Baia Sprie, Breb and Sighet.
Accommodation	See Appendix B for options in Breb, Cavnic, Baia Sprie and at Bodi Lake.
Water	Plenty of streams crossing the path during the first half of the route; or, if starting from Baia Sprie, fill flasks at Cabana Mogoşa. The last opportunity to fill water bottles is halfway up the slope to the Creasta Cocoşului. After that, no water until the descent towards the Neteda Pass.
Note	The red cross trail is a recently marked trail; at the time of writing, the start of it wasn't included on the 2013 edition of the Dimap map.

Two approaches are offered to the Gutâi Mountains. The first is from the beautiful village of Breb, where people are still largely self-sufficient and continue to choose tradition over the comforts of modern life. As you walk out of the village surrounded by haystacks and apple trees, you will soon see the Creasta Cocoșului ('Cock's Comb') loom large in front of you. This is the massif's most defining feature and makes for some fine scrambling off-route (there are climbing routes as well). The second approach to the Gutâi Mountains and the Creasta Cocoșului is from the town of Baia Sprie, just west of Baia Mare.

Both routes end at the Neteda Pass, although it is also possible to go from Baia Sprie to Breb or vice versa. Both routes offer beautiful views of the western Maramureș Depression.

The routes overlap with the red 'C' mountain-biking route. You can rent mountain bikes at Cabana Mogoșa, or at the other end at the campsite in Breb.

From the Babou Maramureș campsite, follow the blue 'C' marks southwest until you reach a junction after 500 metres. Turn right here; you are now on the red cross trail. You will soon see the Creasta Cocoșului ('Cock's Comb') almost right in front of you. At the next junction, continue south towards Creasta Cocoșului, not to Tăul Morărenilor. When the path forks, keep right (the left path would take you to the village of Budești).

Pass through a clearing, with a valley and a sheepfold to the right. When you get to the woods again, keep left. You will see a map of the Creasta Cocoșului park here. Now follow the red stripe/blue cross marks up to **Creasta Cocoșului** (1450m). You can scramble to the top if you like; there is no trail (although there are many climbing routes). Retrace your steps back down to the path if you do.

The majestic Creasta Cocoșului – 'Cock's Comb' – lives up to its name

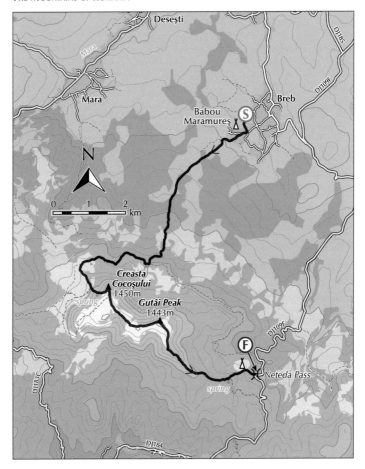

From Creasta Cocoşului the path swings to the right (southeast). Although the red stripe path continues from here, it is no longer marked. You should be able to distinguish, vaguely, three paths; stick to the middle one. At times the path may disappear altogether in the juniper shrubs; just make sure you keep heading east over the ridge towards the Gutâi Peak, which you will be able to see at all times.

After summiting the **Gutâi Peak** (1443m) around 30min later, descend into a forested area. When you get to a clearing, turn left immediately and continue on the red stripe trail, which is now a cart track. Soon you will reach a junction; keep right here. Continue descending towards the Neteda Pass; you should find some water on or next to the path here. You can either camp in the clearing just before the pass or hitchhike the final 8km from **Neteda Pass** to the skiing town of Cavnic.

To continue to the Rodna Mountains
The map suggests there is a red stripe trail from the Neteda Pass east towards the Rodna Mountains; in reality, this trail disappears halfway. If you want to continue to the Rodna Mountains it is best to take a bus to Sighetu Marmaţiei from Cavnic (or try to flag it down from Neteda Pass) and then from there, another bus (or train, but that would take much longer) to Săcel or Dealu Ştefăniţei. See Route 1.

Alternative approach to the Creasta Cocoşului from Baia Sprie
From the centre of Baia Sprie, either walk or hitchhike 5km northeast up the DN18 road until you reach the junction with the DJ183C road that leads to Cabana Mogoşa. From here it's a 3km walk or hitchhike to **Cabana Mogoşa** and **Bodi Lake**.

From the back of the cabana, turn left and walk around the lake. Turn left at the circular orange building, pass underneath the ski lift and cross the picnic area. Follow the red triangle waymark down into the woods. When you get to another ski slope, cross it and keep left; you will see a red 'C' on a tree on your right. At the asphalt road, turn right.

When you meet the DJ183C road, turn right towards Poiana Boului. Very soon you will see a rock marked with a red triangle on your left. Turn left into the woods here; the waymarking suggests you can also keep going up the road, but this will take you off the route. After about 20 metres, keep left; the waymarks aren't always easy to spot.

When you get to a meadow with a clump of trees in the middle after perhaps 10min, cross it to the northeast. Cross the stream and keep heading northeast. Very soon you will meet a cart track; turn right onto it. You are now on the blue stripe trail, and the track gradually ascends to 1200m. When you see a sheepfold to your right and a faded signpost to your left, the blue stripe trail becomes a red stripe trail. Ultimately, the red stripe trail becomes a red cross trail, joined by the red 'C' MTB route. When you get to a junction, turn right up the slope towards **Creasta Cocoşului** (1450m). Follow the red stripe and blue cross waymarks to the foot of the ridge. You can scramble to the top of the ridge (no path/marks) if you like.

From here you can either head for the Neteda Pass, or you can continue to the village of Breb. See description above.

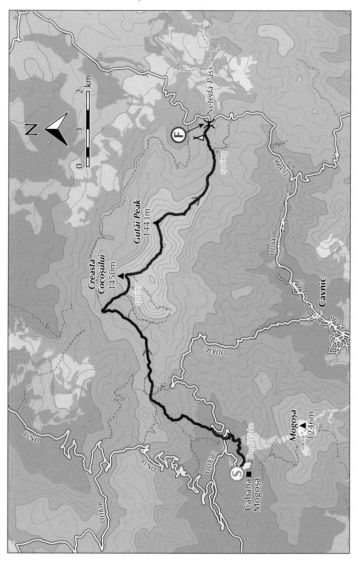

ROUTE 3
Groşii Ţibleşului to Arcer, Ţibleş and Bran Peaks

Start	Pensiunea Schilacy (pension), Groşii Ţibleşului
Finish	Arcer Refuge or Groşii Ţibleşului
Distance	23.5km to Arcer Refuge; another 17km to return to Groşii Ţibleşului
Total ascent	1690m
Total descent	750m
Grade	Difficult
Time	7hr to Arcer Refuge; 40min to descend back to the unpaved road, then another 2–3hr back to Groşii Ţibleşului
Maximum altitude	1840m (Ţibleş Peak)
Maps	Munţii Ţibleş, to be downloaded from http://bit.ly/TiblesMap
Access	Take a minibus from Baia Mare to Groşii Ţibleşului via Târgu Lăpuş. These depart from the parking lot at Strada Mihai Eminescu 20 in Baia Mare, just south of Piaţa Izvoare, and are operated by Versav Trans. There should be one early in the morning and one around noon; it is best to check and ask around the day before your departure. The journey takes around 2hr.
Accommodation	Pensiunea Schilacy in Groşii Ţibleşului and Arcer Refuge (which is fine to use even in a non-emergency). Officially they don't serve meals at Schilacy but they will if you call and order beforehand. (The owners do not speak English, so you may want to ask a Romanian to do this for you.)
Water	Several springs along the approach road; spring on the blue stripe trail between Arcer Refuge and Ţibleş Peak

The remote and little-visited Ţibleş Mountains form a volcanic mountain range that lies to the southeast of the Gutâi Mountains and west of the Rodna Mountains. Its three main peaks, all over 1800m, lie close together; a circuit can be made in one day. However, since this hike requires a long approach walk and an equally long return, it is best to tackle it in two days and spend the night at Arcer Refuge – unless you can find someone to drive you up the forest road for the first 14km and pick you up there at the end of the day. In theory it is possible to cross over into the Rodna Mountains (Route 1) in one long day (about 10 hours' walking); however, at present the route is sparsely marked and there is a large bear population in the forested area in between the two ranges, so under the current circumstances this is not to be advised.

From Pensiunea Schilacy, turn left onto the main road and follow it for 1.3km, then turn right onto an unpaved road, marked blue stripe. Walking past the last scattered houses, dogs and haystacks of Groşii Țibleşului, follow this road east for 12.5km. You'll be walking along the Bradu Stream the entire time; there are several springs and taps alongside the route as you head towards the massif's three main peaks: Țibleş, Arcer and Bran.

At the end of the road, turn right and head up a track. There are various short-cuts to be made, always to the left, but if you want to be sure just keep following the track. After 4km of steady climbing you arrive at a fork: bear left (northeast) on the combined blue stripe and blue circle trail. After another 1.3km and 200m of climbing you'll arrive at **Arcer Refuge** (1450m), where you can leave any surplus luggage behind – you will return here at the end of the day.

From Arcer Refuge head north and up through the forest initially. As the trail swings to the right it becomes rockier and more exposed; you can see the peaks

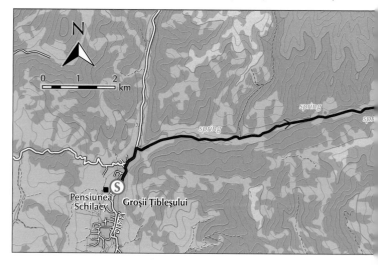

First view of Arcer Peak

ahead of you. Climb to **Arcer Peak** (1829m), gaining almost 400m over a distance of slightly more than a kilometre. From the peak turn right (east) onto the red stripe trail to **Ţibleş Peak** (1840m), which you reach after 1.3km. The slope is strewn with pock-holed rocks. From the monument on the peak, continue southeast to **Bran Peak** (1839m).

To return, retrace your steps towards Arcer Peak, but descend to the left (west) in the saddle 400 metres after Ţibleş Peak. Steeply descend on the blue stripe trail; after 600 metres or so a stream joins the path. After another kilometre you are back at Arcer Refuge. To return to Groşii Ţibleşului from the refuge, retrace your outward route.

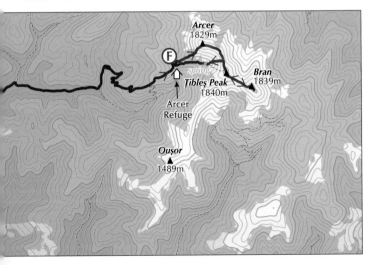

THE MUNŢII MARAMUREŞULUI

ROUTE 4
Repedea to Prislop Pass

Start	Repedea
Finish	Prislop Pass
Distance	88.5km (including 17km by train or railcar)
Total ascent	5270m
Total descent	4600m
Grade	Moderate-difficult
Time	4–5 days
Maximum altitude	1961m (Farcău Peak, Stage 1)
Maps	Either Parcul Natural Munţii Maramureşului/Maramures Mountains Nature Park, 1:50,000 or Maramureşului, 1:65,000, Munţii Noştri. Try to pick up the first one from the national park office in Vişeu de Sus; it is more accurate than the Munţii Noştri one (although it isn't exactly compact).
Note	A compass or GPS is recommended for a navigationally tricky section on Stage 3.

The Munţii Maramureşului, simply meaning 'The Mountains of Maramureş', are Romania's northernmost mountain range and form the natural border with the Ukraine. They are difficult to access and hence few tourists find their way here. Traversing the main ridge makes for a delightful four- or five-day trek from west to east. On the way, you will meet shepherds and blueberry pickers, and cross through tiny villages with hospitable inhabitants, who might well speak Ukrainian rather than Romanian. In terms of technicality this is not a difficult route; the ridge mostly consists of gently undulating grassy slopes with only a few steep ascents and descents – most notably the descent of Pietrosul Bardăului Peak on Stage 3. Be prepared for encounters with livestock guardian dogs – you may want to bring an ultrasonic device to fend them off, as well as trekking poles. (Ultrasonic devices are sold at Liliacul in Sighetu Marmaţiei, Str. Ioan Mihaly de Apsa 15.)

If you'd rather do a shorter trek it is possible to take the narrow-gauge train up the Vaşer Valley from Vişeu de Sus, and either hike westwards to Repedea from Bardău Station (Stages 1–3 in reverse) or eastwards to Prislop Pass (Stage 4). If opting for the latter it is best to take the logging train which departs from Vişeu de Sus as early as 6am and ride on it as far as it goes. Another shorter option would be to hike to the wonderful Vinderel Lake from Repedea (Stage 1) and return the way you came the next day – or continue to Poienile de Sub Munte (see Stage 2) and take the bus back to Sighetu Marmaţiei from there.

Note that Stage 4 begins with a somewhat adventurous journey by train or railcar on a narrow-gauge railway, possibly followed by a further section on foot, in order to reach the described walk start. All in all this is a very Romanian hike!

Access

Take a bus from Sighetu Marmaţiei to Repedea. The journey takes less than 1hr 30min. There are two buses a day in the direction of Poienile de Sub Munte; at 1.15 and 4.45pm (but check schedule at https://autogari.ro for changes). They leave from Autogara Jan, near the train station. This is not the bus station opposite the station; it is about 200 metres further east.

To get away from Prislop Pass at the end of the trek, take a bus west towards Borşa and Sighetu Marmaţiei (around 3.15pm and 9.30pm) or east towards Vatra Dornei (around 8.15am and 3.30pm). Departure times are approximate; buses don't officially stop at Prislop Pass but they will if you flag them down (there's a big parking lot where you can wait).

Camping at Vinderel Lake (Stage 1)

Accommodation, food and facilities

There are two pensions in Repedea, right next door to each other, on the corner of the main DJ187 road and Strada Bisericii, which is also where the blue stripe route starts. The cheapest one is above the corner shop called SC Longa Prod Com SRL (shop open 8am–9pm); otherwise try Laver next door. Vinderel Lake makes for an excellent camping spot; there are springs nearby and you can even go for a swim in the lake. Cabana Coşnea is abandoned; however, you can camp in the yard. There is a grill, a fireplace (with a good supply of wood) and a sheltered picnic table. It's possible to camp in the yard of Canton Silvic Bardău (the foresters' hut at Bardău Station), or if you ask nicely the foresters may even offer you a bed in the hut. Then there's Camping Faina (a camping spot along the narrow-gauge railway, about 6.5km further east from Bardău Station) and Cabana Fântâna Stanchii (camping spot); and at the Prislop Pass there's Cabana Alpina and Cabana Dacilor.

There are several bars and shops but no restaurants in Repedea and Poienile de Sub Munte; at best you can order some *mititei* (garlicky meat rolls) at one of the bars. There is an ATM in Repedea.

STAGE 1

Repedea–Vinderel Lake and Farcău Peak

Start	Strada Bisericii, Repedea
Finish	Vinderel Lake
Distance	13km
Total ascent	1520m
Total descent	350m
Grade	Moderate
Time	5hr
Maximum altitude	1961m (Farcău Peak)
Water	Water from a pipe after about 1.7km from the start; a couple of springs after 8km; more springs at the lake

From the corner shop/pension on the main DJ187 road in Repedea, turn up Strada Bisericii. Walk past the church and the Liceul Tehnologic school (both on the right). You should see blue stripe marks on the concrete electricity poles on the right. After 500 metres, turn right (east) onto a forest road, just before a terracotta plastered house; there is a blue stripe waymark on a pole on the right. The track enters the trees immediately (it is unmarked, but the blue stripe

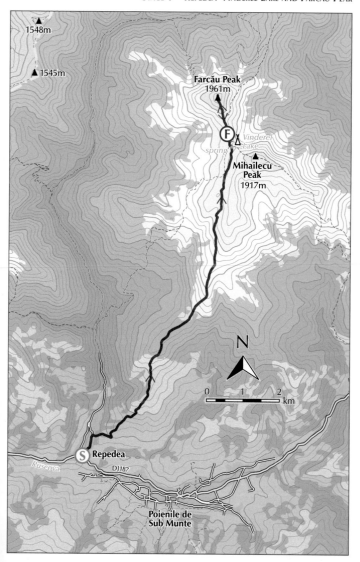

waymarks will reappear after about 1.5km). After 1km, the path forks. Keep right (northeast).

After a further 5km, stay on the blue stripe trail as it departs from the road and goes left (northwest) to bypass a peak. You might well meet some cows here. Keep following this grassy (but marked) trail until you get back on a path. After another 3km the trail becomes grassier and bends to the left again. You should be able to see **Vinderel Lake** after about 1km. Descend to it, pitch your tent at the lake and continue onto the unmarked but easy-to-follow trail to **Farcău Peak** (1961m) and head back again (1hr up, 30min down). (It is possible to continue to Cabana Coşnea on the same day, but camping at the lakeside is highly recommended.)

STAGE 2
Vinderel Lake–Cabana Coşnea

Start	Vinderel Lake
Finish	Cabana Coşnea
Distance	11km
Total ascent	340m
Total descent	1410m
Grade	Moderate
Time	3hr 30min
Maximum altitude	1917m (Mihailecu Peak)
Water	Springs at Vinderel Lake and around Stâna Stânişoara; stream at Cabana Coşnea

Walk along the eastern shore of **Vinderel Lake** and pick up the red stripe trail from here. Turn right (southeast) up the slope towards Mihailecu Peak. There isn't much of a path but you should see the occasional red stripe waymark, and the peak is clearly visible. From **Mihailecu Peak** (1917m), which you should reach in 30–40min, the path goes down a grassy, friendly slope, southeast.

After about 2km the descent becomes slightly more challenging: the path is quite steep and goes through blueberry bushes and clumps of trees. There are waymarks, but since the path isn't exactly obvious it is easy to miss them. Keep right, steering clear of the trees, and keep heading southeast. When you get to a meadow you should see a signpost in the middle of it; cross the meadow to the southwest towards **Stâna Stânişoara** sheepfold. There are several springs and streams here. There is a bit of clambering involved; you will have to cross the bed of a dry stream.

After the sheepfold, the path descends into the forest. After about 3km you will start seeing houses again – these are the outskirts of Poienile de Sub Munte, where many of the villagers are Ukrainian. When you get to the DJ187 road, turn left. After about 500 metres you will come to **Cabana Coşnea** on your right.

Exit route
If you do not intend to make a full traverse of the Munţii Maramureşului, you can exit via the DJ187 road. Either hitchhike or take a bus from Poienile de Sub Munte back to Sighetu Marmaţiei or Vişeu de Sus. The bus journey to Sighet takes 1hr 30min.

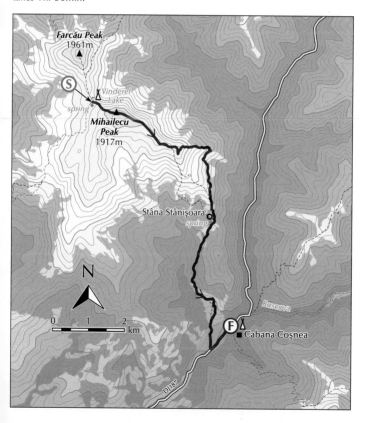

Looking back at Vinderel Lake and Farcău Peak from Mihailecu Peak

STAGE 3

Cabana Coşnea–Bardău CFF Station

Start	Cabana Coşnea
Finish	Bardău CFF Station
Distance	20.5km
Total ascent	1830m
Total descent	1780m
Grade	Difficult
Time	8hr 30min
Maximum altitude	1850m (Pietrosul Bardăului Peak)
Water	Coşnea Stream at the start; several springs cross the path during the first 2km; troughs for cows after 5km; after that, no water until well after the descent of Pietrosul Bardăului Peak.
Note	There may be aggressive dogs at Dosul Bardăului; keep your trekking poles handy.

From the Munţii Maramureşului map board at the bottom of the path leading up to **Cabana Coşnea**, follow the red stripe waymarks southeast along the Coşnea Stream. You will soon leave the Coşnea behind in the valley. After about 4.5km the path forks; keep left (southeast). This section of the path isn't marked. After about 400 metres you will hit the main path again; turn right. You should see a red stripe waymark on your right immediately.

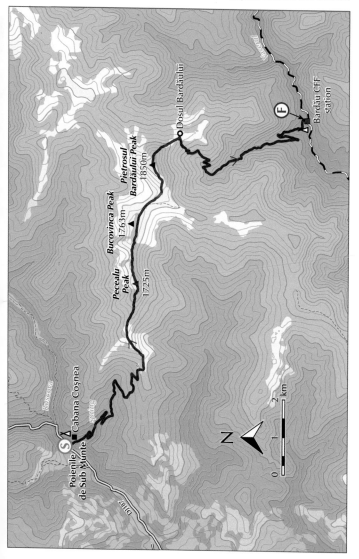

Soon you will come upon a *stâna* (sheepfold) with a herd of cows and several barns. The forest track deteriorates into a narrow trail that takes you northeast up towards Pecealu Peak through juniper trees and blueberry bushes. The path forks almost immediately; turn right (southeast) and reach **Pecealu Peak** (1725m) after 600 metres or so. A grassy marshy clearing marks the start of a tricky section. You will see some old, faded waymarks to the left. Do not follow these; they will only lead you up an unnamed peak and the path disappears eventually. Instead, bear right and follow the new waymarks – you should see a signpost to the right from the clearing. This path allows you to bypass an unnamed peak and **Bucovinca Peak**.

After bypassing Bucovinca Peak you will come to a signpost pointing to Dosul Bardău. The path swings to the south here. Although a waymark suggests you go this way, do not follow this; instead, head up the slope of Pietrosul Bardăului Peak (east). There are signposts on the slope but they are not visible from down below. (It is possible to follow the path south for a bit and then head up left to Pietrosul Bardăului Peak, but this is something of a detour – although you may find a fountain pen here that the author sadly lost!)

On top of **Pietrosul Bardăului Peak** (1850m), which you reach after 1km or so, the marks deteriorate into white squares. Descend the southeastern slope; this is very steep and difficult. The descent goes through juniper and blueberry bushes; the path is marked but the marks are hard to find. Sometimes you will have to go on all fours. Keep heading southeast until you reach another *stâna* (sheepfold) with cows and often ferocious dogs at **Dosul Bardăului** (1534m). There is a well for the cows here, but the water is very murky.

Just before the sheepfold, turn southwest into the forest. The waymarks disappear here; ask the shepherd if you are not sure where to head down (you will have to use Romanian though; saying something along the lines of *Unde este poteca spre halta CFF Bardău?* should help). There is a trail, but it is barely visible and unmarked and soon disappears; you will have to make your way down into the valley with the help of a compass or GPS. Keep heading southwest for about 1km/30min until you can't go any further (the forest becomes too dense and the slope too steep); then head west until you come upon a bigger trail that leads you to the Bardău Stream.

Follow the stream down into the Vașer Valley. You will have to cross the stream almost immediately to stay on the path. You will soon see red stripe waymarks again. After about 1km, the path heads up into the forest, but soon goes down to the stream again. Cross it once more – the stream flows down into the valley and the trail turns into a forest road. When you meet the Bardău again, cross the stream and turn right (southeast). You will soon see and hear the Vașer River roaring in the valley and arrive at **Bardău CFF Station** and foresters' hut.

STAGE 4
Bardău CFF Station–Prislop Pass

Start	Bardău CFF Station
Finish	Prislop Pass (or Cabana Fântâna Stanchii)
Distance	17km from Bardău Station to Catarama halt by train or railcar; 27km from Catarama halt to Prislop Pass on foot
Total ascent	1580m
Total descent	1060m
Grade	Difficult
Time	10–12hr
Maximum altitude	1690m (below Strungi Peak)
Water	No springs, but several rivers and streams along the route

GETTING TO CATARAMA HALT (BY RAIL AND ON FOOT)

This is another long stretch. The best thing to do is make your way north-east up the Vaşer Valley by railcar (*drezina*) or steam train (*mocăniţa*) on the narrow-gauge railway. It makes for a very enjoyable experience. The logging train passes Bardău Station around 8am; best to ask the foresters or rail workers what time the train or railcar is expected to pass by, and what the final station is on that particular day. You could phrase this as follows: *La cât ora vine trenul sau drezina? Până la care haltă merge?* (If you're not doing a full traverse of the Munţii Maramureşului, it is of course also possible to start from Vişeu de Sus CFF Station; in that case the train will leave as early as 6am.) You may have to pay a small charge. You will pass several *pepiniere* (tree nurseries) on the way. Whether you take the train or the *drezina*, there is no guarantee that it will stop at either Valea Babei (after 15km) or the former Catarama halt (after 17km); it may stop earlier or continue further – you're dependent on the foresters' schedule here – so you may have to walk along the railway to the point at which the Catarama River flows into the Vaşer (GPS coordinates: 47.744238, 24.801593), from where this route description starts. Or, if you're very lucky, you may get a ride in a four-wheel drive if one happens to pass by, which is the only other mode of transport here.

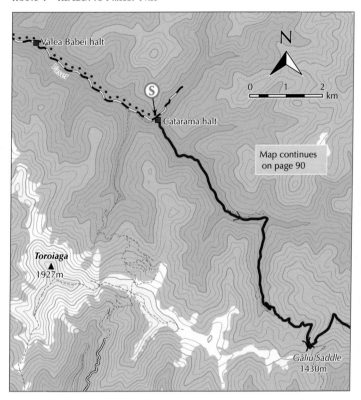

From **Catarama halt**, turn right onto the forest road and ascend along the Catarama River for about 4km. When the road splits into three, take the middle path. This quickly brings you to **Gâliu Saddle** (1430m). You will find a red stripe signpost here; turn left (north) towards Tarniţa Bălăsânii, marked 3hr 30min. After 500 metres the path forks; keep left.

After a further 3km the path leads you through mostly dead forest and over a grassy clearing; the path is unmarked here but marks will reappear as soon as you enter the forest again, although they are sparse and faded initially. You will see one on a tree from the clearing; then soon another one on a tree on the left. Head up this narrow trail (southeast). This trail takes you up to a T-junction; turn right (south). Soon, a stream will cross your path.

Turn left when you see this crucifix

When you see a crucifix on your left and a red stripe waymark on a tree on the right, do not continue down the obvious track. Instead, go up a barely noticeable grassy trail to the left, about 50 metres after the crucifix (the grassy area is about half a metre higher than the forest road); it initially leads south, then east. This grassy section is unmarked; the red stripe waymarks will reappear after about 200 metres. Please note that there are also red stripes without a white background; do not follow these, since these are foresters' marks.

Cross several streams and continue on what's called the 'war path' (Drumul Războiului), where several battles took place during World Wars 1 and 2. To reach the **Tarnița Bălăsânii** saddle (1481m), cross a meadow to the south for the last 500 metres or so; head towards a cross. Cross the road and head up the gravel road (southwest) to reach **Cabana Fântâna Stanchii** (1672m). This is a privately owned cabana and cattle farm (beware of the dogs), but you can camp around here if you want. To continue to the Prislop Pass, continue southeast, descending mostly; the waymarks are red circles initially, but are soon joined by the red stripe. You will reach the **Prislop Pass** (1419m) after about 9km.

Every year, the **Hora de la Prislop festival** is held on the pass; a traditional festival involving lots of music and dancing in traditional attire, as well as plenty of food. There doesn't seem to be an official website, but some googling should help you find the date.

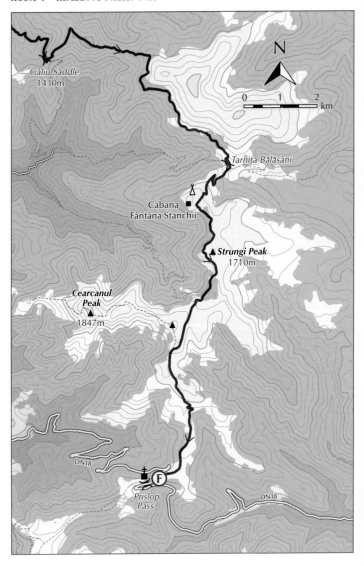

THE EASTERN CARPATHIANS

Looking down towards the Schitul Sfânta Cruce hermitage (Route 5, Stage 1)

The Carpaţii Orientali are a collection of smaller massifs that together separate Moldova in the east from Transylvania and Maramureş in the west. Five of these massifs are presented below.

Three mountain ranges rise up around Vatra Dornei, at the heart of Ţara Dornelor, 'land of the Dorna River': the gentle and pastoral **Suhard** (Route 5) to the northwest, the forested **Rarău-Giumalău** (Route 6) with its white crags to the northeast and the higher, volcanic **Călimani** (Route 7) to the south. The latter boasts a caldera with a diameter of 10km. It is also the site of a (now closed) sulphur mine. North of the Rarău-Giumalău lies the Bucovina, the land of the painted monasteries which were constructed in the 15th and 16th centuries under the patronage of Stephen the Great, voivode of Moldavia, and his successors.

The spa town of Vatra Dornei makes the perfect base: all three ranges can be accessed by simply walking out of town. Vatra Dornei can be reached by bus from Bucharest (9hr 40min) or Braşov (6hr 25min). Buses are operated by Şincarom (www.sincarom.ro – Romanian website). Vatra Dornei has two train stations, the most central being Vatra Dornei Băi; there is a night train from Bucharest and there are direct connections with Cluj, Suceava and Iaşi. The nearest airport is Suceava.

Of all the mountains of Romania, the **Ceahlău** (Route 8) seems to have given birth to the most legends. Panels along the trails enlighten you about the stories that are tied to the many spectacular and bizarrely shaped rock formations. The central Ceahlău is made up of a 500–600m thick layer of conglomerate, with impressively steep drops to many sides. Several rows of limestone cliffs and oddly shaped calcareous rocks give this massif a fantastic aspect. The Ceahlău is a

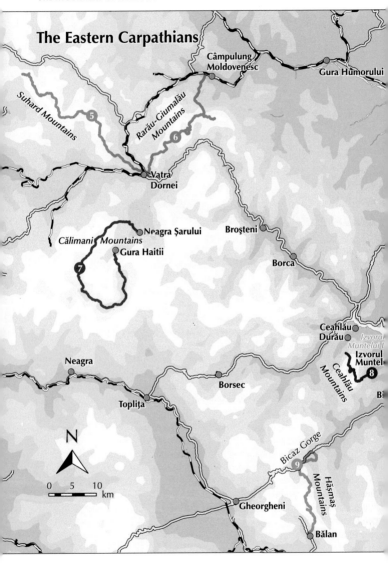

The Eastern Carpathians

Suhard Mountains

Câmpulung Moldovenesc

Gura Humorului

Rarău-Giumalău Mountains

Vatra Dornei

Neagra Şarului

Broşteni

Călimani Mountains

Gura Haitii

Borca

Ceahlău

Durău

Izvoru Muntelui L

Ceahlău Mountains

Izvorul Muntel

Neagra

Borsec

Topliţa

N

0 5 10 km

Bicaz Gorge

Gheorgheni

Hăşmaş Mountains

Bălan

View from Piatra Singuratică towards Hășmașul Mare Peak (Route 9, Stage 2)

well-maintained national park and a popular destination with Romanian mountain lovers. It harbours many protected wildflowers, including the great yellow gentian, globeflower and edelweiss.

The **Hășmaș Massif** (Route 9) is best known for the Bicaz Gorge – a 5km-long gorge with limestone walls rising up as high as 300m on both sides of the road that winds through it. Its accessibility and proximity to Lacu Roșu – a lake created by a landslide in the 19th century – make it a popular tourist resort. However, the Hășmaș has more to offer. Piatra Singuratică ('the lonely rock') offers some fine scrambling and/or climbing; from there a lonely and wild route (Route 9, Stage 2) leads you to Lacu Roșu via Hășmașul Mare Peak (1792m).

The northeast of Romania is difficult to access to say the least; if heading directly to this area, Suceava is the nearest airport. Of the areas dealt with in this chapter only the Călimani and Ceahlău are national parks, which means in these ranges camping is only permitted in designated areas. In the other ranges you are free to pitch your tent anywhere. Finally, a word of warning: if you decide to visit the spa town of Baile Tușnad and the nearby Sfânta Ana Lake, please be aware that there is a large bear population in this area. These bears are familiar with people and even venture into town. Although they don't usually attack people, incidents have occurred in the past, so extreme caution is advised.

THE LAND OF DORNA

ROUTE 5
The Suhard

Start	Vatra Dornei
Finish	Rotunda Pass
Distance	49km
Total ascent	2110m
Total descent	1610m
Grade	Moderate
Time	2–3 days
Maximum altitude	1932m (Omu Peak, Stage 2)
Maps	Țara Dornelor, 1:53,000, Discover Eco-Romania, 2010; or Bazinul Dornelor, 1:80,000, Dorna Ecoturism, 2014. The latter can be acquired from the Salvamont Base in Vatra Dornei, Strada Gării 5. Neither of these maps covers the entire Suhard; the only one that does can be downloaded from www.carpati.org (select 'Ghid', then 'Ghid montan' and 'Suhard', and then 'Hărți' from the right-hand menu).

The little-visited Suhard is a gently undulating and largely forested massif to the southeast of the Rodna Mountains. It makes an excellent connecting walk to the latter but is also worth exploring on its own. Because the terrain is not difficult, you can cover a lot of distance in one day while enjoying the scenery – you can see the Rodna as well as the Călimani and Rarău-Giumalău. You are unlikely to meet other tourists on this trail. A hermitage occupied by a monk offers a welcome rest in between the two stages of this hike. From Cabana Croitor near the end of the route it is possible to cross over into the Rodna Mountains, which are covered in Route 1.

Access
Access to the Suhard is straightforward; it involves simply walking out of the town of Vatra Dornei.

From Rotunda Pass at the end of the trek, walk or hitchhike 4.5km down to the DN18 road and the hamlet of Fluturica, then hitchhike or take a bus eastwards to Vatra Dornei or westwards to Borşa. Eastbound buses should pass around 8.45am and 4pm; westward bound buses around 12.15pm and 2.30pm. They do not officially stop in Fluturica; you can try to flag them down, although hitchhiking is often the best bet – it isn't the easiest place for a bus to stop. Borşa and Vatra Dornei are both a 45min–1hr ride from Fluturica.

Accommodation
Plenty to be found in Vatra Dornei; Serban Cottage is good and affordable. If you prefer camping, try Camping Autoturist. The hermit and his mother at Schitul Sfânta Cruce are not used to taking in visitors, but they will let you pitch your tent. At the end of Stage 2 you can expect a warm welcome at the wonderful Cabana Croitor, or there is also Cabana Rotunda. There is a camping spot just west of the pass too.

STAGE 1
Vatra Dornei–Schitul Sfânta Cruce

Start	Vatra Dornei Băi Station
Finish	Schitul Sfânta Cruce hermitage
Distance	21km
Total ascent	980m
Total descent	470m
Grade	Easy
Time	5hr
Maximum altitude	1571m (near Izvorul Rece)
Water	Springs below Ouşoru Peak, Izvorul Rece and at Schitul Sfânta Cruce (from a tap)

From the railway station in **Vatra Dornei**, walk west on Strada Dornelor for 600 metres, following the blue stripe waymarks. Cross over to the church and climb the steps at the back of it. Cross the road at **Camping Autoturist** and continue climbing the stairs to the AZM building. Continue northeast on Strada Runc. After 100 metres turn left and head north into the forest, which soon opens up again. After a further 800 metres cross a fence and continue west on a forest road. Sadly, much of the waymarking is missing due to deforestation.

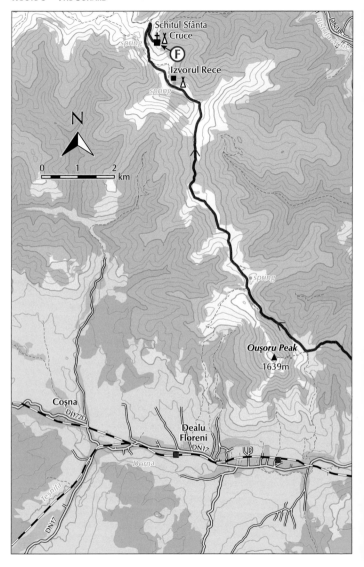

After 4km on the forest road, keep right as another road comes in from the left. After a further 2.5km the blue stripe is joined by the blue cross. The peak with the bald patch ahead of you is **Ouşoru Peak** (1639m); the Dorna Valley is down to the left. At a sheepfold and signpost after another 600 metres turn right (northwest) to stay on the blue stripe trail. There is a **spring** soon after. Follow the fence of the sheepfold northwest into the forest. When you meet another forest road after 2.7km turn right onto it – you can see the Rodna Mountains ahead of you now. After the best part of a kilometre the road forks; turn right, then left at the next fork after 2km.

Continue for 4.4km until you come to a good spring; this is **Izvorul Rece**. It makes a good camping spot if you do not want to continue all the way to Schitul Sfânta Cruce. After 100 metres the trail veers to the left, off the road and uphill – there are waymarks on stones. You can follow the road if you prefer, but it's longer. The trail looks like it is frequented more by wild boar than by humans. After 800 metres you're back on the road. At the signpost, walk down the red circle trail to **Schitul Sfânta Cruce** in 20min.

Although there are various unused buildings on the premises, the hermit and his mother at Schitul Sfânta Cruce are not used to taking in visitors. They will let you pitch your tent – you will want to befriend the dogs first though. If you don't feel comfortable with this, pitch your tent at the last signpost; there is a spring 650 metres down the red circle trail.

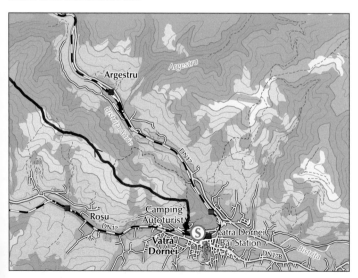

STAGE 2

Schitul Sfânta Cruce–Rotunda Pass

Start	Schitul Sfânta Cruce
Finish	Rotunda Pass
Distance	28km
Total ascent	1130m
Total descent	1140m
Grade	Moderate
Time	9hr
Maximum altitude	1932m (Omu Peak)
Water	At Schitul Sfânta Cruce and Rotunda Pass

This is a long stretch so you will have to rise early. However, once you've descended from Omu Peak the descent to Rotunda Pass is straightforward, over a dirt road.

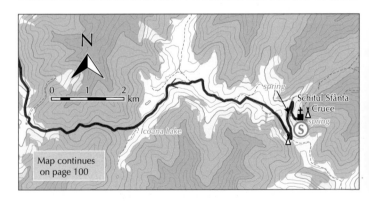

From **Schitul Sfânta Cruce** hermitage, walk back up to the signpost and continue northwest on the blue stripe trail to Omu Peak, signed 5–6hr. After 750 metres the path forks; turn right. At the next fork after 900 metres keep left and head southwest initially, then continue northwest on the white gravel road that joins

Climb towards this rock when you see it to your left

the grassy track you are on. After 1.5km turn left (west-southwest). The next time the path forks, 2km further up, turn right (west) onto a grassy trail into the forest, past the modest **Icoana Lake** – a perfect spot for a break.

Traverse the forest for 1.5km until you come to a deforested area; keep right at an inconspicuous fork, heading west. There is a mark on a fallen tree and a mark on a tree a bit further up. After 2km on a grassy track turn right (north-northeast) onto a gravel road. After 100 metres turn left, up a grassy slope when you see a waymark on a rock. Head northwest towards a large rock with an arrow on it and an old shed next to it.

Continuing on the blue stripe trail, ascend to **Pietrele Roşii Peak** (1772m) which you will reach after 2.8km. Continue northwest towards Omu Peak, descending slightly on a narrow trail lined with dwarf pine. After 1.4km turn left onto a grassy track. When you reach a gravel road after 600 metres turn right, then almost immediately turn left onto a grassy trail to Omu Peak – but first, climb a much peakier, rockier but unnamed summit. From there it's an easy 850-metre walk to **Omu Peak** (1932m).

From the rusty signpost at Omu Peak, descend west on what is presumably the red circle trail – it is unmarked. After 1.3km you reach a gravel road. Don't follow it though; continue west-southwest on the middle path towards the ridge of the Rodna Mountains. The three most prominent peaks you can see are, from left to right, Roşu, Ineuţ and Ineu Peaks. Continue for perhaps 800 metres until you reach a gravel road, which is occasionally marked with a faded red circle or stripe. Continue down the winding road for some 8.5km, cutting corners as you see fit. The charming **Cabana Croitor** is one of the first buildings on the left as you enter the hamlet of Pasul Rotunda (Rotunda Pass); **Cabana Rotunda** is a bit further up to the right.

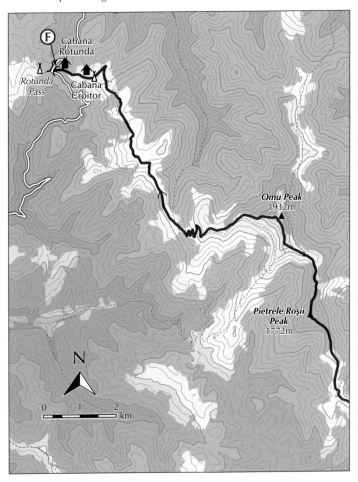

ROUTE 6
The Rarău-Giumalău

Start	Vatra Dornei
Finish	Câmpulung Moldovenesc
Distance	46.5km
Total ascent	1885m
Total descent	1975m
Grade	Easy-moderate
Time	3 days
Maximum altitude	1857m (Giumalău Peak, Stage 1)
Maps	Giumalău, Rarău, Tarnița, 1:60,000, Munții Noștri, or Rarău-Giumalău Mountains and Bucovina Monasteries, 1:70,000, Erfatur-Dimap

One of the perks of the Rarău-Giumalău is that, like the Suhard, they can be accessed straight from the town of Vatra Dornei. To the north they are bordered by the historical region of Bucovina, famous for its painted monasteries. A three-day trek in these mountains can be easily combined with a visit to one or more of these monasteries. Humor and Voroneț are among the most famous ones. Crossing the Rarău-Giumalău isn't difficult; the trail mostly goes over cart tracks, through forests and grassy slopes. The only major ascent is to Giumalău Peak (1857m); a stay at Cabana Giumalău is very rewarding. Rarău Peak itself is uninteresting, but the nearby Pietrele Doamnei ('ladies' rocks') more than make up for this. Descending to the town of Câmpulung Moldovenesc, through flowery meadows and past sheepfolds, is wonderful and gives a good idea of how harmoniously nature and culture intermingle in this part of Romania.

Access
The Rarău-Giumalău can be accessed straight from the town of Vatra Dornei. At the end of the trek you can return to Vatra Dornei from Câmpulung Moldovenesc by train or bus (30min–1hr), or take a bus westwards towards Borșa (3hr).

Accommodation
There are plenty of hotels and pensions to be found in both Vatra Dornei and Câmpulung Moldovenesc. En route, there's Cabana Giumalău on Stage 1, and Cabana Rarău (very expensive) and the camping spot at Salvamont Rarău on Stage 2.

STAGE 1
Vatra Dornei–Cabana Giumalău

Start	Vatra Dornei Băi Station
Finish	Cabana Giumalău
Distance	20.5km
Total ascent	1255m
Total descent	495m
Grade	Moderate
Time	5hr
Maximum altitude	1857m (Giumalău Peak)
Water	Spring at Cabana Giumalău

From the railway station in **Vatra Dornei**, walk northeast to the end of the platform and cross the tracks towards Kaufland. Turn left onto Strada 22 Decembrie, then right onto Strada Schitului and follow the red cross marks. After 200 metres cross a footbridge over the Bistriţa Aurie River. Turn right, then left onto Strada Bârnărel. After 200 metres keep left. Walk to the end of the now unpaved street, then head towards a green electricity pylon with a red cross mark on it, and continue on a well-marked dirt road through fields and forests.

The trail follows a wide cart track most of the time

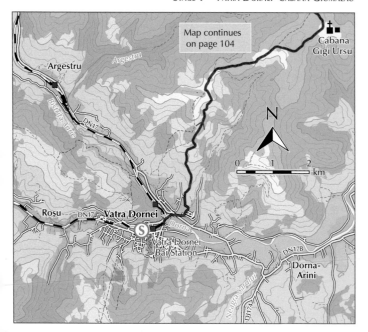

Map continues
on page 104

When the path forks after about 3.5km, keep right. At the crossroads 500 metres further up, keep going straight ahead. After a further 2km the road forks again at a picnic bench with a sign that says 'Loc de odihna şi fumat' ('Place for resting and smoking'). Continue straight ahead for Cabana Gigi Ursu on what is now the blue stripe route. After 1.5km you'll reach the privately owned **Cabana Gigi Ursu** and a small hermitage.

Continue northwest for 1.8km until you come to a signpost. Turn right onto the red stripe route for Cabana Giumalău. After 3.8km the landscape opens up as you leave the forest behind. The trail is now marked with bus stop-type signs and you begin to gently ascend. After 1km or so you reach another signpost, pointing ahead to Giumalău Peak and right to Cabana Giumalău. Continue for another 500 metres to reach the actual fork to which the signpost relates. You can leave your pack behind here as you climb to **Giumalău Peak** (1857m). To reach the peak, either follow the narrow trail to the left or continue on the track; then retrace your steps to the southwest and turn left at the fork to reach the wonderful **Cabana Giumalău** (1641m) in 20min via the yellow stripe trail.

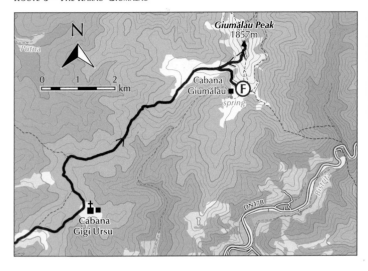

STAGE 2

Cabana Giumalău–Salvamont Rarău

Start	Cabana Giumalău
Finish	Salvamont Rarău
Distance	11km
Total ascent	400m
Total descent	445m
Grade	Easy
Time	3hr
Maximum altitude	1663m (shortly after Cabana Giumalău)
Water	Springs at Cabana Giumalău and Salvamont Rarău. Several springs in between.

This easy walk bridges the gap between the Giumalău and Rarău Peaks. The Rarău Peak itself is uninteresting, but the Pietrele Doamnei ('ladies' rocks') more than make up for it.

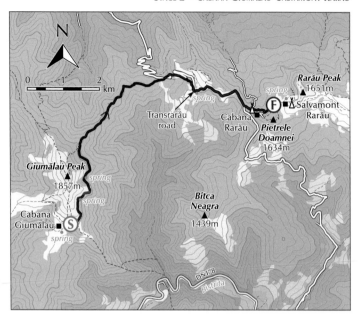

From **Cabana Giumalău**, head east up the red cross trail which contours the eastern flank of the Giumalău Peak. At the signpost after 350 metres, turn left towards Polița Caprelor and Cabana Rarău. The Bistrița Valley can be seen to the right. At the signpost 3km further up, turn right onto the red stripe trail towards Cabana Rarău. After a further 2km you come to a clearing from where you can see the Pietrele Doamnei rocks and the Transrarău road. The path swings to the right and becomes a dirt road.

After 1km you reach the Transrarău; cross it, cut off a hairpin, cross again and walk on the right side of the road until you reach the next hairpin. Then turn right into the forest. Cross a stream and continue southeast for 400 metres. Cross the road at the signpost and walk along the road until it forks after almost 2km. Turn left and walk past the camping spot (unless you want to camp here).

After 500 metres you have the option to turn right to the expensive **Cabana Rarău** (a hotel really) or turn left to the Salvamont base, which is a 15min walk from here. You can't stay in the **Salvamont building** but there is a camping spot next to it and a spring just north of it; follow the orange dots on trees and rocks to find it. The Rarău Peak (1651m) itself can be reached by following the gravel road for 1km or so but is not really worth seeing.

Excursion: Pietrele Doamnei circuit (1.8km, 170m ascent/descent, 1hr)
To climb to Pietrele Doamnei, retrace your steps towards Cabana Rarău for 200 metres then turn left onto the yellow and red triangle trail, which runs parallel to the road. Follow it southwest to Cabana Rarău for 300 metres, then turn left (southeast) onto the blue cross trail. After 1.2km from the start, scramble up to the plateau from which the Doamnei rocks protrude (signed Platou Belvedere), which you will quickly reach, then descend back down and continue on the blue cross until you're back at the start.

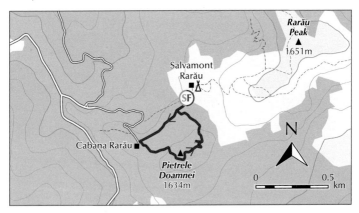

STAGE 3
Salvamont Rarău–Câmpulung Moldovenesc

Start	Salvamont Rarău
Finish	Câmpulung Moldovenesc
Distance	15km
Total ascent	230m
Total descent	1035m
Grade	Easy
Time	3hr 30min
Maximum altitude	1532m (Salvamont Rarău)
Water	Spring north of Salvamont Rarău; another 500 metres off the Transrarău road

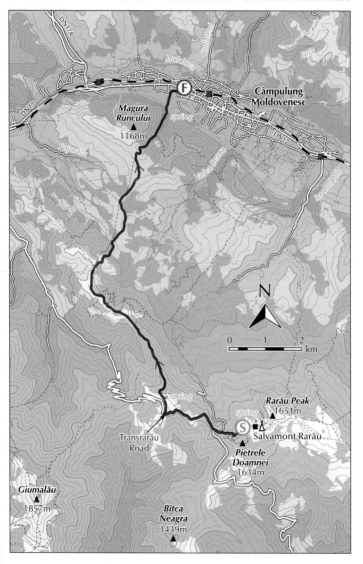

From **Salvamont Rarău**, walk back down the Transrarău road for 3km, then turn right (north) onto the blue stripe gravel road to Câmpulung. There is a spring after 500 metres. The gravel road deteriorates into a narrow trail and passes through trees and fields.

After 4km, after a *stâna* (sheepfold), you meet the gravel road again. Walk past another sheepfold and head north towards the next one. After 500 metres there is a signpost up a tree. Turn right to stay on the blue stripe route.

When you come to a meadow after 1km, stay to the left and pass through the fence of another sheepfold. Continue north-northeast through gloriously flowery fields for about 3km until you meet another gravel road. Descend into **Câmpulung Moldovenesc** alongside the Mesteacănul Stream, reaching the main road after about 2km.

Floral beauty in October

ROUTE 7
The Călimani

Start	Gura Haitii
Finish	Neagra Şarului
Distance	51.5km
Total ascent	2350m
Total descent	2365m
Grade	Easy-moderate
Time	3 days
Maximum altitude	2100m (Pietrosul Peak, Stage 2)
Maps	Călimani, 1:70,000, Munţii Noştri, or Căliman Mountains, 1:60,000, Dimap

The volcanic Călimani Mountains are situated to the southeast of the town of Vatra Dornei. They are perhaps best known for the 12 Apostles Reserve: a group of volcanic rock formations, some of which have anthropomorphic shapes, huddling together below the massif's highest peaks. As with the Suhard and Rarău-Giumalău, it is possible to walk out of town to access these mountains, but this would require a rather long approach walk, adding an extra day to the itinerary described below. Instead, it is best to take a bus to the village of Gura Haitii and start from there.

A remarkable feature of the Călimani is its caldera with a diameter of 10km, which is also the site of a former sulphur mine. Another interesting aspect of these mountains is the ancient Via Maria Theresia road which runs right through them; info panels along the way tell the history of the 18th-century Habsburg Empress, and that of the 19th-century Emperor Franz Joseph, giving insight into the history of the Austro-Hungarian Empire and Romania's role in it.

The terrain varies wildly; from semi-deforested areas and paths overgrown with dwarf pine that are a little challenging to navigate through, to the pastoral meadows below Tămău Peak (1862m). The most challenging section is around the two highest peaks which can be seen from afar: Negoiu Unguresc Peak (2081m) and Pietrosul Peak (2100m), characterised by scree slopes and schist. The Călimani is a national park; camping is only allowed in designated areas.

Access
Take a Şincarom bus from Vatra Dornei to Gura Haitii. There are five buses a day, departing from the Kaufland parking lot.

The blue circle trail starts about 1km before the end of the 174F road in Gura Haitii, despite what the Eco-Romania map on the info panel at the end of the road suggests – so ask the bus driver to drop you off a little earlier.

There is a small entrance fee for entering the Călimani National Park, to be paid at the visitor centre in the nearby village of Saru Dornei or to the park rangers. In practice the first is off route and you may not encounter the latter; you can also pay at the bar/shop of Pensiunea Perla Călimanilor in Gura Haitii, at the start of the blue cross and blue circle trail to 12 Apostoli – if it's open, that is.

The bus leaves Neagra Şarului at the end of the trek from the town hall, just to the right of where you meet the road. Very occasionally, there is a bus from Şărişor to Vatra Dornei too, allowing you to miss the final 4km – check https://autogari.ro to see if you're in luck, or ask the locals.

Accommodation
Pensiunea Poarta Călimanilor and Pensiunea Perla Călimanilor in Gura Haitii; the meteo station at Reţiţiş Peak offers beds (with use of the kitchen) as does the adjacent Cabana Roza Vânturilor, where you can also pitch your tent. The latter is not open year-round; in both cases you will have to make a reservation. There is a camping spot near Negoiu Saddle as well as a refuge, one out of four that were built in 2018 – the other three are not en route. Camping at Poiana Pietrele Roşii. There is one pension in Neagra Şarului, called Pensiunea Off Road Călimani.

Sunny morning at Poiana Pietrele Roşii (Stage 2)

STAGE 1

Gura Haitii–Rețițiş Peak

Start	Blue circle trail head, Gura Haitii
Finish	Rețițiş Peak
Distance	17.5km
Total ascent	1390m
Total descent	380m
Grade	Moderate
Time	5hr 20min
Maximum altitude	2032m (Iezerul Călimanului Peak)
Water	Bring plenty of water with you on this stage. The only reliable water source is at Iezer Lake, which is a 45min descent from Rețițiş Peak towards Toplița. The tap water at the meteo station isn't drinkable but you could filter it. If you're lucky there'll be a bucket of fresh water there which you may be able to take some from.

From **Gura Haitii**, head southeast up a dirt road marked with a blue circle. When it forks after 1.5km, keep left. After 300 metres the trail inconspicuously veers to the right (south) and becomes a grassy trail. After 700 metres you are back on a dirt road. The terrain becomes grassier; parts of the main ridge can be seen to the right.

When you see an arrow on a tree after just over 1km, turn left (south, about 160°) and head up a grassy slope. There are few marks here due to deforestation. After about 170 metres you should find a clear and marked trail into the forest. After a further 1km you arrive at a grassy plateau with juniper, dwarf pine and spruce. Cross it to the left of the rocky outcrop you see at the far end.

Continue past **Călimanul Cerbului Peak** (2013m), after which you will have beautiful views of the main ridge to the right. Cross the plateau to the southeast. When you come to a signpost, continue on the combined red circle and red stripe trail towards Pietrosul Peak. The trail is marked with black and white poles that are quite far apart – there are a few faded waymarks on rocks. From here you will have a pretty good view of the huge caldera and former sulphur mine as well.

You'll reach **Iezerul Călimanului Peak** (2032m) after 3km of very gentle ascending. Then descend to 1800m over the next 2km, and continue for a further 3km through tall grass and shrubs to reach a gravel road. Turn right onto it; look out for an arrow on a rock after 1.4km and turn right up a narrow trail through dwarf pine until you reach **Rețițiş Peak** (2021m) and the meteo station.

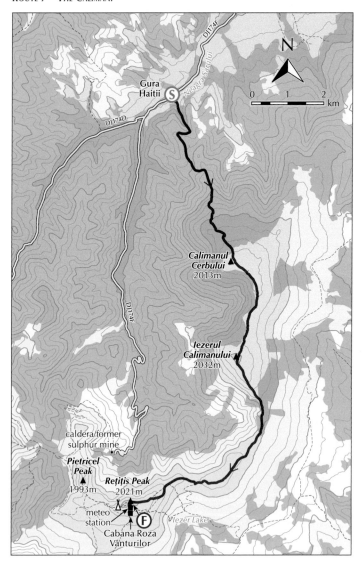

STAGE 2
Reţiţiş Peak–Poiana Pietrele Roşii

Start	Reţiţiş Peak
Finish	Poiana Pietrele Roşii
Distance	18km
Total ascent	710m
Total descent	1075m
Grade	Moderate
Time	5hr 15min
Maximum altitude	2100m (Pietrosul Peak)
Water	Springs at Poiana Izvoarele and Poiana Pietrele Roşii; several springs in between

From the meteo station at **Reţiţiş Peak**, head southwest, following the ubiquitous poles down to a gravel road. You are now on the Via Maria Theresia.

> The **Via Maria Theresia**, named after 18th-century Habsburg Empress, was built hundreds of years ago. Initially it served to supply the Austro-Hungarian frontier guards with food and ammunition. It has now been turned into a thematic path.

After 900 metres you come to a crossroads; head down westwards on the red stripe trail, off the road. After 1km you are back on the gravel road; after a further 700 metres follow the trail as it bends to the left (northwest), off the road again. Continue for 1km to reach **Negoiu Saddle**; there is a camping spot here and a refuge 20min down the blue cross trail to the left.

Climbing Negoiu Unguresc Peak

ROUTE 7 – THE CĂLIMANI

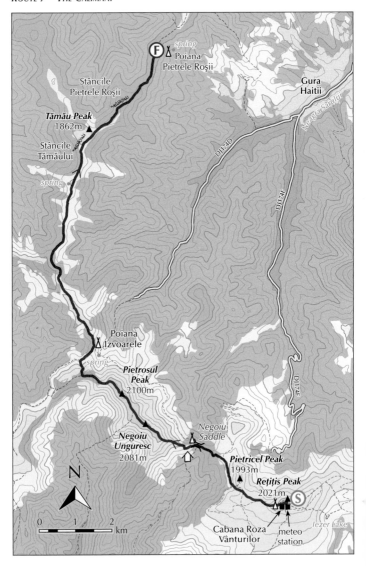

114

From the saddle, continue ahead on the red stripe trail and climb to **Negoiu Unguresc Peak** (2081m) over a slope covered in schist. You will reach the first – nameless – peak after 1.3km; the Negoiu is 400 metres further up. (Confusingly, on some maps they both carry the same name.) Looking back, you can now see another quarry.

Continue over the ridge for 1.7km to reach **Pietrosul Peak** (2100m). There is some scree but the terrain is mostly grassy. Some of the rocks on the trail have perfect round holes in them; they look man-made but are in fact created by round shells that have dissolved. Descend for 1km to reach a signpost and turn right onto the red cross trail towards Gura Haitii. After 30min you reach the camping spot at **Poiana Izvoarele**. The spring is 5min down the red circle and cross trail.

From the camping spot, continue northwest on the red circle trail and climb to an unnamed peak (1830m). Meadows and trees alternate but the terrain remains fairly open and calls for little ascending and descending. After 5km the first rock formation comes into view: **Stâncile Tămăului**. The path becomes rockier too as you pass below **Tămău Peak** (1862m).

After a further 1.6km you pass by the group of rock pillars called **Stâncile Pietrele Roşii**, and 1km later you reach the meadow named after it. Cross it to the northeast, past the blue cross exit to Dornişoara and the sheepfold – although outside of summer, when there is no flock here, this makes the perfect camping spot because of the splendid views. The official camping spot is just 800 metres further up at **Poiana Pietrele Roşii**; the spring is 50 metres down to the right.

STAGE 3
Poiana Pietrele Roşii–Neagra Şarului

Start	Poiana Pietrele Roşii
Finish	DJ174F road, Neagra Şarului
Distance	16km
Total ascent	250m
Total descent	910m
Grade	Easy
Time	3hr 30min
Maximum altitude	1771m (12 Apostles Reserve)
Water	Springs at Poiana Pietrele Roşii and Poiana Apa Rece, and after Stâncile lui Lucaciu

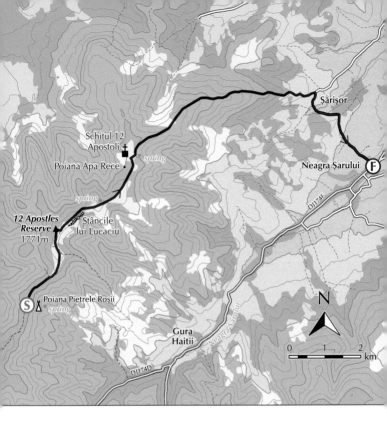

From the camping spot at **Poiana Pietrele Roșii**, continue northeast on the red circle trail. After 1.9km the blue circle descends to the right; this is an exit route to Gura Haitii. Continue ahead on the red circle to the **12 Apostles Reserve**. After 350 metres you are greeted by the first of them (although there are definitely more than 12 sculptures and they don't all look human): the Marshall. The trail actually passes over and through some of the rock sculptures, and some can be climbed fairly easily. After you've passed through a gate-like structure, turn right and walk down the blue circle trail for about 150 metres, then turn left onto the combined red and blue circle.

After 1km you'll pass stone pillars much like the ones at Pietrele Roșii; these are called **Stâncile lui Lucaciu**. After a further 800 metres you'll reach a point where there's a spring about 150 metres down an unmarked trail to the left. From here, continue for 1.5km over an easy and almost level path until you arrive at the signpost in **Poiana Apa Rece** meadow. There is a small hermitage, **Schitul 12 Apostoli**, just down to the left. To continue, turn right (east), down the red circle trail towards Neagra Șarului. After 200 metres turn left at the **spring** and continue on the blue triangle trail for Șărișor.

According to the signpost the red circle trail to Neagra Șarului is closed due to fallen trees. Of course, this situation may change over time but the blue triangle trail is the safer option. Please note that there is another blue triangle trail departing from Poiana Apa Rece; this leads to Vatra Dornei. The signpost to Șărișor deceptively points north whereas you'll want to head northeast.

After 3.3km of descending, the forest road forks; keep right. After a further 1.3km the road forks again; there is an arrow on a tree. Climb over the fence and continue on the narrow, unkempt path to the right of the road. Cross another fence after 500 metres. After that you're on a gravel road. You are now in **Șărișor**. When you meet the asphalt road after 1km, turn right and walk down the road for 3km until you reach the DJ174F road in **Neagra Șarului**.

12 Apostles Reserve, with the distinctive Marshall in the foreground

117

THE CEAHLĂU

ROUTE 8
Izvorul Muntelui to Durău

Start	Izvorul Muntelui
Finish	Durău
Distance	22.4km
Total ascent	1575m
Total descent	1615m
Grade	Moderate
Time	3 days
Maximum altitude	1900m (Toaca Peak, Stage 1 extension)
Maps	One of these three: Munţii Ceahlău, 1:50,000, Bel Alpin; Ceahlău Massif, 1:50,000, Dimap; Ceahlău Mountains, 1:50,000, Munţii Noştri

The 25m-high Duruitoarea Waterfall near Durău (Stage 2)

The Ceahlău Mountains are an absolute delight to explore. Compact and moderate in altitude, they can be tackled in two days, although the itinerary below presents a three-day trek to do justice to all its beautiful rock formations, such as Clăile lui Miron; two tall haystack-shaped rocks surrounded with myth. Cabana Dochia is one of the best huts in the country; it serves excellent food, including homemade jam and bread. From its terrace you have memorable views over the 30km-long Izvorul Muntelui Lake. Toaca Peak (1900m), with its iconic staircase, is only about 30min away. The descent to Durău leads past the beautiful Duruitoarea Waterfall.

Access

The Ceahlău is best accessed from the south. Take a bus from Braşov to Bicaz (5hr 30min–6hr 30min) and from there a taxi to Cabana Izvorul Muntelui (14km). The Ceahlău can be tackled as an extension of the Hăşmaş (see Route 9); in that case, take a bus from Lacu Roşu. Many people start in Durău, but if you don't have a car it is particularly hard to reach because the only bus comes from faraway Iaşi.

At the end of the trek, buses from Durău to Iaşi depart at 4.30am, 10.15am, 1.15pm and 6.45pm. Duration: 4hr. However, Iaşi is not a particularly useful destination – it's in Romania's 'far east' – hence it's more practical to hitchhike from Durău to the DN15. From there it's possible to hitchhike onwards, northeast, to Vatra Dornei. This should take no more than 2hr.

Don't forget to buy a ticket to access the park before you walk through the gate at the start. It's definitely worth stopping by the very informative visitor centre. If you plan to include the excursion to Ocolaşul Mare Peak, you will need to ask for permission from the park staff since this is not a marked trail, and ideally, find a local (guide) to accompany you.

Accommodation

Cabana Izvorul Muntelui; Cabana Dochia; plenty of pensions and hotels in Durău.

STAGE 1

Cabana Izvorul Muntelui–Cabana Dochia

Start	Cabana Izvorul Muntelui
Finish	Cabana Dochia
Distance	6.8km
Total ascent	1000m
Total descent	105m
Grade	Moderate
Time	2hr 40min
Maximum altitude	1750m (Cabana Dochia)
Water	Springs after 2km, at Poiana Maicilor, at the meadow below Ocolaşul Mare, and at Cabana Dochia

Three trails to Cabana Dochia depart from the park gate at **Cabana Izvorul Muntelui**; follow the red stripe waymarks. This trail veers off the road to the right after 130 metres, and cuts off sections of the road several times. Cross the Maicilor

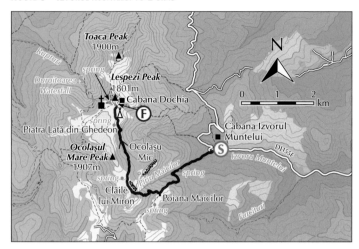

Stream twice. After just under 3km you will reach **Poiana Maicilor**. Continue west and up on the combined red stripe and blue cross trail. You can see the sheer rock wall and spires of Ocolaşul Mic shimmering through the trees now. Another 1km of ascending brings you to **Clăile lui Miron**; two tall haystack-shaped rocks surrounded with myth.

> **Legend** has it that a shepherd called Miron played his flute so mesmerisingly here that everyone flocked to him; birds, animals and rocks alike. It is said his flute can still be heard when the wind blows through the haystacks.

Immediately after Clăile lui Miron, turn left to arrive at a meadow after 500 metres. To the left are **Ocolaşul Mare Peak** (1907m) and various impressive rock formations, the most striking of which is Coloana Dorică. You can admire these from a closer range on Stage 2, below. Cross the Ocolaşul Mic Plateau to the north; you can see the 30km-long Izvorul Muntelui Lake to the right.

Traverse the forest for about 2km, then climb the steep rocks of **Piatra Lată din Ghedeon**. Cross the camping meadow and continue for 400 metres to reach **Cabana Dochia** (1750m), where often you will find yourself above a tapestry of clouds rising from the lake. Clouds or not, the views are stunning and the cabana itself is well provided: there is electricity, a reception, the dorms are spacious, there are indoor toilets and the homemade bread and jam are excellent, as is the rest of the food.

Extension: Cabana Dochia–Toaca Peak and back

From Cabana Dochia you can reach the iconic Toaca Peak (1900m) in 30min or so. A 500-step staircase leads up to the peak, but it can also be reached via a trail. From the cabana, simply walk north on the red stripe trail past the barely noticeable Lespezi Peak – there are several parallel trails, all running south–north – and return the way you came.

Toaca Peak is named after the semantron which monks used to strike on the peak to announce the time of prayer – semantron in Romanian being *toacă*. A small hermitage can still be found just west of Cabana Dochia.

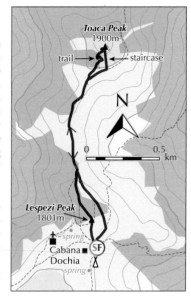

EXCURSION

Cabana Dochia–Ocolașul Mare Peak–La Pălărie–Cabana Dochia

Start/finish	Cabana Dochia
Distance	7km
Total ascent/descent	400m
Grade	Moderate
Time	2hr 30min
Maximum altitude	1890m (just below Ocolașul Mare Peak)
Water	At Cabana Dochia
Note	If you plan to do this walk you will need to have permission from the park staff, since this is not a marked trail; see www.ceahlaupark.ro (English-language option available) for contact details. Ideally, find a local (guide) to accompany you.

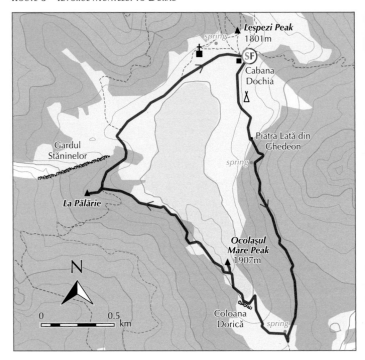

From **Cabana Dochia** walk south on the red stripe trail until you arrive at the Ocolaşul Mic Plateau again. From the picnic table and spring, head west up an unmarked trail towards **Coloana Dorică**. You will also find the Masa Dacică (Dacian Table) here, as well as various other wondrously shaped rock formations.

Continue north to **Ocolaşul Mare Peak** (1907m); there is no trail up this steep side but you can clamber up as far as you feel comfortable with, and take a peek into the deep cave hidden in its innards. Return to the trail and continue northwest alongside the steep rock wall of Ocolaşul Mare; many edelweiss (*flori de colt*) grow here undisturbed.

After 1.2km you reach the junction with the blue stripe route; follow the short trail to the left to **La Pălărie** ('the hat') for the best views of Gardul Stăninelor – a rock wall that looks like a fence because of its pattern of lines. Then return and continue north on the blue stripe trail back to **Cabana Dochia**, reached in about 45min.

STAGE 2
Cabana Dochia–Durău

Start	Cabana Dochia
Finish	Salvamont base, Durău
Distance	7.8km
Total ascent	175m
Total descent	1110m
Grade	Moderate
Time	2hr 30min
Maximum altitude	1781m (near Piatra Lăcrămată)
Water	At Cabana Dochia

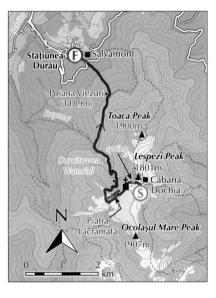

From **Cabana Dochia**, head southwest on the red cross trail. There is a parallel trail past the little **monastery** if you'd like to visit it. Walk past **Piatra Lăcrămată** ('the weeping stone'), then turn right (northwest) to Durău to stay on the red cross trail. After 700 metres of descending you'll arrive at **Polița cu Ariniș** (1622m).

Descend a potentially very slippery trail for 1.5km, then cross a stream to arrive at **Duruitoarea Waterfall**. Turn right, then after 350 metres keep right to stay on the red cross trail. The trail goes up and down through the forest for 1.5km. At **Poiana Viezuri** (1189m), keep left and descend to a road in 25min. Cross it and continue until you reach the visitor centre and the Salvamont base in **Durău**. The best way to leave Durău is by hitchhiking to the DN15 and onward from there, since the only buses are to the somewhat remote Iași.

THE HĂŞMAŞ MASSIF AND LACU ROŞU

ROUTE 9
Bălan to Lacu Roşu

Start	Bălan
Finish	Lacu Roşu
Distance	34km
Total ascent	1680m
Total descent	1530m
Grade	Easy-moderate
Time	3 days
Maximum altitude	1792m (Hăşmaşul Mare Peak, Stage 2)
Maps	Giurgeu and Hăşmaş Mountains, 1:60,000, Dimap; Zona Lacul Roşu şi Cheile Bicazului, 1:15,000, Dimap for a more detailed overview of Lacu Roşu (but not absolutely necessary)

The Hăşmaş Massif is best known for what is perhaps Romania's most famous gorge: the 5km Bicaz Gorge with steep 300m-high walls, situated just north of Lacu Roşu ('the red lake'), a natural dam lake that was created by a landslide in the 19th century. A national road runs through the gorge, making this area very accessible to tourists and rather busy during the summer months. This route combines these famous spots with a trek through the remoter parts of the massif, including Piatra Singuratică ('the lonely rock'), popular with Romanian climbers but also accessible to walkers, and Hăşmaşul Mare Peak (1792m), as well as the lesser-known Bicăjel Gorge. It is possible to just visit the gorges or only hike to Piatra Singuratică and back.

Access
Take a bus from Braşov to Miercurea Ciuc (1hr 45min). They leave at 8am, 11.30am and 5.15pm from Autogara 1, next to the main station. In Miercurea Ciuc, change to a bus to Bălan (1hr 10min) – there are 10 of these daily. Alternatively, take the aforementioned bus from Braşov (in the direction of Gheorgheni) but stay on it for about 30min longer and get off in Sândominic (not an official stop – ask the driver to drop you off there). From there, hitchhike the final 11km to Bălan.

From Lacu Roşu at the end of the trek, if you'd like to continue into the Ceahlău (Route 8), take a bus north to Bicaz (20min–1hr) – see https://autogari.ro for the schedule. Enter Braşov as a departure point to see which northbound buses pass through Lacu Roşu towards Bicaz. Otherwise, take the bus south from Lacu Roşu to Braşov – in that case enter Bicaz as a departure point to get an overview of all southbound buses.

Accommodation

Cabana Piatra Singuratică (self-catered); plenty of pensions and hotels in Lacu Roşu. It's possible to pitch a tent at Cabana Piatra Singuratică, but don't store food in it – this is bear territory.

STAGE 1

Bălan–Piatra Singuratică

Start	Bălan church
Finish	Cabana Piatra Singuratică
Distance	4km
Total ascent	620m to the cabana; another 80m up Piatra Singuratică
Total descent	Negligible
Grade	Easy (with optional difficult climb of Piatra Singuratică)
Time	1hr 30min
Maximum altitude	1587m (Cabana Piatra Singuratică) or 1608m (Piatra Singuratică)
Water	There is a spring on the trail after 3.4km, and one 300 metres north from Cabana Piatra Singuratică

Piatra Singuratică ('the lonely rock') is popular with Romanian climbers but can be accessed by walkers too thanks to a route fitted with cables.

From the church in **Bălan**, walk up Strada Pârâul Fierarilor, following the blue stripe waymarks. After 800 metres the road forks; cross over a bridge to the right. Continue on the blue stripe trail as it immediately veers off to the left, up into the forest. After 2.2km the blue cross trail departs to the right; continue straight ahead on the blue stripe trail. When the path forks at the foot of a big rock after 350 metres, keep left to stay on the blue stripe trail. After 100 metres, when the trail is

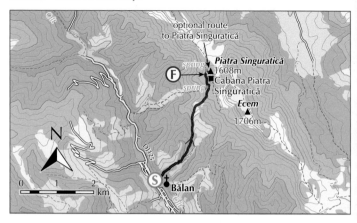

joined by a red triangle, turn left and continue up for 350 metres until you arrive at **Cabana Piatra Singuratică**. The challenging climb up **Piatra Singuratică**, which is right next to the cabana, takes 15–20min. Descend the same way you came up.

To visit Moara Dracului

To see 'the devil's mill', retrace your steps along the blue stripe trail for 250 metres, then turn left (east) and head down the blue cross trail for 1.25km. Return the same way you came.

According to legend, the devil himself had to grind the Ecem Mountain into walnut-sized pieces within one year to gain the hand of an impoverished widow's beautiful daughter. He didn't succeed – at least, not quite, because there is a lot of rubble to be found at **Moara Dracului**, 'the devil's mill', although the rocks are not quite walnut-sized…

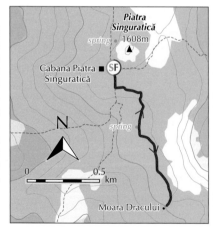

Moara Dracului – a place of legend

STAGE 2

Piatra Singuratică–Lacu Roşu

Start	Cabana Piatra Singuratică
Finish	Lacu Roşu
Distance	20km
Total ascent	530m
Total descent	1080m
Grade	Moderate
Time	5hr
Maximum altitude	1792m (Hăşmaşul Mare Peak)
Water	Spring 350 metres north from Cabana Piatra Singuratică; another one at the Salvamont refuge after 8km

This trail leads through the heart of the Hăşmaş to Lacu Roşu ('the red lake'), a natural dam lake that came into existence following the collapse of a slope caused by an earthquake in 1838. The flooded trees still rise above the surface. The lake lies just south of the famous Bicaz Gorge, making this a popular spot. Expect to encounter lots of cattle on this hike, so be prepared for the accompanying dogs.

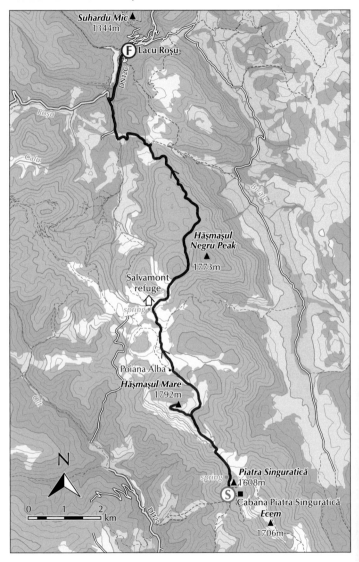

From **Cabana Piatra Singuratică** head north on the red stripe trail. After 700 metres cross a large meadow to the northwest, staying on the left – there are waymarks on trees. After 1.5km enter the forest. After a further 450 metres turn left up the red circle trail to **Hăşmaşul Mare Peak** (1792m). It's 850 metres to the summit. You can leave your pack at the junction if you like. Retrace your steps and continue on the red stripe trail.

After 2.5km, continue northwest from the signpost in Poiana Alba. Just as you start to descend into another meadow, the trail swings sharply to the left (west) and brings you to the **Salvamont refuge** and a spring after 500 metres. Shortly after, you reach a remarkably informative signpost. Continue on the blue circle trail for Lacu Roşu, signed 4hr 30min. (If you're strapped for time you can opt for the blue stripe trail, signed 3hr.)

Cross a meadow northeast; there are no waymarks until you enter the forest on the other side. There are a great many fallen trees on this trail – at times the walk turns into a bit of a limbo dance. Waymarks are not always easy to find. The trail up Hăşmaşul Negru Peak no longer seems to exist.

When the trail forks after 8.5km, keep right. After another 600 metres turn right onto a cart track alongside a meadow. Turn left onto the red circle trail after 230 metres, and then after 1.4km turn right onto a gravel road. Continue on it for 1km until you reach the DN12C road. Turn right onto this and walk the last 2km to **Lacu Roşu** village.

Grazing cows – a common sight on this route

STAGE 3
The Bicaz and Bicăjel Gorges

Start/finish	Pensiunea Stefania, Lacu Roşu
Distance	10km
Total ascent/descent	450m
Grade	Moderate
Time	2hr 30min
Maximum altitude	1018m (Lacu Roşu Monastery)
Water	In Lacu Roşu. Pensiunea Stefania has a tap with spring water by the side of the road.

The Bicaz Gorge is teeming with tourists during the summer months. Few people seem to be aware, though, that there are various other gorges nearby. One of them is the Bicăjel Gorge. Combining the two makes for a rewarding circular hike, allowing for plenty of time to explore the environs of Lacu Roşu itself on the same day.

From Pensiunea Stefania in **Lacu Roşu**, head northeast on the DN12C through the **Bicaz Gorge**. Follow its hairpins through the gorge past stalls selling tourist merchandise for 3.8km, then turn right over the remains of a bridge – no more than a few concrete beams. The yellow stripe trail starts here. After 250 metres comes your main challenge on this trail: cross a footbridge in a deplorable state. At the end both boards and beams are missing for several metres, so you will have to balance yourself on the supporting cables.

Once you've overcome this hurdle, continue southeast on the trail through the **Bicăjel Gorge**. Cross the stream once more; soon the trail bends to the right (southeast). Almost immediately turn right again; an arrow on a tree points you to a cart track with a fence on it after 100 metres. Walk south alongside the fence until you hit another one. Walk further south over a muddy road which soon bends to the right – you might want to avoid the first muddy 100 metres by jumping the aforementioned fence and walking through the field alongside the road.

When you hit the **Bicăjel Stream** after 1km, turn left – not right despite the treacherous waymark. Follow a grassy track for a bit, then wade through the stream and cross a meadow west-northwest on the other side – there is a mark on a concrete electricity pole. Then follow an inconspicuous trail to the left. After

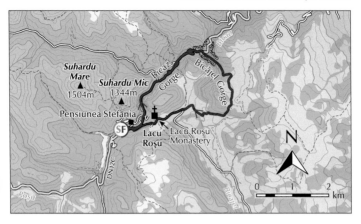

850 metres turn right onto a gravel road, then right again after another 300 metres; this is Strada Bicăjel. Continue for 1.8km, past Lacu Roşu Monastery, until you are back on the DN12C road into **Lacu Roşu**. Turn right to arrive back at Pensiunea Stefania after 700 metres.

The Bicaz Gorge is one of the region's most popular attractions

THE MOUNTAINS AROUND BRAŞOV

The Tigăile Mari rocks, seen here from the trail, are typical of the interesting formations found in the Ciucaş Massif (Route 15, Stage 2)

There is no doubting that Braşov is one of the best bases in Romania for mountain lovers. The Saxons called it Kronstadt for good reason: the city is quite literally crowned with a ring of forested hills that develop into mountains as you venture further south. Braşov is worth a visit on its own: must-dos are a walk over the medieval city walls, a climb to the citadel, and a visit to the Black Church (Biserica Neagră/Schwarze Kirche) where services are still held in German and organ concerts are frequently organised during summer. Concerts and open-air film festivals are also held at Piaţa Sfatului, the central square, against the beautiful backdrop of the forested Postăvaru Massif. Braşov also lies close to some of Romania's most popular attractions, including Bran Castle (inseparably tied to the Dracula myth), the citadel towns of Râşnov and Rupea and some of the best-preserved fortified churches, such as the ones in Prejmer and Viscri.

From the charming old town you can walk straight into the **Postăvaru Massif** (Route 10) via the popular Tâmpa Hill that can be accessed by a cable car too. From the Postăvaru it's possible to continue ahead into the **Bucegi** (Route 16); the most accessible and perhaps also the most popular massif in Romania. Its impressive craggy peaks rise up steeply to the west of the Prahova Valley (Route 17). Behind

this rocky façade, however, lies a plateau that makes for very easy walking
along the length of the Bucegi. Many
tourists come here only to spend the
day around the natural rock sculptures
at Babele, which can be reached by
cable car from the town of Buşteni
– which, consequently, tends to get
very busy during weekends and the
summer months. However, if you venture beyond this popular spot there
are plenty of lesser-visited and more
challenging trails to be explored.
The Bucegi is scattered with cabanas
so you can leave your tent behind

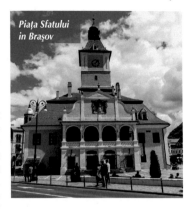

Piaţa Sfatului
in Braşov

(although it is possible to camp next to cabanas if preferred) – they do need to be
booked well in advance though. The towns of the Prahova Valley are all popular
skiing resorts, so there is plenty of accommodation. Sinaia is also home to the Peleş
Castle, an elegant and elaborate neo-Renaissance palace built for King Carol I.

A stone's throw from Braşov but east of the Prahova River lies the **Piatra Mare**;
a small massif that can be easily reached by bus or taxi which makes for some
fine day walks (Routes 11 and 12). The best-known route goes through the Seven
Ladders Gorge (Route 11), requiring the walker to climb ladders over (and sometimes through) the Şipoaia Stream. Routes 11 and 12 are shorter walks and although
both can be tackled in one day, you might want to stay at Cabana Piatra Mare.

Also east of the Prahova River are the **Baiului Mountains** (Route 13), a largely
unforested, gently undulating grassy ridge that offers beautiful views to the
Bucegi in the west and the Ciucaş in the east. It also offers a fine connecting walk
between these two ranges, traversing the **Grohotiş Mountains** (Route 14).

The remoteness of the **Ciucaş** (Route 15), away from any public transport
connections, makes it more difficult to access than the other mountains around
Braşov. For that reason it gets a lot less crowded than the Bucegi for instance –
although apparently during weekends Cabana Vârful Ciucaş gets frequented by
locals who drive up the access road from Cheia in their four-wheel drives. The
Ciucaş is best known for its iconic karst formations.

Among the most challenging and exciting ranges in Romania is the **Piatra
Craiului**, 'King's Rock' (Routes 18 and 19). It bears its name with pride: the
22km saw-like limestone ridge is majestic indeed. The Piatra Craiului is a compact range, but allows for plenty of good walking, scrambling and climbing. The
ridge walk is spectacular: you can actually walk on the ridge's knife edge, with

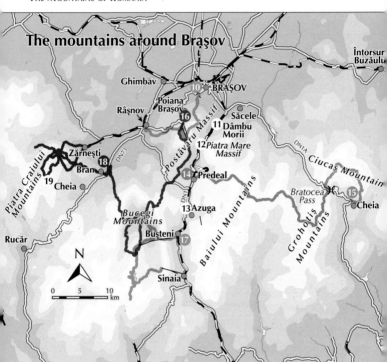

stunning views to the Bucegi to the southeast, the Iezer-Păpuşa to the west and the Făgăraş to the northwest. Climbing can be done in the Zărneşti Gorges (Cheile Zărneştilor), which also wall in one of the entrance routes into the Piatra Craiului proper. The Piatra Craiului ridge lies just 30km southwest of the city of Braşov and 10km from the railway station of Zărneşti, making access very easy.

The Piatra Craiului National Park is home to as much as 30% of all floral species in Romania – the extremely varying climate conditions make this mountain range a favourable place for many species to flourish. The park hosts many endemic species of plants and flowers. The *garofita pietrei craiului* (*Dianthus callizonus*), otherwise known as Piatra Craiului pink, a bright pink flower with frilled petals, is the emblem of these mountains. On top of that, it is home to wolves, bears, lynxes and chamois. Of these four, you stand a good chance of seeing the latter on the steep western face of the ridge.

THE POSTĂVARU MASSIF

ROUTE 10
Braşov to Râşnov

Start	Braşov
Finish	Râşnov
Distance	24km
Total ascent	1400m
Total descent	1330m
Grade	Easy-moderate
Time	2 days
Maximum altitude	1604m (Cabana Postăvaru, Stage 1)
Maps	One of the following: Postăvaru, Piatra Mare, Baiului, 1:45 000/50 000, Munţii Noştri; Postăvaru – Poiana Braşov, 1:25 000, Discover Eco-Romania; 'Five mountains from the Carpathians' bend', 1:70,000, Erfatur-Dimap

The beauty of this easy route is that it takes you from one glorious medieval city centre to another. It starts in the old centre of Braşov and ends at the foot of the miraculously well-preserved citadel in Râşnov. It leads through the heart of the densely forested Postăvaru Massif and offers views to the higher surrounding mountains: the Bucegi, the Piatra Craiului and the Făgăraş. Stage 1 can also be used as a precursor to Route 16 (Poiana Braşov to Bran).

The Schwarze Kirche in Braşov

Access

Braşov is served by many trains from Bucharest. Most trains take about 2hr 45min from Bucureşti Nord Station. From Braşov Station, take the no. 4 bus to Livada Poştei bus station, or no. 51 to Primărie stop and walk a few minutes south to reach Piaţa Sfatului, Braşov's historic main square. You can easily get the train back to Braşov (or elsewhere) at the end of the second day if you don't want to spend the night in Râşnov.

Accommodation

Cabana Postăvaru; Club Rossignol and many other places in Poiana Braşov; plenty of options in Râşnov.

STAGE 1

Braşov–Cabana Postăvaru

Start	Piaţa Sfatului, Braşov
Finish	Cabana Postăvaru
Distance	11km
Total ascent	1100m
Total descent	100m
Grade	Easy
Time	3hr 15min
Maximum altitude	1604m (Cabana Postăvaru)
Water	In Braşov and at Cabana Postăvaru

From Piaţa Sfatului in **Braşov**, walk down Strada Republicii and turn right onto Strada Michael Weiss. Turn right again onto Strada Castelului and almost immediately right onto Suişul Castelului, which will take you up to the old city walls. Turn right onto the promenade (Aleea Tiberiu Brediceanu) and choose the upper path. Turn left onto the blue stripe route towards Cabana Postăvaru. After 500 metres, turn right at the signpost to Poiana Braşov/Postăvaru. Very soon you will come upon a muddy cart track; turn left onto it and after about 200 metres turn left again.

After about 3.5km, turn left to stay on the blue stripe route (the path to the right is marked blue triangle and leads to Poiana Braşov). Turn left again when you see a signpost to Cabana Postăvaru on a tree. Pass a basin and cross two ski slopes to arrive at **Cabana Postăvaru**. If you want you can continue to Poiana Braşov, which is less than 3km down from here (see Stage 2).

To continue to the Bucegi Mountains

It is possible to continue to the Bucegi Mountains from either Poiana Braşov or Cabana Postăvaru. See Route 16, Stage 1.

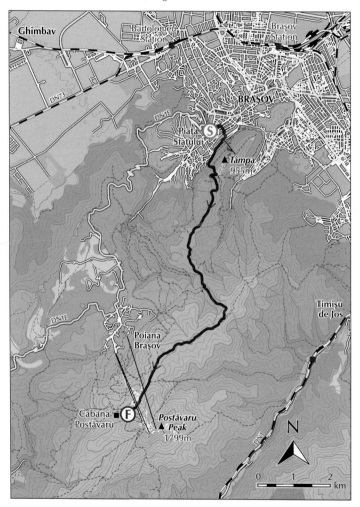

STAGE 2
Cabana Postăvaru–Râşnov

Start	Cabana Postăvaru
Finish	Central Râşnov
Distance	13km
Total ascent	300m
Total descent	1230m
Grade	Easy
Time	4hr 30min
Maximum altitude	1604m (Cabana Postăvaru)
Water	Fill bottles at Cabana Postăvaru or in Poiana Braşov

Start following the red cross trail, which departs from the back of **Cabana Postăvaru**. When you meet another path, turn left (southwest) to stay on the red cross trail. Cross the ski slope and turn right (northeast). Very soon, turn left (west), then left again. When you get to an unpaved road, either turn right (east) to continue on the red cross trail or go down the ski slope; the red cross trail will cross the slope and ultimately goes down the slope too.

From Telegondola Postăvarul Express in **Poiana Braşov** (plenty of restaurants here if you need refreshment), walk down the grassy trail that leads westwards. When you get to the junction in the asphalt road, turn left onto the combined blue stripe/yellow cross trail for Râşnov. Continue on the unpaved road to Telescaun Pârtia Lupului and pass underneath the ski lift. Soon, the path splits; keep right (southwest). Walk along the stream. When you get to a bridge, turn right (west) onto the yellow cross trail for Râşnov.

When you get to the main (**DN1E**) road, turn left onto it and continue on the yellow cross trail towards Râşnov and Cristian. Walk down the main road for a little while, then just before you get to the hairpin, turn left onto a grassy trail that leads southwest. It is marked blue stripe, red triangle and yellow cross. When you get to a forest road, turn left (south) onto the blue stripe route to *bisericuta* (little church) Paginilor, *peştera* (cave) and *oras* (town) Râşnov. Keep right to stay on the blue stripe route. When the path forks, keep right. For the last 500 metres or so to the road, the path is unmarked; there is a marked grassy trail to the left but it is barely visible. It is best to stay on the main path until you get to the gravel road, where the waymarks will reappear.

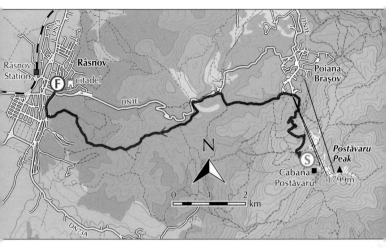

Turn left onto the road; this leads you into **Râșnov**. When in the town, turn right onto Strada IL Caragiale to make your way towards the centre. From here you can either walk up to the magnificent citadel or take the cable car. It is a short walk down to Râșnov Station; you can easily travel back to Brașov on the same day if you don't want to spend the night in Râșnov.

Râșnov's impressive citadel

139

THE MOUNTAINS OF ROMANIA

THE PIATRA MARE MASSIF

ROUTE 11

Şapte Scări Gorge and Piatra Mare Peak from Dâmbu Morii

Start/finish	Dâmbu Morii
Distance	17.5km
Total ascent/descent	1100m
Grade	Moderate
Time	4hr 40min
Maximum altitude	1844m (Piatra Mare Peak)
Maps	Postăvaru, Piatra Mare, Baiului, 1:45,000/50,000, Munţii Noştri
Access	The easiest way to get to the trailhead is to take a taxi from Braşov (about 10km). Alternatively, the 17B bus to Timişu de Jos stops at Dâmbu Morii. There's a small fee for accessing the Seven Ladders Gorge, taken at the entrance.
Accommodation	Best to find something in Braşov; see Appendix B and www.booking.com. There are several pensions in Dâmbu Morii if you want to be right at the start in the morning – Vila Canionul 7 Scari and Vila 7 Scari among them. Although both this route and Route 12 can be tackled in one day, you might want to stay at Cabana Piatra Mare (15 beds). If going during the weekend, do make a reservation. It is open throughout the year; meals are served on Saturdays and Sundays only.
Water	Drinks (and small snacks) are sold at Cabana Şapte Scări; spring at Cabana Piatra Mare; plenty of streams cross the trail

This circular walk takes you through the fabulous Şapte Scări (Seven Ladders) Gorge, where the Şipoaia Stream cuts through Jurassic limestone. From 1 May to 1 September the gorge is open daily; outside the season it is open on Saturdays and Sundays only, although it is closed during or after heavy rain.

Do check the gorge's Facebook page (www.facebook.com/7Scari) before you set out. Access to the gorge costs 10RON, to be paid at the tax point at the entrance.

This walk can be adapted to anyone's needs: it is possible to return at the end of the gorge via another trail, making this a very short and easy walk, or to continue to Cabana Piatra Mare, as suggested below. The excursion to Piatra Mare Peak is optional.

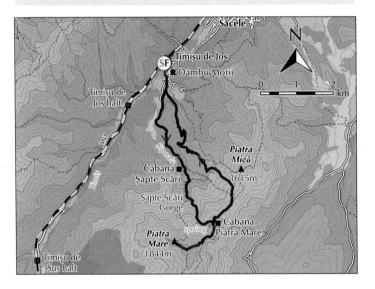

From the DN1 road in **Dâmbu Morii**, walk south up Strada Piatra Mare until you get to the trailhead; there is an info panel marking the start of the trail towards the gorge and a signpost. Follow the yellow stripe waymarks for 3km alongside the Şipoaia Stream until you get to **Cabana Şapte Scări**; then make your way up through the gorge by means of seven ladders; the tallest one is about 15m. (There are actually 10 ladders if you count the smaller ones too.) You might get wet, especially if you're doing this in spring. Getting through the gorge itself only takes 15–20min. It is about 230 metres long; the Şipoaia makes a drop of about 60m.

At the end of the gorge there's a signpost. It is possible to go back down to Dâmbu Morii immediately via the red circle trail, bypassing the gorge (25–30min). Another option for a quick return would be to turn left onto the blue triangle trail.

The gateway to Piatra Mare Peak

However, if you want to continue to Piatra Mare Cabana and Peak, continue on the yellow stripe trail. Cross the stream and head up into the forest. There are several forks, but all paths seem to lead up the same way (south-southeast). There are several red stripe signposts along the way. After about 3km in the forest you will arrive at Poiana Sura de Piatra and **Cabana Piatra Mare** (1635m). The peaks of the Ciucaş Mountains can be seen to the southeast. (This section of the route, including the 3km to the gorge and the gorge itself, can actually be done in little over 2hr, rather than the 3hr stated on the first signpost.)

To continue to Piatra Mare Peak, head southwest up the red stripe trail. After about 400 metres you arrive at a meadow at the foot of a rock mass. Scramble up the rocks until you get to a gentler path through grassy meadows – although there is a steep drop to the right. After a further 400 metres the red cross trail departs to the left; from this point you have splendid views of the Bucegi, Baiului and Piatra Craiului to the left and Braşov to the right. Continue on the red stripe trail until you reach **Piatra Mare Peak** (1844m), which also marks the end of the trail. Return to Cabana Piatra Mare the way you came.

To return to Dâmbu Morii, head north on the red stripe trail (also called Drumul Familiar). This needs little description; the waymarking is straightforward enough. The blue stripe trail departs after 1km. Descend through the forest for 7km to return to the forest road you started on, and from there walk back to the DN1 road in **Dâmbu Morii**.

Alternatively, you could go down the red circle trail from Cabana Piatra Mare to Dâmbu Morii; see Route 12.

ROUTE 12
Timişu de Sus to Dâmbu Morii via Tamina Gorge

Start	Timişu de Sus
Finish	Dâmbu Morii
Distance	17km
Total ascent	1100m
Total descent	1245m
Grade	Moderate
Time	5hr
Maximum altitude	1787m (just beyond Piatra Scrisă)
Maps	Postăvaru, Piatra Mare, Baiului, 1:45,000/50,000, Munţii Noştri
Access	The easiest way to get to the trailhead is to take a taxi from Braşov (about 20km). First make sure the taxi has a Rovinieta (vignette for national roads), otherwise it will not be allowed to take you there. You are most likely to find these at Braşov's main station. Alternatively, take a train from Braşov or Bucharest (the latter takes between 2hr 15min and 3hr 15min): get off at the Timişu de Sus halt and walk south for 1km to the start of the trail. At the end of the walk, the 17B bus to Braşov stops at Dâmbu Morii.
Accommodation	Best to find something in Braşov; see Appendix B and www.booking.com. Although both this route and Route 11 can be tackled in one day, you might want to stay at Cabana Piatra Mare (15 beds). If going during the weekend, do make a reservation. It is open throughout the year; meals are served on Saturdays and Sundays only.
Water	Spring at Cabana Piatra Mare and in the forest after the Şirul Stâncilor section

This different approach to the Piatra Mare massif takes you through the lesser-known Tamina Gorge. It is definitely worth exploring and although shorter, it's more exciting than the Şapte Scări Gorge (Route 11) simply because it's wilder and has rickety ladders. The route described here does not go over Piatra Mare Peak but you can easily do so if you want to; it may take about 30min longer than the route described below.

The blue stripe trail departs east from the DN1 road in between Timişu de Sus railway halt and Timişu de Sus village, signed 1hr to Cascada Tamina and 3hr to Cabana Piatra Mare. The trail almost immediately departs from the forest road; keep right or follow the narrow path in between the two main paths initially – it will soon merge with the main path again.

The Tamina Gorge makes for a short but interesting section

After about 1km the path briefly merges with the forest road; continue east. The trail cuts off good chunks of the forest road. When you meet the forest road again after 1.2km, stay on it for about 50 metres, then turn right when you see an info panel. Follow a path down to the west; there are no marks here but this path takes you down into the **Tamina Gorge**. Cross the stream over a tree trunk with footholds and enter the gorge. It is short but sweet: making your way up involves walking over slippery planks, climbing rickety ladders and hands-on rock work while the stream thunders down underneath you.

When you come to the end of the gorge, follow the trail to the right of the stream. This brings you to a meadow. Cross the stream to the right (south); you will see waymarks again here. This path takes you back to the forest road. When you reach it, continue east on the blue stripe route. Just before you reach a foresters' lodge after 400 metres, the trail swerves to the right (east), off the forest road and into the forest. After about 1.5km, the forest opens up; head north towards a signpost, up a grassy slope. Behind you, you can see the Bucegi, Piatra Craiului and Făgăraş.

When you reach the shepherd's hut at **Piatra Scrisă** you have the option to continue straight ahead to Piatra Mare Peak (1844m) via the red cross trail and then descend to Cabana Piatra Mare via the red stripe trail (allow 30–45min for this detour). However, the route described here passes underneath it. At the signpost after the shepherd's hut and corral, turn right onto the red cross route, then turn left onto the blue triangle trail. The spring shown on the Munţii Noştri map is no more than a muddy pool in spring, let alone in summer. The trail takes you through a cool forest and past the steep southern face of Piatra Mare; you can see how it got its name (Big Rock). About 2km after Piatra Scrisă, turn right (east) onto the red stripe trail to **Cabana Piatra Mare** (1630m), signed 10–20min.

From the cabana, continue northeast towards Dâmbu Morii down the red stripe route. After 800 metres, start following the blue stripe waymarks which depart to the right (east); you will soon see a signpost pointing to Dâmbu Morii, signed 2hr 30min from here (but it can really be done in about 1hr). After 1.3km on this trail there is the option of a little detour to **Peştera de Gheaţă** to the right – it takes less than 30min there and back. However, although the name means 'ice cave' it is more of a large cleft in the rocks and cannot be accessed without major clambering (so you might as well skip it).

From the signpost, turn left (west) and follow the red circle waymarks for Dâmbu Morii along the stunning overhanging rocks of **Şirul Stâncilor**. The first kilometre down this trail is quite steep and the soil is loose, so tread with care. After 1km there is another signpost – continue northwest into a fir forest. The path soon widens and becomes considerably easier and less steep. After 2km the forest opens up; the waymarks become scarce here but the trail is mostly visible and all you have to do from here is aim for Dâmbu Morii down below. You will have to jump over a stream once or twice before you're back on the access road to Şapte Scări. Turn right onto it and walk back down to the DN1 road in **Dâmbu Morii**. The 17B bus stop is immediately to your right.

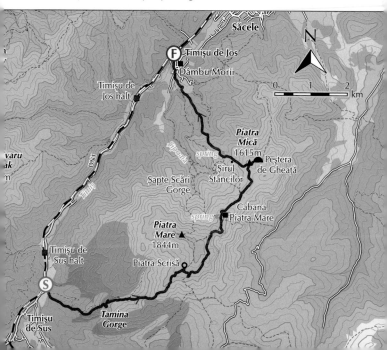

THE BAIULUI AND GROHOTIŞ

ROUTE 13

A north–south traverse of the Baiului

Start	Azuga Station
Finish	Posada railway halt
Distance	28km
Total ascent	1360m
Total descent	1680m
Grade	Moderate
Time	6hr 30min
Maximum altitude	1895m (Baiu Mare Peak)
Maps	Postăvaru, Piatra Mare, Baiului, 1:45,000/50,000, Munţii Noştri
Access	Azuga is served by multiple trains a day from both Bucharest and Braşov. There are also several buses from Braşov. See Appendix C.
Accommodation	Plenty to be found in Azuga or one of the neighbouring towns, or stay in Braşov and take an early train or bus. There is Florei Refuge near the end of the route; search for 'Refugiul Florei' on Facebook. It is open year-round, sometimes staffed and admission is free. Plenty of good camping spots on the route but no water.
Water	Spring on the DN1 just beyond the start of the trail, and another one on the same road when you cross the bridge towards Posada halt. No water on the trail itself but there is water about 30min from Florei Refuge – ask the owner for instructions.

This long but gentle walk takes you along the length of the Baiului, parallel to the Bucegi, offering beautiful views and lush green scenery. It is perfect for a spring day – all the snow will have melted away here long before it has done so in the Bucegi. For much of the time the trail follows a dirt road, cutting off corners wherever possible. This also makes this route quite suitable for mountain biking, although perhaps the first few kilometres to the chairlift station slightly less so. The walk can be tackled in a day if you leave early; there are plenty of good camping spots though so you could split it in two. You would have to carry enough water though, since there are no springs on the trail.

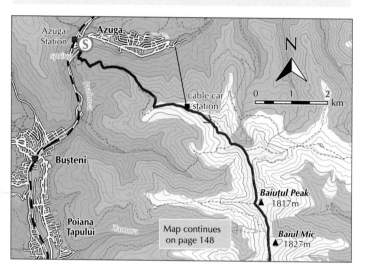

From **Azuga Station**, walk to the DN1 and turn right onto it. Follow it for a few hundred metres until you see the signposted start of the blue triangle route to your left. Head southwest up this trail. After 2.8km the trail forks; take the option that swings to the left (east). Another 800 metres brings you to a meadow, where the trail swings to the right (south). After 300 metres turn left onto a gravel road and walk up the Sorica ski slope. Walk past the **cable car station** and adjacent hut; there is a signpost on a fence to the right.

From here, follow the red stripe trail onto the main ridge. Keep right; walk past the outdoor toilets, not up to the mast. After 2.7km of ridge walking you will see a signpost; from here the waymarks on the ridge will be red cross until it departs to Buşteni via Culmea Zamora after 850 metres (you can reach Buşteni in 3hr–3hr 30min if you want or need to). Red stripe waymarks will reappear after this junction.

Continue south, past **Baiuţul Peak** (1817m). When the red stripe reappears it is joined by the blue circle for a while. After 1.6km there is a fork; keep left

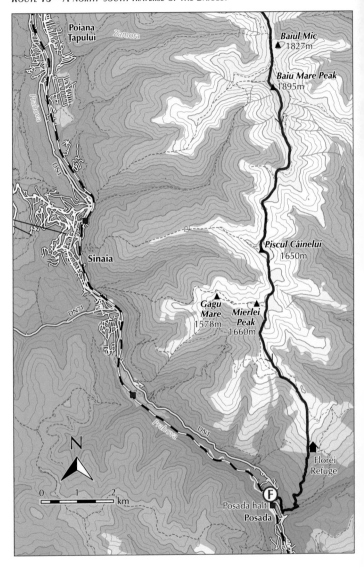

Looking towards the Bucegi from the Baiului ridge

to continue to **Baiu Mare Peak** (1895m), which you will reach after 900 metres. About 5km of gentle ascending and descending follows. At **Piscul Câinelui Peak** (1650m) the blue circle trail departs to the right, towards Predeal; turn left (east) to continue on the red stripe trail to Posada. After 2km the trail bypasses Mierlei Peak – the trail goes over the road not over the peak here, but in case of emergency there is an unmarked exit trail west from Mierlei Peak.

From here the road goes steadily down. The Prahova Valley widens; you can see further afield, and the Bucegi has been reduced to forested hills. There is a fork after some 700 metres; keep left. After a further 2.6km the trail very inconspicuously veers off to the right and leaves the track; follow a grassy unmarked trail south. After 1.3km you will reach **Florei Refuge**, which was rebuilt in 2018. From here, head down into the forest, following red stripe waymarks, although they will soon disappear again – this section of the red stripe trail is marked in mysterious ways.

After 1km the path forks – turn left onto a grassy trail, then after about 500 metres red stripe waymarks reappear; head south. When the path forks, keep left (southeast). After 600 metres turn left onto a forest road, then almost immediately make a sharp right turn onto a narrow path (marked again). Follow it down to the DN1 road and turn right onto the road. Cross a viaduct, then immediately afterwards make a U-turn and descend an inconspicuous rickety concrete staircase which leads down to **Posada halt**, past a few houses.

ROUTE 14
Across the Baiului and Grohotiş

Start	Predeal
Finish	Bratocea Pass
Distance	42km
Total ascent	2165m
Total descent	1990m
Grade	Easy-moderate
Time	2 days
Maximum altitude	1840m (below Paltinu Peak, Stage 1)
Maps	Postăvaru, Piatra Mare, Baiului; 1:45,000/1:50,000, Munţii Noştri, combined with 'Five mountains from the Carpathians' bend', 1:70,000, Erfatur-Dimap

This route takes you through the little-visited territory between the Bucegi and Ciucaş Massifs. It makes an interesting connecting walk but is enjoyable enough to tackle on its own. Much of the route follows the border between Braşov and Prahova Counties. The going is fairly easy – the trail leads through forest and mostly over cart tracks until Gavan Lake, then rises above the tree line to the Baiului's characteristic grassy slopes, offering grand views of the Bucegi behind and the Ciucaş ahead. Expect encounters with sheepdogs who are not used to tourists and might be more on guard because of that – you might want to bring an ultrasonic device. This can be bought at Ultra Armory, Strada Roşiorilor 21, Braşov (www.arme-poligon.ro – Romanian website).

The bucolic main ridge of the Baiului (Stage 1)

Access

Predeal is served by multiple trains a day from both Bucharest (2hr) and Braşov (40min). Cabana Susai can also be reached by car over the road, cutting out the first part of Stage 1.

From the Bratocea Pass you can continue into the Ciucaş, either by crossing the pass and continuing on the red stripe trail, or by turning right onto the blue stripe trail to Cheia, signed 1hr, and heading up the Zăganu-Gropşoarele spur. See Route 15. There is no public transport from the pass; in order to hitchhike back to Braşov you should do so as early as possible because lorries are redirected via the DN1 after 6pm and there is little other traffic on this road.

Accommodation and food

Vila Veveriţa in Predeal has affordable rooms and comes with a kitchen. Cabana Susai is officially only a restaurant now but has three rooms. Cabana de Vanatoare Ritivoi should be open but is a hunters' lodge so should only be used as a refuge. There are eight berths but only two mattresses.

Samicom supermarket near Predeal Station has a good range of hiking food (dried fruits, protein bars, etc). The Camin Militar Predeal serves cheap meals.

You will need to camp at Predeluş Pass at the end of the first stage. (Camping is also permitted throughout the route.)

STAGE 1
Predeal–Predeluş Pass

Start	Predeal Station
Finish	Predeluş Pass
Distance	19km
Total ascent	1145m
Total descent	935m
Grade	Moderate
Time	5hr 40min
Maximum altitude	1840m (below Paltinu Peak)
Water	In Predeal; at Cabana Susai; spring at Ritivoi hunting cabin; spring just after Predeluş Pass

From **Predeal Station**, cross the tracks east, turn left onto Strada Eroilor, then make a sharp right onto Strada Muncii. Keep left towards Hotel Robinson; after 350

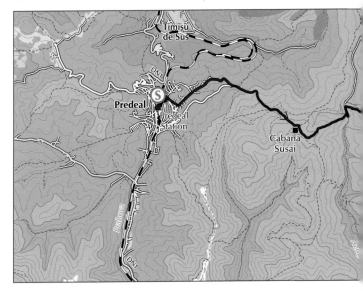

metres turn left onto Bulevardul Libertății, and walk past a plethora of hotels and pensions. After 1.2km, when you see the Office Lounge, keep right; after 150 metres you'll reach the start of the marked trail. Follow the red stripe waymarks for Cabana Susai. The trail is also marked red cross and blue circle. After about 600 metres stay on the trail as it splits off the forest road to the left.

After 200 metres the blue circle trail to Piatra Mare Peak veers off to the left, signed 4hr. Ignore this. After another 800 metres the trail merges with a gravel road. The red cross route departs left to the Piatra Mare Massif. After 100 metres on the road, turn left (east) to continue on the red stripe trail, which is joined by the blue cross here. After about 800 metres a large white building rises up in front of you as you exit the forest. Turn left in front of it and follow the signs to Cabana Susai. Very soon, the red stripe and blue cross trails depart left to Cabana Rentea, signed 5hr 15min; continue southeast to **Cabana Susai** which you reach after 150 metres – the waymarks are still red stripe.

Walk around Cabana Susai and continue on the red triangle trail. Head east and descend on a cart track to the left of the forest road. After 1.3km turn right onto a road, then left almost immediately, crossing the Azuga Stream over a concrete bridge. Stay on the red triangle route as it veers off the road into the forest to the right. The trail now climbs southeast alongside a gully. After 250 metres

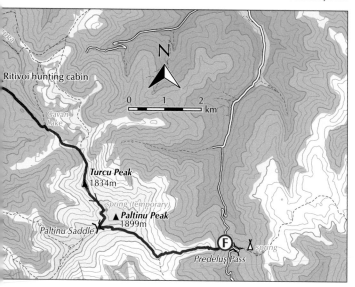

turn left onto a track, then right immediately. The waymarks disappear for a while. After 500 metres there is an arrow to the right on a tree; ignore this and stay on the road to keep heading east. Behind you is the Bucegi (west), while the Piatra Mare can be seen to the left (north).

Continue through a relatively open area with re-emerging forest. The trail gradually swings northeast. After about 1km you reach Poiana Ritivoi. The **Ritivoi hunting cabin** is 800 metres further on, and there is a spring a little bit further up. After 1km, having crossed a small stream, stay on the red triangle trail as it veers to the right (southeast) and off the road, into a grassy area. After 250 metres you reach the rather unremarkable **Gavan Lake**.

Here the path splits into three: the red triangle departs left (northwest); the middle path presumably leads down to the audible stream (northeast). Take the rightmost path (southeast). This is an unmarked and narrow grassy trail. It forks immediately – keep right. At the next fork, keep left. After 1km the trail merges with the red stripe trail again, which has made rather a detour. It is alternately marked red and yellow stripe.

Continue south and steadily ascend the gentle grassy slope to **Turcu Peak** (1834m). The peaks of the Ciucaș can be seen to the left (east). After 1.2km the track you are on goes up east to Paltinu Peak (1899m); instead follow the marked

153

trail which bypasses it to the right (south) over a grassy trail. There is a (possibly temporary) spring to the left after 250 metres. After 500 metres make a sharp left in **Paltinu Saddle** (1790m). It is possible to pitch a tent around here but it would mean camping near a flock and hence dogs.

A steady descent east follows; continue east for 4km along the straightforward marked and mostly grassy trail until you reach **Predeluş Pass** (1250m). The pass does not make the greatest of camping spots with its buzzing electricity pylons. There are a few flat grassy spots about 100 metres further up the red stripe trail though, and there is a stream after another 500 metres.

STAGE 2

Predeluş Pass–Bratocea Pass

Start	Predeluş Pass
Finish	Bratocea Pass
Distance	23km
Total ascent	1020m
Total descent	1055m
Grade	Easy
Time	6hr 20min
Maximum altitude	1769m (just before Bobul Mic Peak)
Water	Springs after 10, 16 and 17.5km
Note	There is no public transport from Bratocea Pass and little or no traffic after 6pm. An early start is recommended in order to hitchhike back to Braşov.

From **Predeluş Pass**, head east up a dirt track, which is the continuation of the red stripe trail – it is still marked. The path heads steeply up along the stream – 900 metres of walking brings you to the source. The forest opens up and gives way to grassy slopes. After a further 50 metres a trail splits off to the left (north), but stay on the marked trail as it swings to the right (south) briefly, then north again. After 2.5km the trail bypasses the unremarkable **Sloeru Mărcuşanu Peak** (1592m) and swings to the right (southeast). The Ciucaş Massif now lies ahead of you, but the trail temporarily leads away from it – it makes a large V-shaped detour through the Grohotiş Mountains. The trail is marked with sturdy painted branches.

Descend southeast through dwarf pine, passing by a *stâna* with some 10 dogs after about 1km – but make sure you attract the attention of the shepherd before

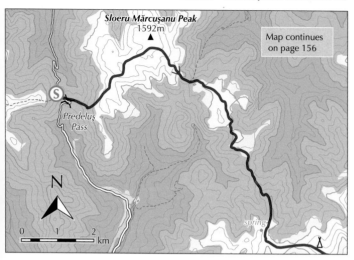

you pass. Some 250 metres later the trail veers to the left (east), off the main track. After a further 900 metres there's another *stâna*, this time with cows, at some distance to the right of the trail. The poles that mark the trail are a bit harder to find here; head southeast initially. Soon the trail swings to the right (south). After 800 metres the trail briefly passes through a wooded area; there are fewer waymarks here. Head southeast as you emerge from the forest, towards a marked rock, after which the trail swings to the right (south) again.

The trail is marked with wooden stakes

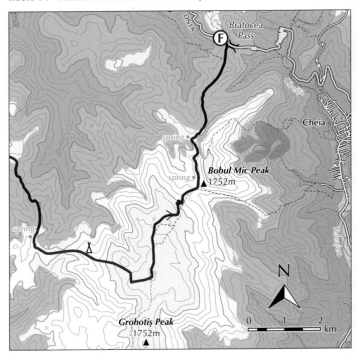

Cross a large meadow to the south and head up into the forest after 1km. After another kilometre, cross a meadow to the southeast; there is a pole at the far end. Exit the forest. When the path forks after 300 metres, keep left (south), bypassing an unnamed peak. There is a **spring** 100 metres further on. After 750 metres the trail splits off the track and climbs to the right (east); there is a corral in the valley to the right. This area makes a good camping spot, provided that you stay away from the sheep.

About 2.5km later the trail bends to the north; you are now finally heading straight for the Ciucaş. There is a tarn to the right after 200 metres. The trail is now also marked with a red cross. After a further 3km the trail swings again to the left (north), bypassing **Bobul Mic Peak** (1752m) with its gigantic rounded boulders – a prelude to the Ciucaş. After 100 metres there's a **spring**; then another one after 1.2km. The first trees appear; the trail alternately ascends and descends until you reach **Bratocea Pass** on the DN1A road after about 3km.

THE CIUCAŞ MASSIF

ROUTE 15
Cheia to Bratocea Pass

Start	Cheia
Finish	Bratocea Pass
Distance	22km
Total ascent	1685m
Total descent	1435m
Grade	Moderate
Time	1–2 days
Maximum altitude	1954m (Ciucaş Peak, Stage 2)
Maps	Ciucaş, 1:25,000, Munţii Noştri, or Munţii Ciucaş, 1:30,000, Bel Alpin

The Ciucaş Mountains lie in the eastern extremity of the Carpathians' Bend. They are best known for their iconic karst formations that stir the imagination, shaped over time by wind and rain. They carry names such as Babele la Sfat ('old women talking'), Turnul Goliat ('Goliath's tower') and Mâna Dracului ('the devil's hand'). The Ciucaş consists of two main spurs – the Zăganu-Gropşoarele and the Bratocea spur – which roughly meet at the massif's highest point, Ciucaş Peak (1954m). The terrain is very varied: forest and grassy meadows are followed by steep rocky climbs to Poarta de Arama and Ciucaş Peak – in between these two points the route follows an easy trail over a mostly grassy ridge. If you set out early, both stages can be tackled in one day.

Access
There is no public transport directly to Cheia. If you have a car, access is easy enough: simply drive down the DN1A from Braşov, or up from Bucharest via Ploieşti, to the village of Cheia. If not, you can try to hitchhike, or hike across the Baiului and Grohotiş Mountains; see Route 14. If you decide to hitchhike, make your way out of Braşov first; there is a bus to Săcele (35min) from the Roman bus station in the Astra quarter of Braşov – departure times are displayed on the platform. Alternatively, take the 17B bus to the Aurora stop on the DN1 road and then walk to the start of the DN1A road (1km) and hitchhike from

157

First rhododendrons of the season on the trail-side slopes of the Ciucaş (Stage 1)

there; or take a train from Braşov to Dârste railway halt (9min) and do the same. Alternatively, Sorin Rusu, the owner of Coronensis Apartment in Braşov, is more than happy to drive hikers to the start of the route for a very reasonable fee – or to any place in the Braşov area that is difficult to access without a car of your own. See Appendix B for his contact details.

Another access point would be the village of Vama Buzăului to the north; this is served by various buses from Braşov. From here it's a 5hr (15.5km) hike to Ciucaş Peak via the red cross trail.

Since there is no public transport from the Bratocea Pass, hitchhiking back to Braşov is your only option. Try to do so as early as possible because lorries are redirected via the DN1 after 6pm, and there is little other traffic on this road.

Accommodation
Cabana Vârful Ciucaş – not to be confused with Complex Cabana Ciucaş in Cheia itself. You can also camp within the bounds of the cabana (do contact the cabana first to check whether there is space), but not elsewhere. Several other properties can be found in Cheia through www.booking.com.

STAGE 1

Cheia–Cabana Vârful Ciucaş

Start	DN1A road, Cheia
Finish	Cabana Vârful Ciucaş
Distance	11.7km
Total ascent	1320m
Total descent	705m
Grade	Moderate
Time	3hr 30min
Maximum altitude	1883m (Gropşoarele Peak)
Water	At Cabana Vârful Ciucaş

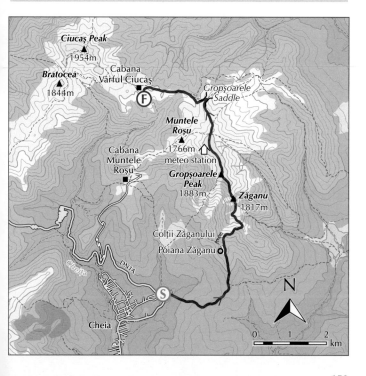

The red cross trail to Cabana Vârful Ciucaş via the Zăganu-Gropşoarele spur departs east from the DN1A road in **Cheia**, signed 5–6hr. (You will find that it can be done much faster than that; all the timings on the signposts are rather generous.) The red cross is initially joined by the blue stripe route. After 1.5km the trail sharply bends to the left (northeast). After another kilometre the blue stripe departs to the right; stay on the red cross trail. After a further 1.3km, exit the forest and cross a meadow to the north, towards the ridge – this is **Poiana Zăganu** (1336m).

Walk past a sheepfold; after this the path swings to the right, past the **Colţii Zăganului** rocks. The path goes steadily up and brings you to a saddle after 1km. The Bucegi and Baiului are behind you. Turn left (northeast) towards Zăganu Peak, and climb to some of the rounded rock sculptures that are so characteristic of the Ciucaş. The trail takes you past some brilliant rock formations; when you've passed these you'll be able to see the Bratocea spur ahead of you (Stage 2), as well as the road leading up to Cabana Vârful Ciucaş from Cheia. Continue north towards Gropşoarele Peak via the wonderful gate-like Poarta de Arama, past **Zăganu Peak** (1817m). There's a short section with a rusty cable here which you probably won't really need.

Almost 1km after Poarta de Arama you'll reach **Gropşoarele Peak** (1883m). You can see Cabana Vârful Ciucaş and Ciucaş Peak from here. Continue north towards them, past a **meteo station** and tiny shelter. After 1.7km there's an option to turn left to Cabana Muntele Roşu (3km), should you need it. Continue for a further 15min to arrive at **Gropşoarele Saddle**, then bear left to stay on the red cross route to **Cabana Vârful Ciucaş** (1595m), signed 30min from here – you will find it just to the left of the main path.

Poarta de Arama is a natural gate in the Ciucaş Massif

STAGE 2
Cabana Vârful Ciucaş–Bratocea Pass

Start	Cabana Vârful Ciucaş
Finish	Bratocea Pass
Distance	10.3km
Total ascent	365m
Total descent	730m
Grade	Moderate; easy after Ciucaş Peak
Time	2hr 30min
Maximum altitude	1954m (Ciucaş Peak)
Water	At Cabana Vârful Ciucaş
Note	There is no public transport at Bratocea Pass, and little or no traffic after 6pm. In order to hitchhike back to Braşov you will need to arrive at the pass with time to spare.

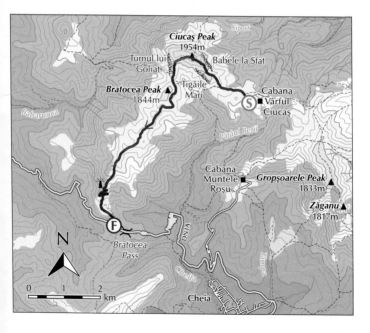

Babele la Sfat ('old women talking')

From **Cabana Vârful Ciucaş**, walk northwest up to the signpost, then continue on the combined red stripe and red cross trail for Ciucaş Peak, signed 1hr 15min. Ahead of you are the splendid **Tigăile Mari rocks**. Walk around these, first on a path, then up a rocky gully for about 200 metres. After this, the path bears to the left and goes up, past the famous **Babele la Sfat** rock formation. There is a fork here; keep right. **Ciucaş Peak** (1954m) is just 400 metres on from here.

From the peak, the path leads southwest to Bratocea Pass, signed 3hr 30min–4hr (again, very generous timings). It leads past the **Turnul lui Goliat** and Turnul Roşu rock formations over the Bratocea spur. After almost 5km from Ciucaş Peak the path swings sharply to the left, then leads past a satellite tower after 800 metres. Turn left onto a gravel road here; this will take you all the way down to **Bratocea Pass** (1263m) which you will reach after 2km.

THE BUCEGI MOUNTAINS

ROUTE 16
Poiana Braşov to Bran

Start	Poiana Braşov
Finish	Bran
Distance	64.5km
Total ascent	4480m
Total descent	4775m
Grade	Moderate
Time	5 days
Maximum altitude	2507m (Omu Peak, Stage 2)
Maps	One of the following for the Bucegi proper: Erfatur-Dimap; Munţii Bucegi, 1:33,000, Discover Eco-Romania/Zenith; Bucegi–Leaota, 1:70,000/1:25,000, Munţii Noştri; Munţii Bucegi, 1:50,000, Bel Alpin. For the approach walk to Cabana Diham, use either 'Five mountains from the Carpathians' bend', 1:70,000, which also offers an overview of the entire route, or Postăvaru–Poiana Braşov, 1:25,000, Discover Eco-Romania.

This chapter presents two itineraries through the Bucegi, each with their own merits. This first one approaches the Bucegi from Poiana Braşov; this lets you cross the Postăvaru Massif to the south. It is also possible to start in Braşov – see Route 10.

The Bucegi is perhaps Romania's most popular massif; it is easily accessed by car or train from the towns of the Prahova Valley (Buşteni and Sinaia), from where it is possible to take a cable car up the ridge. This route avoids the busiest areas and offers a less-frequented route to the highest peak in the Bucegi, Omu Peak (2507m), before descending to Bran with its famous castle through the lush Gaura Valley, from where it is possible to call it quits or cross over into the Piatra Craiului.

Whether you take this approach or the Prahova Valley approach described in Route 17, you can make your way to Omu in two days. The itineraries are far from rigid; you will see that you can essentially pick and mix from the two. Once you've arrived at Cabana Babele (see Route 17), Omu or Padina, you have several options open to you. The most important thing is to decide what sort of approach

163

Waterfall in the Ialomiţa Valley (Stage 4)

you prefer; a lengthy, quiet and easy one across the Postăvaru Massif or a much quicker, busier and steeper one from one of the towns in the Prahova Valley. The route described here includes a couple of short tricky sections that are equipped with cables, but is on the whole the more straightforward and peaceful option.

There is a significant population of bears in the Bucegi, but if you take the usual precautions (make some noise on the trail; do not store food in your tent) they are more than likely to stay away.

Access

To reach Poiana Braşov from Braşov, take bus no. 20 from Livada Poştei's bus station. The ride takes about 25min; buses depart every hour or half-hour, depending on the day of the week. Visit www.ratbv.ro for the timetable (English-language option available).

At the end of the trek, there are numerous buses from Bran to Braşov. The journey takes between 45min and 1hr; buses depart from various locations in Bran. The bus stops in Râşnov as well, from where you could do Route 10 in reverse or just visit the citadel. See https://autogari.ro for timetable and stops. Alternatively, you can take a bus in the opposite direction, to Câmpulung Moldovenesc, and continue into the Iezer-Păpuşa Massif (Routes 20 and 21).

Accommodation
Club Rossignol (pension and restaurant) in Poiana Braşov is good. On the route are Cabana Postăvaru, Cabana Secuilor, Cabana Trei Brazi, Cabana Diham, Cabana Padina and Cabana Omu. Plenty of lodgings are to be found in Bran; if you want to camp, Vampire Camping is very good despite its unimaginative name. You can camp next to every cabana on this route, but be aware of the presence of bears in the Bucegi: do not store food in your tent (ask the hut warden to store it in the cabana overnight) and do not camp below the treeline – although bears have been known to go all the way up to Omu Peak. It can get quite windy (not to mention very cold) at Cabana Omu and the camping space is rather limited, so you might prefer a bed in the heated cabana instead.

Note that Cabana Omu is closed from September/October to May/June (depending on weather conditions) and you should phone to check that it is open before you set out. Facilities at Cabana Omu are rather sparse; meals are pricey and portions small. There is no water and the outdoor toilet is no more than a hole in the ground in a wooden cabin.

STAGE 1
Poiana Braşov–Cabana Diham

Start	Strada Poiana Soarelui, Poiana Braşov
Finish	Cabana Diham
Distance	18.5km
Total ascent	1480m
Total descent	1170m
Grade	Moderate
Time	6hr 30min
Maximum altitude	1604m (Cabana Postăvaru)
Water	At the cabanas; there's a spring shortly after the start of the red cross route and one at Cabana Diham

In **Poiana Braşov**, turn right out of the car park where the bus has dropped you off, onto Strada Poiana Soarelui. Walk to the end of the main road, past Capra Neagra restaurant, the police station and the wooden church. At the **AnaTeleferic Express chairlift**, turn left onto the ski slope. This is where the red cross route starts. Either follow the red cross marks to the left of the ski slope or walk straight up the ski slope until you see the red cross marks again – the route crosses the ski slope to the right.

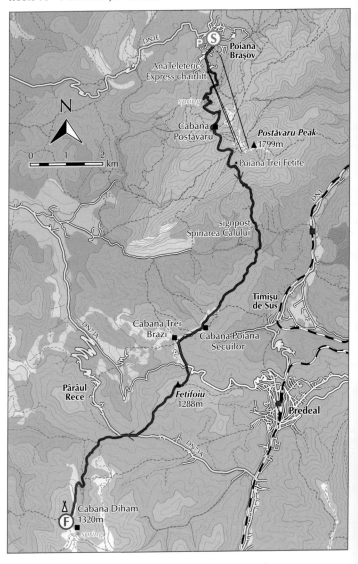

After almost 2km, turn right, then left. Walk up the Drumul Rosu ski slope for about 700 metres (there is a shortcut). Then turn right (southwest) to arrive at **Cabana Postăvaru** (1604m), also known as the Julius Römer Hutte, after about 300 metres. From the cabana, turn southeast onto the yellow stripe route towards Predeal (see the signs on the cabana wall). You will arrive at **Poiana Trei Fetite** in less than half an hour. (Note that Cabana Cristianu Mare has burnt down but there are still signposts pointing to it.)

When you reach the signpost at the end of what is called **Spinarea Calului** (a spur called 'the horse's back'; 1020m), keep heading south. From here it is 1hr to **Cabana Poiana Secuilor** and no more than 1hr 15min to **Cabana Trei Brazi** – not 2hr as the signpost suggests. You will pass an intersection with the red triangle trail coming from Timișu de Sus railway halt to the Cheile Râșnovului (Râșnov Gorge).

From Cabana Trei Brazi, the blue triangle departs west (across the meadow). This is probably the easier route; however, for the more interesting route turn left (south) onto the main road to Predeal. Follow it for 500 metres (blue cross/yellow stripe waymarks), then turn right up into the forest (blue cross waymarks). Walk for 2.5km on the blue cross trail, over the **Fetifoiu** spur and peak (1288m) to reach the **DN73A road**.

Turn right (west) and follow the road for 300 metres. Turn left when you see 'Diham' written in large red letters on a concrete electricity pole. The trail is marked red circle and blue stripe. From here it is 1hr 30min to Cabana Diham. Follow the red circle trail into the woods. Once back on the forest road, turn left. After you cross a bridge, the path goes steeply up into the woods, to the right. Soon you will arrive at a meadow; cross it to the left and follow the path (along a gravel road) to the left until you arrive at **Cabana Diham** (1320m), where you can either camp or ask for a bed in a dorm. Hot meals and drinks are available. There's a spring nearby; there are outdoor toilets and there are two sockets in the dining room.

The Postăvaru seen from Cabana Trei Fetite

STAGE 2
Cabana Diham–Cabana Omu

Start	Cabana Diham
Finish	Cabana Omu
Distance	8km
Total ascent	1390m
Total descent	240m
Grade	Moderate
Time	4hr 30min
Maximum altitude	2507m (Omu Peak)
Water	Fill flasks at spring at Cabana Diham; buy water at Cabana Omu

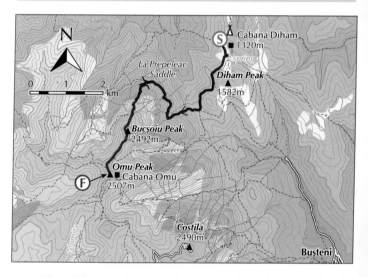

From **Cabana Diham**, head south-southwest on the dirt road marked red circle. After about 300 metres turn right. After a further 2km turn right (west) onto the red stripe/red triangle trail to Cabana Omu – 4hr 30min according to the signpost but quite a bit less in reality. Please note that there is no water after this point until you reach the cabana.

View of the ridge at the start of the trail

After 1km the path swings northwest. At **La Prepeleac Saddle** (1760m) the path forks; veer left to stay on the red stripe route. After a challenging, steep and rocky section with cables between 1900m and 2000m you will be rewarded with glorious views from the ridge. Continue on the red stripe trail until you reach **Bucșoiu Peak** (2492m). From here, all that separates you from **Omu Peak** (2507m and not very peaky at all) is about 100m of descent and 120m of ascent. You should arrive at Cabana Omu in less than 1hr.

STAGE 3

Cabana Omu–Cabana Padina via Bătrâna Saddle

Start	Cabana Omu
Finish	Cabana Padina
Distance	12km
Total ascent	300m
Total descent	1280m
Grade	Easy
Time	3hr
Maximum altitude	2507m (Cabana Omu)
Water	At and around Cabana Padina

This is a wonderful leisurely walk that will show you an entirely different side of the Bucegi. You will essentially be walking along the county border between Braşov and Dâmboviţa. This route can be combined with the next; that way, you can leave most of your luggage at Cabana Omu and return on the same day.

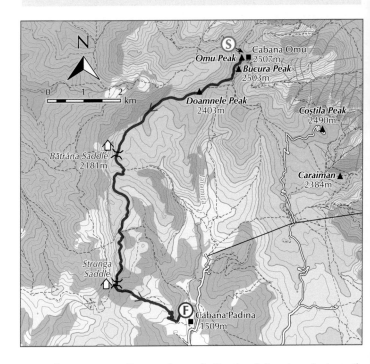

From **Cabana Omu**, set off in a southwesterly direction. Follow the red stripe trail. Bypass **Bucura Peak** (2503m) to the right and the next one to the left; this section is also marked yellow stripe. Do not follow the stone arrow up; this seems to be a bit of a practical joke (there's another stone drawing up there).

After **Doamnele Peak** (2403m), about 30min from the start, the landscape changes dramatically; the area to the west of the main ridge is as green and gentle as the ridge is rocky and barren.

This path is known as the **Drumul Granicerilor**: Guard's Route. It marked the border between the Austro-Hungarian Empire and Romania until 1918. From here, you have views of the Piatra Craiului to the west, and the villages between the Bucegi and Piatra Craiului in the valley down below.

About 2.5km after Doamnele Peak the path goes through dwarf pine for a while, after which you will reach the **Bătrâna Saddle refuge** (2170m). From there, almost 5km of gentle descending brings you to the refuge at **Strunga Saddle** (1893m); turn left (southeast) onto the combined red stripe/red cross trail here. Please note that the red stripe trail splits here; the one to the right departs towards the Leaota Mountains. From here it's another 45min to **Cabana Padina** (1509m), where you can treat yourself to decent food and plenty of water (or beer).

STAGE 4
Cabana Padina–Cabana Omu via the Ialomiţa Valley

Start	Cabana Padina
Finish	Cabana Omu
Distance	9km
Total ascent	1050m
Total descent	75m
Grade	Moderate
Time	2hr 30min
Maximum altitude	2507m (Cabana Omu)
Water	At Cabana Padina, and many springs along the way

This walk back to Omu Peak takes you through the wonderful Ialomiţa Valley; the river that cuts the Bucegi in half. It involves a 1000m climb, but it is a very gentle ascent most of the time. Along the way, you may meet donkeys, sheep and cows: it is a very pastoral route, avoiding any serious climbing but with beautiful views of the ridges to the left and right. It can be done on the same day as the previous stage, although it is definitely worth spending a day in the Padina area and paying a visit to the Ialomiţa Cave.

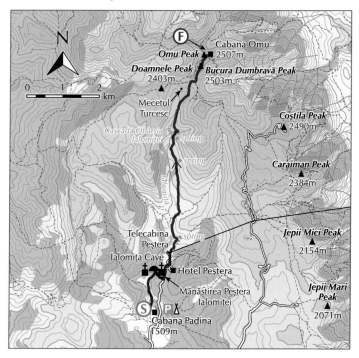

From **Cabana Padina**, walk down to the car park, where the Padina Fest sign is. Turn left (north) towards Cabana Valea Dorului; the path is marked red stripe and blue cross. After 1km you will find the **Ialomiţa Cave** to your left.

> The **Ialomiţa Cave** (Peştera Ialomiţei) is situated on the right flank of the Ialomiţa Gorge. The monastery at the cave's entrance was built in 1993, but the place has been a sanctuary for much longer: the first hermits are reported to have lived here as early as the 15th century. The hermitage has burnt down and been rebuilt a number of times. The site is considered an important spiritual place and is even deemed to be the energetic centre of the earth by some. The cave itself is intriguing: visitors can climb staircases to explore the enchanting galleries and magnificent rock formations. There's a refreshing spring in the courtyard at the entrance. The cave is open from 9am–9pm, last entry at 6pm. More information, including a virtual tour, can be found at http://pesteraialomitei.ro/en.

Continue on the blue cross route which veers to the right. Cross the river and go up the staircase, past the **Mănăstirea Peştera Ialomiţei**. Then turn left (north) onto the asphalt road, past **Hotel Peştera**, and follow it to its end (about 1km); turn right after the **Telecabina Peştera**.

After about 200 metres turn left onto the blue stripe route, signed 3hr to Cabana Omu. There are a sheepfold and a couple of **springs** at the start; several streams will cross your path. After about 3km you will be treated to some beautiful waterfalls. After a bit of ascending, cross the grassy plateau past a huge boulder called **Mecetul Turcesc**; another short ascent on a scree slope brings you to a junction with a signpost. Turn left (red and blue stripe) to make your way back to **Cabana Omu** in about 25min.

STAGE 5
Cabana Omu–Bran

Start	Cabana Omu
Finish	Vampire Camping, Bran
Distance	17km
Total ascent	260m
Total descent	2010m
Grade	Moderate
Time	5hr
Maximum altitude	2507m (Cabana Omu)
Water	Stream in the Gaura Valley
Note	Bears may be encountered on the approach to Bran; make noise as you walk and they'll stay away.

From **Cabana Omu**, set off in a northwesterly direction, following the red cross waymarks. The path forks almost immediately; bear left (west) and descend the path marked red and blue stripe, red cross and yellow triangle. After almost 1.5km, turn left (southwest) onto the red cross route which takes you down into the Gaura Valley. Much of the stream is dry in August and part of it runs underground. During this part of the descent you will have views of the Piatra Craiului and the Făgăraş looming large behind it.

Cross the stream after 2.5km, passing a **waterfall** to the right. A tricky section with loose rocks and narrow gullies follows; tread carefully. The cables should help. After 1km, the path forks: the yellow triangle trail veers to the left, to Şimon

173

village. Keep right to stay on the red cross trail. Head up into the forest until you come to a small clearing; from here the path will descend again. You have a good chance of meeting bears here, so make sure you make some noise.

After about 5km turn left onto the forest road to Poarta and Bran, which turns into an asphalt road after 1.3km. Walk or hitchhike the last 5km or so from **Poarta** to Bran (or call a taxi), unless you want to stay in one of Poarta's pensions. Once in **Bran**, turn right onto the DN73 road, to find Vampire Camping on your left after 1km.

For an onward route into the Piatra Craiului, see the alternative start to Route 18: 'Bran–Cabana Curmatura'.

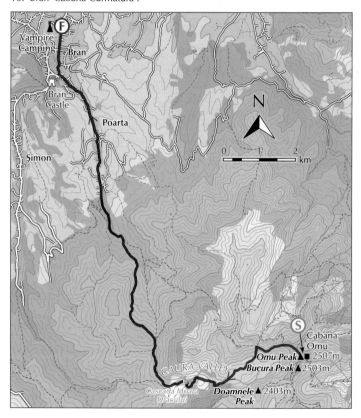

Looking west from the red cross trail just before it dips into the Gaura Valley

BRAN CASTLE

Despite its reputation as 'Dracula's castle', Bran Castle was never the 15th-century Vlad the Impaler's home – although he was locked up there for a while. Vlad Țepeș (his family name) has very little connection with Bram Stoker's *Dracula*. In fact, Stoker hadn't ever been to Transylvania – he conjured up the story after having spent much time in libraries. However, Stoker's description of Dracula's castle is strikingly similar to the appearance of the imposing Bran Castle – perched on a steep cliff – and indeed he seems to have based it on an illustration of the castle at Bran. Bran Castle does have an intriguing history: erected in the 14th century, it saw many empires pass by and ended up being the residence of Queen Marie (the last Queen of Romania; also known as Marie of Edinburgh) in the 20th century. A historical timeline and information on visiting hours and tickets can be found at http://bran-castle.com. Be aware that there is often a very long queue to enter the castle; you may want to avoid weekends.

ROUTE 17

Into the Bucegi from the Prahova Valley

Start	Buşteni
Finish	Cable car to Sinaia
Distance	51.5km
Total ascent	3750m
Total descent	2620m
Grade	Moderate
Time	4 days
Maximum altitude	2507m (Omu Peak, Stage 2)
Maps	One of the following: Erfatur-Dimap; Munţii Bucegi, 1:33,000, Discover Eco-Romania/Zenith; Munţii Bucegi, 1:35,000, Munţii Noştri; Munţii Bucegi, 1:50,000, Bel Alpin; Bucegi-Leaota, 1:70,000/1:25,000, Munţii Noştri

The second of the two routes through the Bucegi described in this guide (the other being Route 16) starts from Buşteni's railway station, right at the foot of the majestic Caraiman Peak (2384m) and its neighbours. From Buşteni and neighbouring Sinaia, cable cars go up to the ridge, which means this side of the massif can get very crowded, especially during weekends and in August. The ascent to the ridge is steep and challenging, but once you are on top you will find yourself on a plateau that makes for easy walking. This route combines both sides of the horseshoe of the Bucegi, and traverses the Ialomiţa Valley that separates them as well. It is possible to combine stages of this route with stages of Route 16. The route ends above Sinaia; you can either take the cable car down or walk. While you are there, do visit the magnificent Peleş Palace. Please be aware that the Bucegi has a large bear population; be sure to make some noise in the forest and they'll stay away.

Access
Buşteni is served by no fewer than 20 trains a day from Braşov and 15 from Bucharest. The journey takes between 50min and 1hr from Braşov, and about 1hr 50min from Bucureşti Nord.

It is possible to enter the Bucegi by car from Sinaia (for example), via the DJ713A and DJ714 roads that lead past Cabana Zănoaga and all the way up to Cabana Padina. This gives the option of starting at Cabana Padina and doing several day walks from there.

Horses near the Transbucegi road (Stage 4)

From the end of the trek there are several onward options. These include taking the '2000' cable car down to Sinaia (operates daily 9.30am–6.30pm – check details at https://www.sinaiago.ro/en); walking down to Sinaia via the red stripe trail (9km, about 3hr); or closing the loop and heading back to Cabana Babele via the yellow stripe trail and going down to Bușteni from there (6km, about 2hr) – but bear in mind that the Babele–Bușteni cable car is unreliable. A third alternative would be to hike north on the yellow stripe trail to Cabana Piatra Arsă and descend via the blue stripe trail to Sinaia (11km, about 3hr 30min).

Accommodation
The Bucegi is scattered with cabanas. The ones on this route are Cabana Babele, Cabana Padina, Cabana Bolboci, Cabana Zănoaga and Cabana Valea Dorului. Cabana Babele was closed for an extended period in 2017 but should now be open year-round; resort to the nearby (staffed) Salvamont base or bring your tent if you can't reach it by phone. Otherwise, continue to Cabana Padina (see Stage 3) or Cabana Omu (see Stage 2), both less than 2hr away. There's a campsite just beyond Cabana Zănoaga, and another one in Bușteni (Aviator). You can camp next to any of the cabanas and refuges in the Bucegi, but due to the presence of bears you should not store food in your tent. You'll find plenty of other accommodation in Bușteni and Sinaia. Note that Cabana Miorița (end of Stage 4) is no longer open.

Facilities at Cabana Omu are rather sparse; meals are pricey and portions small. There is no water and the outdoor toilet is no more than a hole in the ground in a wooden cabin. It is possible to pitch your tent on the grassy area next to the cabana but it can get quite windy (not to mention very cold) up there so you might prefer a bed in the heated cabana.

STAGE 1
Bușteni–Cabana Babele via the Jepii Valley

Start	Bușteni Station
Finish	Cabana Babele
Distance	7km
Total ascent	1450m
Total descent	150m
Grade	Moderate
Time	3hr 15min
Maximum altitude	2296m (Cabana Babele)
Water	At Cabana Babele; there is a stream in the Jepii Valley and another one between Cabana Caraiman and Cabana Babele

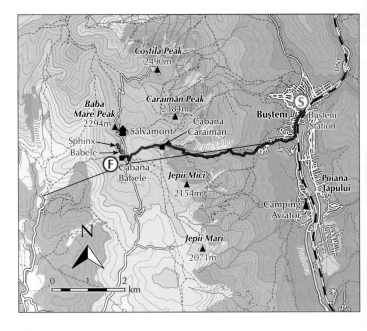

Up into the clouds from the Jepii Mici Valley

As you exit **Buşteni Station** you will immediately see Caraiman Peak and the sheer rock wall of the Bucegi towering above you. Turn left and walk along the DN1 road for 600 metres, then turn right onto Strada Telecabinei. Follow it for the best part of a kilometre, past the visitor centre and *telecabina*. Before long you'll see blue cross, red circle and blue triangle waymarks appearing. It is the blue cross route you want to follow. After about 1km the asphalt road turns into a dirt road. After a further 250 metres the road ends; take the right path to stay on the blue cross trail.

Very soon you'll see a signpost to Valea Jepii Mici, Cabana Caraiman and Cabana Babele. Turn left here. After 2.5km cross the stream. After a steady climb featuring multiple cables and some staircases you'll arrive at the now privately owned **Cabana Caraiman** (2025m).

Stay on the blue cross route for Cabana Babele, which is only 30min away. Pass to the right of the grey derelict building; turn right and you'll see the green-roofed, stone-red **Cabana Babele** and the rock sculptures in front of you. If Cabana Babele is closed, try your luck at the **Salvamont base**, which is 15min further north on the yellow stripe trail.

STAGE 2

Cabana Babele–Cabana Omu via Caraiman Peak and back

Start/finish	Cabana Babele
Distance	15km
Total ascent/descent	850m
Grade	Moderate; second half easy
Time	3hr 45min
Maximum altitude	2507m (Omu Peak)
Water	Fill bottles at Cabana Babele

This circular route can be split in two; you can walk the first 9km to Cabana Omu, stay there and walk back to Cabana Babele the next day – or continue to Cabana Padina or Bran (see Route 16). It is easily tackled in one day though.

From the front door of **Cabana Babele**, turn right (northwest) and follow the yellow stripe waymarks towards the Salvamont base. When you arrive in the valley that lies between Cabana Babele and the Salvamont base, turn right (east) onto the red cross route to **Crucea Eroilor** (2.5km, 1hr). From Crucea Eroilor ('Heroes' Cross'), retrace your steps until the path forks; follow the signposts to the right (west). The path runs almost parallel to the other path. Go up the rocky gully; the waymarks on the rocks are sparse and do not have the usual white background – they can be hard to spot, especially in bad weather.

Make your way up to **Caraiman Peak** (2384m) in about 30min; it is marked with a pile of stones. From here the path is clearly marked with signposts again. What follows is a very straightforward, level walk across the plateau. At the end of it, turn left onto a dirt road. Stay on the marked trail as it soon bends to the northwest, off the dirt road, onto a narrow trail into the valley. The red cross trail ends here; pick up the yellow stripe waymarks from here.

After 1km head up west (left) on the combined yellow/red stripe trail. A marking on a shed tells you Omu Peak is 1hr 30min from here; in reality it can be done in 45min in fair weather. Cabana Omu soon appears on the horizon. The path swings southwest (left), goes down and round the cliffs you were walking on previously. From here it is a short walk to **Omu Peak** and cabana.

To return to Cabana Babele (this should take about 1hr–1hr 30min), retrace your steps down the yellow stripe trail for almost 3km until you meet the start of

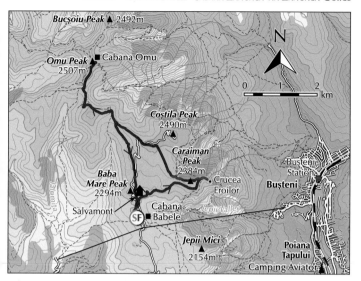

the red cross trail again. Keep right to stay on the yellow stripe trail, and walk the very straightforward and uneventful route back over the plateau to either the **Salvamont base** or **Cabana Babele**.

STAGE 3

Cabana Babele–Cabana Zănoaga via Zănoaga Gorge

Start	Cabana Babele
Finish	Cabana Zănoaga (Complex Turistic Zănoaga)
Distance	21.5km
Total ascent	700m
Total descent	1500m
Grade	Easy
Time	5hr 30min
Maximum altitude	2206m (Cabana Babele)
Water	At Cabana Padina and Cabana Zănoaga. There's a spring in the courtyard of the Ialomiţa Monastery and Cave, and a spring about 12.5km from the start.

181

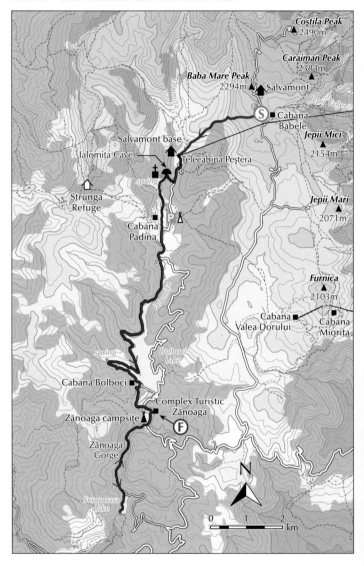

This leisurely walk requires you to walk over the DJ714 road, past Bolboci Lake, for a good while. The section over the road isn't very exciting, but it takes you to the Zănoaga Gorge which is definitely worth it. It makes for a nice restorative walk in between the tougher sections of this route. Zănoaga Gorge can also be reached by car.

From **Cabana Babele**, turn west and head down the blue cross route. It should take about an hour to reach **Telecabina Peştera** and the Salvamont base in the valley, and another 10min to reach the **Ialomiţa Cave** (Peştera Ialomiţei – see http://pesteraialomitei.ro/en for visiting hours and further information). From the cave it is just a 20min walk over a gravel road to **Cabana Padina**.

From Cabana Padina, continue southwest – the gravel road soon turns into an asphalt road, and again into a dirt road as you reach **Bolboci Lake** (3km, 40min) The road winds around the lake; ignore the two roads to the left early on, before you reach the lake. After almost 8km from the northern side of Bolboci Lake you'll reach **Cabana Bolboci** on the southern lakeside – an excellent spot for a break.

Stay on the asphalt road (the DJ714). One more kilometre brings you to **Complex Turistic Zănoaga**. You can leave your pack here. The Zănoaga campsite is 200 metres down the road, on the right. To continue to the Zănoaga Gorge, turn right just after the campsite and follow the blue cross waymarks for Cabana Scropoasa. The path forks almost immediately; keep right, then bear left, following the stream. A sign saying 'Reservaţia Naturală Zănoaga-Lucăcilă' marks the entrance to the **Zănoaga Gorge**. When the path forks, keep left and descend towards the waterfall.

The Ialomiţa Cave and Monastery

After 2km you'll get to **Scropoasa Lake**. There is a hydro power station to the left, over the bridge; however, the path continues south, hugging the shore. (The abandoned Cabana Scropoasa is on the trail that goes up to the right.) At the far end of the lake you can get a peek of Scropoasa Gorge. The path ends here though; retrace your steps to return to Complex Turistic Zănoaga. Not only will you be able to order a good meal at Cabana Zănoaga, but there's also a whole sweet stall with homemade treats inside!

STAGE 4
Cabana Zănoaga–Cabana Miorița

Start	Cabana Zănoaga (Complex Turistic Zănoaga)
Finish	Cable car to Sinaia
Distance	8km
Total ascent	750m
Total descent	120m
Grade	Easy
Time	2hr 30min
Maximum altitude	1960m
Water	At the cabanas
Note	Bears may be encountered on or near this route; be sure to make noise as you're walking and they'll stay away.

From **Cabana Zănoaga**, turn right onto the DJ714 road. After 300 metres the road forks; keep right. After 400 metres on this road, turn right onto a dirt road; there's a signpost to Cabana Miorița. Soon, the path forks again; keep left, even though the trail to the right looks like the obvious continuation. The trail is marked with yellow cross and red triangle waymarks, and leads through an absolutely enchanting pine forest; it is very quiet except for the sound of a trickle of water, and has a wonderful mossy floor. This is definitely bear territory too – paw prints have been spotted.

The path soon swings to the left and goes up. When you come to a clearing with a yellow cross signpost, cross it to the northwest, then turn right. Cross another, larger clearing, again northwest. Turn left onto the path at the other end; it is initially unmarked. After about 20 metres, turn right, up the rocky path, to find the waymarks again. You will soon emerge out of the forest; for the rest of the way the trail leads over grassy hills.

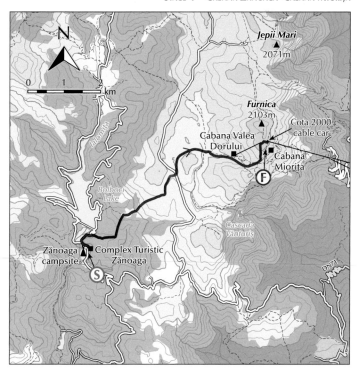

Cross the DJ713 road and continue on the dirt road towards **Cabana Valea Dorului** (1.820km from here, according to a very precise signpost). There is a stream to the right here. After 1.3km on this road you'll see a signpost; it's possible to make a 3km detour via the Vânturiș Waterfall at this point, but this is only worthwhile in spring/early summer.

If not opting for the detour, continue on the same road and walk past **Cabana Valea Dorului**, then turn left up the red triangle trail to arrive at the **Cota 2000 cable car**, which will take you down to Sinaia in two stages (tickets are to be bought after the first ride). Cabana Miorița (now closed) is a 5min walk south from the green *telecabina*.

THE PIATRA CRAIULUI MOUNTAINS

ROUTE 18
The northern ridge

Start/finish	Zărneşti
Distance	42.5km
Total ascent/descent	3720m
Grade	Moderate-difficult
Time	4–5 days
Maximum altitude	2238m (La Om Peak, Stage 4)
Maps	One of the following: Piatra Craiului, 1:40,000, Munţii Noştri; Piatra Craiului, 1:30,000, Bel Alpin; Piatra Craiului, 1:30,000, Discover Eco-Romania/Zenith. If you can't get hold of any of these, 'Five mountains from the Carpathians' bend', 1:70,000, Erfatur-Dimap will also do.

The Piatra Craiului ridge offers plenty of challenges (Stage 4)

The Piatra Craiului, 'King's Rock', is a paradise for thrill-seeking hikers: the 22km-long saw-like limestone ridge is a gigantic rocky playground where much time is spent on all fours, scrambling up walls that seem impossibly steep, and clambering and leaping from one big rock to the next like a chamois. If you want to take in the beauty of the Piatra Craiului but not venture up the main ridge, you can walk up to Cabana Curmatura (Stage 1, or Stage 5 in reverse) and then descend to Zărneşti Gorge via the Crăpăturii Valley – or descend to the Zărneşti gorges via the blue stripe route. This could be tackled in a day. If you want to test the waters first, try the short Piatra Mică circuit (Stage 2) before you move on to the main ridge – this will give you a good idea of what to expect in just a couple of hours.

This route essentially comprises a number of day walks from Cabana Curmatura, where you can camp (or pay for a bed in a dorm) and then explore the ridge carrying just a day pack. This is particularly useful as these walks contain some very challenging technical sections and carrying a backpack throughout would make things considerably more difficult. It is possible to start from Bran – see alternative start below – and thus to connect this route with Route 16.

Access
There are nine regional trains from Braşov to Zărneşti each day. The journey takes about 40min. See https://regiocalatori.ro for a timetable (select 'Mersul Trenurilor', 'Rute' and 'Braşov–Zărneşti'). Buy tickets at the Regio Călători desk at Braşov Station (on the left as you enter), not the CFR desk. Buses to Zărneşti leave from Autogara 2, Strada Avram Iancu 114, every 30min – the journey takes 1hr.

For the alternative start, there are numerous buses from Braşov to Bran. The journey takes between 45min and 1hr. See https://autogari.ro for timetable and stops.

The Piatra Craiului mountains are a national park. You will have to buy an entry ticket to the park; you can either buy one online (www.pcrai.ro – English-language option available) or from the blue ticket machine at the Zărneşti post office (12A Strada Spârchez Tiberiu). A ticket costs 5RON and gives you access to the park for seven days.

Accommodation
Plenty of options in Zărneşti and Bran. On the route there's Cabana Gura Râului at the start of the dirt road into the gorges; a camping spot just before Fântâna lui Botorog; and camping spot and beds at Cabana Curmatura (the most central hut) and Plaiul Foii Cabana (down in the Bârsa Valley on the western side of the ridge – see Stage 5 alternative finish). There are numerous shelters, mainly on top of the ridge; if you want to make a full north–south traverse you can stay in these – although bear in mind they can fill up quickly and you aren't guaranteed

a place. Facilities at Cabana Curmatura are very basic; there are no bathrooms; there are just outdoor toilets, a spring and a shower which is a basically a trickle of water through a pipe from a stream in a wooden cabin. Electricity is only available in the evening. However, the decent food (apple pie if you're lucky!) and lovely staff more than make up for these austere circumstances. Note that wild camping is not permitted in the Piatra Craiului since it is a national park, and doing so could result in a fine.

A great place to stay before and after hiking in the Piatra Craiului is the village of Măgura, which lies just east of the striking Zărneşti gorges. A selection of pensions is listed in Appendix B. You can also camp in the backyards of all of these.

Water
There's a fountain at the start of the yellow stripe trail (see Stage 1 below) called Fântâna lui Botorog. Once you're up in the mountains you will have to rely on the spring at Cabana Curmatura (although you can also buy bottled water at the cabana if the stream has dried up, which it may do towards the end of summer) – there are no water sources on the ridge. There are a couple of other springs on some of the stages, but all far below the ridge.

STAGE 1
Zărneşti–Cabana Curmatura

Start	Zărneşti Station
Finish	Cabana Curmatura
Distance	9km
Total ascent	800m
Total descent	70m
Grade	Easy
Time	2hr 30min
Maximum altitude	1470m (Cabana Curmatura)

The main route described here is the shortest and easiest route to Cabana Curmatura, the hut that serves as the base for all stages of this route. It does not lead through the gorges; if you want to see these, use the alternative start from Bran, also described below.

Exit **Zărneşti Station** and turn right onto Strada Tudor Vladimirescu. Follow the signs for the centre, Măgura and Plaiul Foii along Strada Mitropolit Ion Meţianu, which becomes Strada Spârchez Tiberiu. After you have passed Strada Stefan cel Mare to the left, you will start seeing blue stripe waymarks. Pass Strada Magurii to the left and continue onto an unpaved narrow road, walking along a stream for 200 metres. At the end of this, turn right (a faded blue arrow points you in the right direction) and immediately turn left onto the main road (DJ112G). Walk along the road for 1km until you get to **Cabana Gura Râului**.

Follow the now unpaved road into the gorge, passing a **camping spot** after 1.2km. Another 400 metres brings you to **Fântâna lui Botorog**. Turn right onto the yellow stripe trail to Cabana Curmatura here. After 2km of ascending, leave the woods behind to arrive at a grassy clearing called **Poiana Zănoaga**, from where you will have beautiful views of the Piatra Craiului ridge ahead and back to the Bucegi Mountains. Cross the clearing and keep following the yellow stripe trail until you get to **Cabana Curmatura** (less than 3km, 1hr).

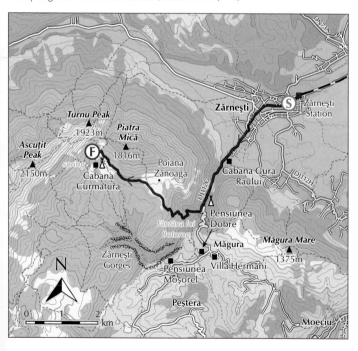

ALTERNATIVE START
Bran–Cabana Curmatura

Start	Vampire Camping, Bran
Finish	Cabana Curmatura
Distance	17km
Total ascent	1700m
Total descent	1000m
Grade	Moderate
Time	5hr 30min
Maximum altitude	1470m (Cabana Curmatura)
Water	Fântâna lui Botorog, Cabana Curmatura

From Vampire Camping in **Bran**, turn right onto the DN73 road. Once in the centre of Bran, pass **Bran Castle** to the right; follow the road that winds around it. Just past the castle you will see a signpost marked red stripe to Cabana Curmatura. Cross the stream to the right of the road over a narrow bridge here, then cross the meadow to the west to get to the start of the red stripe trail.

Two trails start here; take the left one. The path goes up steeply through the woods. After 1km or so it becomes much more gentle and leads through meadows, with scattered birch trees to the left and a pine forest to the right. You can see the Bucegi Mountains behind you and the town of Moieciu de Jos in the valley down below. Soon you will be able to see the eastern end of the Piatra Craiului ridge ahead of you, to the northwest.

The path leads through a sheepfold after about 1.5km – mind the dogs. You soon enter a much cooler beech forest. After a further 1.5km, leave the forest behind you to enter a meadow with scattered rocks – this is **Poiana Măgura Mare**, just below Măgura Mare Peak (1375m). From here you can see the Piatra Craiului ridge in all its glory – an excellent spot for a break.

To continue, walk to the left (southwest) for about 20 metres, then almost immediately turn right to descend into another meadow (more sheep and dogs). Cross it to the northwest, into the forest again. Cross the next meadow to the northwest, towards the Piatra Craiului ridge. There are some waymarks on a wooden shed; after that, the marks are hidden in the grass. Turn left (west) when you arrive at a wooden cross, so that you are facing the ridge again. The trail merges with a forest road very briefly, then plunges into the woods to the right. When you get to a hairpin in the road, either follow the red stripe trail back into

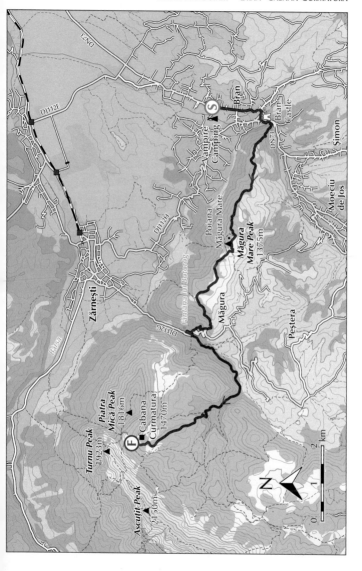

Descending to the Zărneşti gorges in winter

the woods (a shortcut that ultimately joins the road again), or follow the road down to **Fântâna lui Botorog**.

From here you have several options. For the fastest route, follow the yellow stripe trail as described in Stage 1 of Route 18. If, however, you want to explore the gorges, head southwest on the gravel road; follow the wooden signpost for 'Prăpăstiile Zărneştilor'. Before long, blue stripe marks will appear. Pass the barrier that marks the entrance to the gorges; leave the road and turn right after 3.7km.

The trail splits into blue stripe and yellow circle here. Keep following the blue stripe route (although the yellow circle route also leads to Cabana Curmatura and is a bit easier, so you have options). After about 2km, emerge out of the woods to be rewarded with a view of the ridge. Turn right (northeast) onto a dirt road. Turn left (northwest) at the signpost pointing to Cabana Curmatura and walk along a stream. The blue stripe and yellow circle trails merge again here. When you get to another dirt road after 500 metres, turn right onto it and walk the last few steps to **Cabana Curmatura**.

STAGE 2
Piatra Mică circuit from Cabana Curmatura

Start/finish	Cabana Curmatura
Distance	5km
Total ascent/descent	520m
Grade	Moderate
Time	2hr 15min
Maximum altitude	1816m (Piatra Mică Peak)

This excellent short walk explores the Piatra Mică, 'Small Rock'. It is only comparatively small; this mass of rock looks daunting enough when you're standing at the foot of it. It can easily be tackled on the same day as the entry walk, if you're still up to some good scrambling.

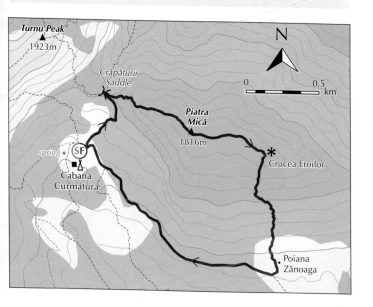

From **Cabana Curmatura**, head northwest up the blue circle trail. After 600 metres you'll arrive at **Crăpăturii Saddle**. From the viewing platform, excellent views are to be had of the Piatra Mică to the right, Valea Crăpăturii down below and Turnu Peak to the left. At the signpost, make a sharp right turn (southeast) to stay on the blue circle trail. After about 200 metres turn right (south) and go up a steep section with cables.

Traverse the calcareous Piatra Mică ridge – only a few hundred metres long – until you come to a grassy meadow, from which you can see Crucea Eroilor ('Heroes' Cross'). Looking back, you can see the main ridge of the Piatra Craiului in all its glory. Make your way through dwarf pine over a well-marked narrow trail to the unmarked **Piatra Mică Peak** (1816m).

Continue ahead, and from **Crucea Eroilor** (1797m) make your way down to **Poiana Zănoaga** through the forest (30–45min). From the signpost in the clearing, turn right onto the yellow stripe trail again to return to **Cabana Curmatura** in about 30min.

STAGE 3

Turnu and Ascuțit Peaks circuit from Cabana Curmatura

Start/finish	Cabana Curmatura
Distance	6km
Total ascent/descent	790m
Grade	Difficult
Time	4hr 30min
Maximum altitude	2150m (Ascuțit Peak)
Note	This route involves a lot of scrambling, aided by cables

From **Cabana Curmatura** head northwest up the blue circle trail. After 600 metres you'll arrive at **Crăpăturii Saddle**. Turn left (southwest) onto the red circle trail from the viewing platform and very soon you'll come to face a sheer rock wall; this mountain is called Turnu ('Tower') for good reason.

The challenging and exhilarating, sometimes almost perpendicular ascent is made with the help of a good many cables. After about 1hr 30min you'll reach **Turnu Peak** (1923m). Another 1hr 30min of craggy ridge walking on the red circle trail brings you to **Ascuțit Peak** (2150m) with its dome-shaped red shelter. Just after the shelter, turn left (southeast) onto the blue triangle route to Cabana Curmatura. The descent is quite steep but not very difficult, but expect lots of scree and some cables. Once you reach the forest road (about 2km/1hr 30min), turn left to reach **Cabana Curmatura** in 10min or so.

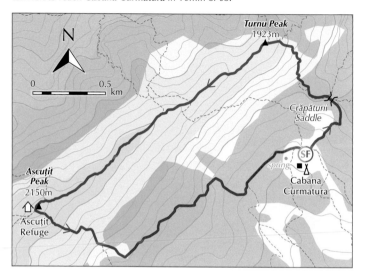

Climbing Turnu Peak

STAGE 4

La Om Peak circuit from Cabana Curmatura

Start/finish	Cabana Curmatura
Distance	14.5km
Total ascent/descent	1420m
Grade	Difficult
Time	6hr 20min
Maximum altitude	2238m (La Om Peak)
Water	Several streams and a spring after La Table
Note	The route involves much scrambling and clambering; proceed with care.

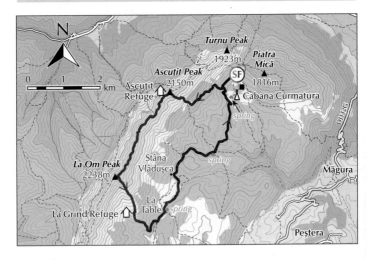

From the front door of **Cabana Curmatura**, turn right. Follow the dirt road for about 500 metres until you get to a signpost marked yellow, red and blue triangle. Follow the blue triangle to the right. Soon you will get to the first scree slope; make your way up it. Very soon you should see a blue arrow to the left – follow it into the woods. For the first 30 metres or so the rocky path runs more or less parallel to the slope; after that it veers to the left. Cross the next scree slope to the southwest – the path will continue southwest for quite a while. A

gentle 20min ascent brings you to a meadow at around 1715m with a signpost, pointing west towards the ridge.

Some 500 metres or so beyond the meadow, go steeply up a rocky slope to the right (northwest); bear left wherever you can to avoid the scree. After some 20min on this slope there's a short section with cables, and another signpost to Ascuţit Refuge, signed 30–45min. When you arrive on the ridge, **Ascuţit Peak** (2150m) and shelter are to your right.

To continue, turn left (southwest) onto the narrow ridge. The ridge trail is marked red circle. The Bucegi and the Piatra Craiului foothills can be seen to the left; the Piatra Mică is now behind you and the Făgăraş Chain to your right. There is a very good chance of seeing chamois on the steep northwestern flanks. The ridge walk involves quite some clambering; this ridge is really a gigantic rocky playground with all its cracks and crevices.

After about 3km of ridge walking you reach **La Om Peak** (2238m), the highest point on the ridge. Turn left onto the red stripe trail to go down the southeastern slope. Be careful – there is a lot of loose, terracotta-coloured rubble on the first, rather steep, section. About 1hr of descending brings you to **La Grind Refuge** (1620m).

From the refuge, follow the combined blue and red stripe trail down through a deforested area to **La Table**; a grassy valley with a spring. The signpost here says it is another 3–4hr to Cabana Curmatura; in reality it's more like 2hr.

Turn left onto the red triangle trail. Pass **Stâna Vlâduşca** (1415m) with its herd of cows to the right (beware of the dogs!) and cross the meadow to the north; red cross merges with red triangle here. The path forks after you've crossed a stream; keep left to stay on the red triangle route and traverse a soggy meadow. After about 3.5km you'll reach a gravel road; there's a spring here. Turn left, off the gravel road, almost immediately – the path leads back into the woods, passing several streams. After 1km descend to the forest road and turn left onto it, and walk the last kilometre back to **Cabana Curmatura**.

STAGE 5
Cabana Curmatura–Zărneşti via Valea Crăpăturii

Start	Cabana Curmatura
Finish	Zărneşti Station
Distance	8km
Total ascent	190m
Total descent	920m
Grade	Moderate
Time	3hr
Maximum altitude	1580m (Crăpăturii Saddle)
Water	Several springs at the bottom of Crăpăturii Valley

This is a rather spectacular route back to Zărneşti, which, of course, can also be used in reverse as an approach walk.

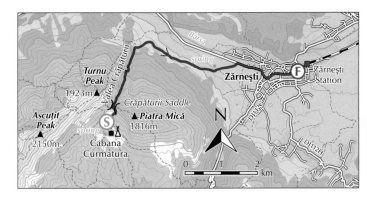

From **Cabana Curmatura**, head northwest up the blue circle trail. After 600 metres you'll arrive at **Crăpăturii Saddle**. From there, go northeast down the yellow stripe trail. The trail descends very steeply down a scree slope. After 1.3km or so, at an altitude of 1100m, the path enters the forest and is joined by a stream.

When you emerge onto a clearing after 500 metres, turn right (east); cross the stream and go up the narrow trail, which is unmarked initially. Yellow and blue

*This is how steep the western face
of the Piatra Craiului really is*

stripe waymarks will appear soon. Do not follow the blue stripe waymarks that
head north from the clearing though: this is the continuation of the blue stripe
route in the opposite direction. The yellow and blue stripe path leads through
the fields, just above the valley to the left. There's a **spring** after almost 3km; very
soon after that you'll meet the asphalt road coming from Plaiul Foii leading into
Zărneşti. Turn right onto it and walk the final 2.5km to **Zărneşti Station**.

ALTERNATIVE FINISH
Cabana Curmatura–Cabana Plaiul Foii

Start	Cabana Curmatura
Finish	Cabana Plaiul Foii
Distance	6.5km
Total ascent	630m
Total descent	1220m
Grade	Difficult
Time	4hr
Maximum altitude	1936m (Padinei Închise Saddle)
Water	At Cabana Curmatura and Cabana Plaiul Foii

This route provides a connection between the Piatra Craiului and the Făgăraş. From Cabana Plaiul Foii you can either explore further – see Route 22 – or head back to Zărneşti by taxi (or by a 13km walk down a dusty road).

From **Cabana Curmatura**, start following the blue stripe trail northwest, into the woods. Just before you get to a scree slope, turn left, passing underneath some large fallen trees, then head steeply up a rocky section with faded waymarks. When you meet another scree slope, keep right; the path hugs the sheer rock wall to the right. Just before you get to the top of the ridge, the path swings to the right (northeast), and you will shortly arrive at **Padinei Închise Saddle** (1936m).

From the saddle, make your way down, northwest, towards Diana shelter and Cabana Plaiul Foii. Prepare for a very steep descent down a scree slope, with a rock wall to the left. There is a small trickle of water and a puddle at La Gavan, but don't rely on this to refill your bottles.

After 450m of descending over a distance of 1.5km you will reach the **Diana shelter** at Poiana Curmătura Prăpăstiilor (1510m). If you want, you can continue straight to Zărneşti from here; in that case, turn right (east) and continue on the blue stripe trail to reach Zărneşti in 2hr–2hr 30min. However, if you want to continue to Cabana Plaiul Foii, descend the yellow triangle trail through the forest. When you reach a meadow, cross it to the west, then turn left onto the road – there is a spring after 300 metres. **Cabana Plaiul Foii** is 1km down the road, situated on the right.

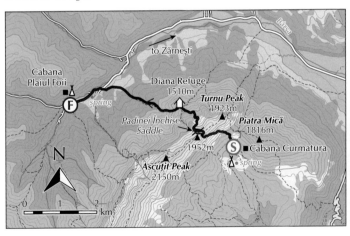

ROUTE 19
The southern ridge

Start	Cabana Plaiul Foii
Finish	Cabana Brustureț
Distance	17km
Total ascent	1555m
Total descent	1435m
Grade	Difficult
Time	7hr 45min
Maximum altitude	2195m (Grindului Saddle)
Maps	One of the following: Piatra Craiului, 1:40,000, Munții Noștri; Piatra Craiului, 1:30,000, Bel Alpin; Piatra Craiului, 1:30,000, Discover Eco-Romania/Zenith
Access	The only transport option to Cabana Plaiul Foii is taxi. The road is unpaved so the driver will likely charge you more than for other destinations (around 50RON from Zărnești). Alternatively, Sorin Rusu, the owner of Coronensis Apartment in Brașov, will drive you to Plaiul Foii in the morning and pick you up at Cabana Brustureț at the end of the walk for a very reasonable fee; see Appendix B for his contact details. See the end of this route description for other options for leaving the area at the end of the walk.
Accommodation	Cabana Plaiul Foii at the start, Cabana Căprioara at the end, and pensions in Dâmbovicioara 5km beyond the finish. It's possible to camp at Cabana Plaiul Foii; however, theft is not uncommon in this area so keep an eye on your valuables and tent at all times. Wild camping in the Piatra Craiului is not permitted. A great place to stay before and after hiking in the Piatra Craiului is the village of Măgura, which lies just east of the striking Zărnești gorges. A selection of pensions is listed in Appendix B. You can also camp in the backyards of all of these.
Water	At Cabana Plaiul Foii; the Tamaș Stream at the start; spring near Cabana Brustureț. No water on or near the ridge.
Note	This route involves a good deal of scrambling with some sections aided by cables – not all of which are in ideal condition.

Without a doubt, this is one of the most exhilarating and most difficult single-day walks in all of Romania. To ascend to the jagged Piatra Craiului ridge you need to brave the near-vertical walls of the western face of the Piatra Craiului via the Lanţuri ('Chains') route. After that feat you have more than 3km of rough ridge walking and clambering ahead of you, followed by an easy but long descent through meadows and woods to Cabana Brusturet (now closed – see end of route description). The southern ridge (Creasta Sudica) is much less visited than the northern half. It is slightly lower but by no means less difficult; you will be spending much time on all fours. The southern half of the Piatra Craiului ridge can be tackled in a long day starting at Plaiul Foii. (If you're willing to carry a full pack and six litres of water, a traverse of the entire ridge can be made in two days: Cabana Curmatura to La Om via Turnu and Ascuţit Peaks – see Route 18, Stages 3 and 4 – then spend the night at Grind 2 Refuge below La Om Peak before continuing onto the southern half of the ridge.) The ridge may be dry but it is by no means barren: especially in spring you will find it adorned with a great variety of alpine flowers, and you may very well spot chamois on its western side.

From **Cabana Plaiul Foii**, walk west along the DC50A road for about 350 metres, then turn left (southwest) onto a gravel road. There's a signpost at the start, according to which it is 5–6hr to La Om Peak via the Lanţuri route. Walk along the Tamaş Stream, passing a barrier after 1.4km. The trail bends slightly to the left; continue south. Red and blue triangle and blue stripe trails diverge to the right here – continue straight ahead (southeast) to stay on the red stripe trail. After 600 metres there's a signpost to Spirlea Refuge (1440m), signed 2hr–2hr 30min from here – in fact it can be reached in under an hour. Climb steeply through the forest; you will reach the **refuge** after 2.3km.

The sheer rock wall of the Piatra Craiului now rises up in front of you; it is so steep that it may well make you wonder how you are ever going to get up there – but you will. After a little more climbing you can see the Făgăraş to the right; you will see much more of it later on. Soon you will see a signpost, where the red stripe trail forks; turn left to continue towards the ridge. The path soon becomes a scree slope, the top of which marks the start of the so-called 'Drumul lui Deubel' trail – named after the 19th-century entomologist Friedrich Deubel, who made significant contributions to the development and promotion of hiking trails in the Carpathians.

With the help of cables, climb a chimney behind the **'La Zaplaz'** rock sculpture, which looks a bit like a lantern. Many more sections with cables follow; in one instance the cable has come loose and has frayed and the rocks are very smooth. Try pulling yourself up by holding onto the end of the cable – this requires some strength (or perhaps a friendly push from behind). The whole climb from La Zaplaz to the ridge is less than 1.5km, but you will ascend a whopping 555m to **Grindului Saddle** (2195m). The trail is mostly well marked though, and during the first half or so you can benefit from the shade of the rock walls beside you.

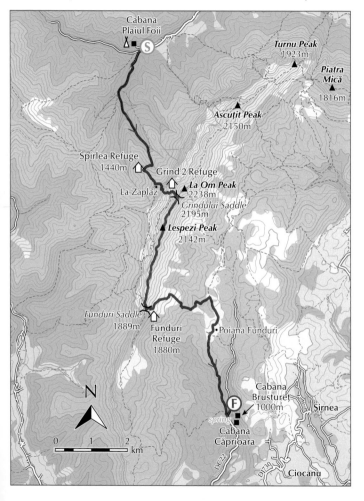

Grind 2 Refuge is just to your left when you arrive at the saddle. La Om Peak (2238m) is a short hike further to the left; it would take around 1hr there and back to climb it. However, from Grindului Saddle, turn right onto the southern ridge, marked red circle and signed 3–4hr to Funduri Saddle. Make a sharp right almost immediately to get right on top of the ridge – this is Colți Grindului.

The trail stays on top of the ridge for a long time; after just over a kilometre it descends a little and continues to the left of the ridge for a while. Clamber up to **Lespezi Peak** (2142m); after this peak the trail becomes a bit smoother for a while, until you start descending towards Funduri Saddle through dwarf pine. About 3.5km of ridge walking brings you to a signpost; turn left (southeast) here and descend to **Funduri Refuge** in about 5min.

Walk past the refuge, then turn left (east) and descend on the blue triangle/red circle trail. When you enter the forest there is a section with fewer waymarks; just continue south (straight ahead) at the same altitude until you see waymarks and an arrow, then turn left (northeast) and continue descending. After 600 metres you will reach a meadow; turn left. The path becomes a pleasant and nearly level forest road. After a further 400 metres cross another meadow east, then turn right (south) onto the blue stripe route, signed 1hr 30min–2hr to Cabana Brustureț. The trail quickly splits off the forest road; keep right.

After 700 metres stay with the trail as it veers to the right (south), off the track – the waymarks are hard to miss – then leads to another track. Cross **Poiana**

Above La Zaplaz, looking towards the Făgăraș

The magnificent southern Piatra Craiului ridge: it is sometimes hard to predict where the trail will go next

Funduri meadow – from here you have perfect views back to the ridge. The trail veers off the track again; cross another meadow to the left (south), where you will find a signpost, signed 1hr to Cabana Brustureţ. Descend through the forest; after 2.5km you will find **Cabana Brustureţ** (1000m) on your left.

Unfortunately, Cabana Brustureţ has closed down. If you want to stay locally there is Cabana Căprioara just a little further up the road (the DC22), and several other pensions in Dâmbovicioara 5km further up the DC22. If you want to make your way out of the area straight away and have not arranged transportation, you can either walk south on the DC22 through the Brustureţ and Dâmbovicioara gorges (7km) or follow the yellow stripe trail east to the village of Ciocanu on the DJ730 road (2km), and then walk over the road to Şirnea (3km) and take a bus to Braşov from there. The last bus departs at 5.14pm (schedule may be subject to change – check www.autogari.ro). Hitchhiking is not really an option since there is very little traffic here. The road back to Braşov is incredibly scenic, through the hills between the Piatra Craiului and the Bucegi, which look glorious under the setting sun.

THE FĂGĂRAŞ MOUNTAINS

Ascending towards Viştea Mare and Moldoveanu
Peaks (Route 22, Stage 3; photo: Dan Govareanu)

The **Făgăraş** is Romania's longest and highest ridge and is often dubbed 'the Transylvanian Alps'. Across the Carpathians, only the Tatra Mountains reach higher altitudes – but the Făgăraş covers a much bigger territory: an area of 3000km². The main ridge extends east to west for over 70km. The eastern end lies just south of Braşov, separated from the Piatra Craiului by the Bârsa Valley. The ridge ends just west of Sibiu – another delightful medieval Saxon city – where the Olt River, which flows along the northern side of the Făgăraş, bends south. Geographically, the Făgăraş is the natural border between Transylvania to the north and Muntenia to the south. It also marked the border of the Habsburg Empire.

Eight of Romania's 14 peaks over 2500m lie in the Făgăraş, including the two highest peaks in the country: Moldoveanu (2544m) in the eastern part, and the rockier Negoiu (2535m) in the western half. As many as 42 peaks are over 2400m. The first and last stages of the 90km-long ridge route proposed in this chapter (Route 22) involve a long, slow ascent to the main ridge through forest and over long, rust-coloured grassy slopes. The middle three stages are more eventful and sometimes require some bravery and stamina, especially when traversing Romania's most difficult scrambling section, Custura Sărăţii, which lies

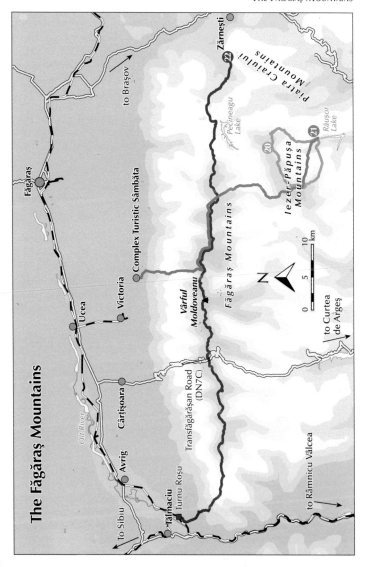

The Făgăraş Mountains

Zărneşti

22

Piatra Craiului Mountains

to Braşov

Pecineagu Lake

Răuşor Lake

21

20

Iezer-Păpuşa Mountains

Făgăraş

Complex Turistic Sâmbăta

Făgăraş Mountains

N

km
0 5 10

to Curtea de Argeş

Ucea

Victoria

Vârful Moldoveanu

Cârţişoara

Transfăgărăşan Road (DN7C)

Olt River

to Râmnicu Vâlcea

Avrig

Talmaciu

Turnu Roşu

To Sibiu

just west of Negoiu Peak (but can be bypassed). The summit path is well marked and, with the exception of some scrambling sections, the path is always clearly visible. There is no shortage of water in the Făgăraş, which mostly consists of igneous rocks; there are plenty of springs on the trail or a short distance from it, as well as a good many glacial lakes and tarns, which make for great camping spots. In fact you can camp anywhere you like: the Făgăraş is not a national park (yet) and therefore bivouacking is not restricted to designated areas. The ridge is dotted with refuges; cabanas can be found in the valleys to the north and require descending to an altitude of 1500m or lower. The climate in the Făgăraş is harsher than in most other mountainous areas in Romania; it receives the highest amount of rainfall and it is often the first to see snow.

Those who do not want to make a full traverse of the main spine, which can be tackled in five or six days if not descending to cabanas, will want to opt for one of the many access routes from the north. The northern side is much steeper than the southern side and hence the approach walks, through glacial valleys, are shorter. Access points from the north (from west to east) are Avrig, Porumbacu de Jos, Ucea de Jos, Voila and Făgăraş, which are all on the railway line from Sibiu to Braşov. In each case though you will have to cover quite some distance (20–30km) before you are really at the foot of the mountains, whereas you will be right at the start if you begin at the eastern or western end in Plaiul Foii or Turnu Roşu respectively. The railway halts in the west are considerably closer to the mountains than the ones in the east. Another option would be to hitchhike (or drive) up the famous Transfăgărăşan Road from Cârţa and start your hike at Bâlea Lake. There is one company that offers bus transfers to Bâlea Lake; see www.bale-abus.ro (reservations only). Note that the Transfăgărăşan is open from late June until September only, with precise dates dependent on snow cover. Check www.transfagarasan.net for up-to-date info. The southern spurs, with gentler and longer slopes, are hardly frequented by tourists, except perhaps for the Rea Valley, which allows tourists to drive up to just a few hours away from the Moldoveanu Peak.

An east-to-west traverse of the ridge is outlined below (Route 22); one of the access routes on the northern slopes, through Valea Sâmbătei, is described in Route 21.

To the southeast of the Făgăraş Chain lies the **Iezer-Păpuşa**; a crescent-shaped massif with several peaks over 2400m. They much resemble the Făgăraş in character. Long grassy stretches alternate with steep climbs over scree slopes; a circuit can be made in as little as two days. The Iezer-Păpuşa is more difficult to access than its northern neighbour and hence sees fewer visitors. It makes for challenging enough hiking though, and offers a great approach walk to the Făgăraş (Route 21). Like the Făgăraş, the Iezer-Păpuşa is not a national park and therefore camping is possible throughout, so long as you leave no trace.

THE IEZER-PĂPUȘA MASSIF

ROUTE 20
Iezer-Păpușa circuit

Start/finish	Cabana Voina
Distance	29km
Total ascent/descent	2130m
Grade	Moderate
Time	2 days
Maximum altitude	2470m (Roșu Peak, Stage 2)
Maps	Făgăraș, 1:75,000, Munții Noștri

The Iezer-Păpușa is the Făgăraș' beautiful smaller cousin. Tucked away to the southeast of it, this crescent-shaped massif is more difficult to access and therefore sees fewer visitors. Travelling towards it is an adventure in itself: a 2hr bus journey from Brașov to the access town of Câmpulung Muscel takes you over the Rucar-Bran Pass, through the breathtakingly beautiful hills of the Land of Bran that lies in between the Bucegi and Piatra Craiului Mountains.

Stage 1 quickly brings you to the main ridge and one of the peaks that gives the massif its name, Păpușa ('Doll') Peak (2391m). Stage 2 brings you to the highest peaks in the massif, Roșu (2470m) and Iezerul Mare (2462m), and back to the start at Cabana Voina. Apart from the ascent to the main peaks, this isn't a very demanding route; on the long stretch in between Spintecătura Păpușii and Roșu Peak the trail crosses a plateau and after Crucea Ateneului it simply follows a cart track.

A lack of accommodation at the end of the first stage means you'll probably need to bring a tent and camp at Curmătura Bătrânei. A compass or GPS may come in handy on the first part of Stage 2 – especially in poor visibility – although in general the route is well waymarked. Please note that there are bears in the Iezer-Păpușa; make some noise while you're in the forest (sing, whistle, talk, use a bear bell) and they'll stay away. Store your food away from your tent if camping below the tree line.

Access
The Iezer-Păpușa lies snugly south of the Făgăraș, Piatra Craiului and Bucegi Mountains, which makes it a bit harder to reach. First, take a bus to the town of

In between Roşu and Iezerul Mare Peaks (Stage 2)

Câmpulung Muscel from either Braşov (2hr) or Bucharest (2hr 30min–3hr). From there, take a taxi to Cabana Voina (23km). Your best option is to make a reservation with Rom Euro Expres; either call 0742 004 832 or contact one of the drivers, Irinel, directly at 0752 020 017, who will transport you in a comfortable BMW. The same applies for the return journey at the end of the trek; reception in the area is poor but the cabana has a phone and you may be able to find somebody who'll make the call for you.

Accommodation
Cabana Voina at the start; Cabana Cuca 1hr up the trail is not always open – make a reservation beforehand. Good camping spots at both, and at Curmătura Bătrânei – the saddle at the end of the first stage.

STAGE 1
Cabana Voina–Curmătura Bătrânei

Start	Cabana Voina
Finish	Curmătura Bătrânei (Bătrânei Saddle)
Distance	14.5km
Total ascent	1645m
Total descent	460m
Grade	Moderate
Time	6hr
Maximum altitude	2391m (Păpuşa Peak)
Water	Springs at Cabana Voina, Cabana Cuca, Grădişteanu Saddle. There is a tarn (possibly seasonal) below Spintecătura Păpuşii.

This walk quickly brings you to the main ridge and one of the peaks that gives the massif its name, Păpușa ('Doll') Peak (2391m). It is shorter and perhaps more challenging than the red stripe alternative over Găinațu Mare Saddle, but definitely also more rewarding and more scenic. If you arrive at Cabana Voina in the course of the day you can walk to Cabana Cuca straight away; this saves you an hour of walking the next morning.

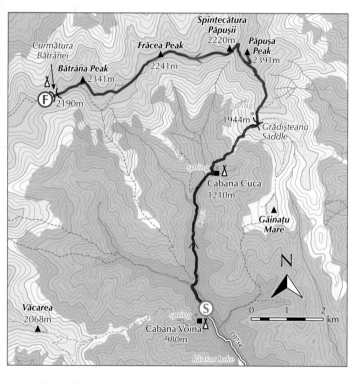

From **Cabana Voina** (980m), head northwest up the gravel road. After 750 metres, cross a bridge over the Bătrâna River and keep right, following the blue stripe and yellow triangle waymarks for Cabana Cuca. The blue circle and cross split off to the left here. After 2.3km the river forks; continue along the Cuca River to the

211

right. You will reach **Cabana Cuca** (1210m) after 800 metres. There are outdoor toilets, a terrace with a roof, picnic tables – and a bear warning.

From Cabana Cuca continue northeast up the blue stripe and yellow triangle trail, signed 4hr 30min to Păpuşa Peak. After just 150 metres another signpost tells you it is just 3hr 30min to Păpuşa Peak; this is more realistic. Turn left (north) here and head up a steep forested slope. After 750 metres exit the forest and climb northeast, up a grassy slope. The western part of the ridge with Iezerul Mare and Roşu Peaks is now behind you.

After a further 1.2km another signpost points to Păpuşa Peak; there is a sheep-fold here and the red stripe trail comes in from the right. This is **Grădişteanu Saddle** (1944m). There is a spring after 100 metres, to the left, marked with two stone crosses. Continue northeast. The trail is now marked with black and yellow poles. Ultimately the trail swings north and winds up towards Păpuşa Peak.

After 1.7km you will reach a signpost to Roşu Peak. To climb **Păpuşa Peak** (2391m), which lies off the main trail, leave your pack here and follow the path to the right for about 500 metres, then make a sharp right and continue for about 150 metres to reach the peak. Retrace your steps (or walk down in a straighter line if you can see the signpost).

Continue on the red stripe route towards Roşu Peak. After 500 metres the trail swings sharply to the left (southwest), underneath **Spintecătura Păpuşii** (2220m). Cross a small boulder field, then bear right (west-southwest), following

212

poles that have been bent over so that they look more like flagpoles. The trail continues on the other side of the ridge. Head up the rocks for a bit; once you're on the ridge the terrain is grassy and almost level – more like a plateau. Râuşorul Lake can be seen to the left, as well as the town of Câmpulung in clear conditions. The Făgăraş rises to the right.

After **Frăcea Peak** (2241m) the trail bends to the southwest. After a further 1.7km turn right (northwest) at the signpost. Straight ahead is the red triangle route which leads back to Cabana Voina; ignore this and continue on the red stripe route, which departs right sooner than the Munţii Noştri map suggests. From above it looks like there's a lower trail too which bypasses Bătrâna Peak, but it is a bit of a detour.

There are fewer waymarks on this section. Keep heading northwest until you reach **Bătrâna Peak** (2341m). You can see the elongated shape of Pecineagu Lake to the right. From here, follow an arrow down to the south-southwest, then continue southwest on the aforementioned lower path, towards **Curmătura Bătrânei** (2190m); a bowl-shaped grassy area which you will reach after about 1km.

STAGE 2
Curmătura Bătrânei–Cabana Voina

Start	Curmătura Bătrânei
Finish	Cabana Voina
Distance	14.5km
Total ascent	485m
Total descent	1685m
Grade	Moderate
Time	4hr 45min
Maximum altitude	2470m (Roşu Peak)
Water	No water except for a small tarn at Crucea Ateneului; if you've run out, descend from Crucea Ateneului to Iezer Refuge (30min) where you'll find a spring.

This stage brings you to the highest peaks in the massif, Roşu (2470m) and Iezerul Mare (2462m), and back to the start at Cabana Voina. It is possible to walk back via the blue circle route instead of the red stripe; see Route 21, Stage 1 in reverse.

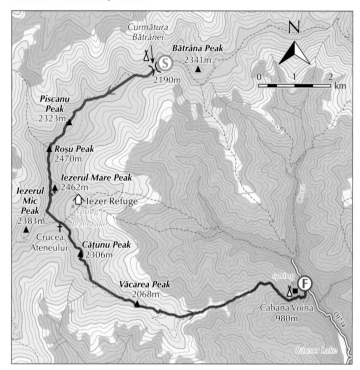

Head southwest from **Curmătura Bătrânei** to stay on the red stripe trail towards Roșu Peak, which is in plain sight. Waymarks are scarce here; a compass or GPS device is no luxury, especially if visibility is low. Occasionally the trail is marked with short wooden stakes. Matters improve after a kilometre or so. After another kilometre, climb to the southwest; when you see a bus stop-type sign after 350 metres bear left (south-southwest). After another 650 metres the ascent of Roșu Peak begins. Bypassing Piscanu Peak (2323m), stay to the left of the low, rocky, dinosaur-shaped ridge and after 700 metres you'll reach **Roșu Peak** (2470m). From here the red triangle trail departs north towards the Făgăraș; see Route 21, Stage 1.

To continue towards **Iezerul Mare Peak** (2462m), turn left (south). In fact Iezerul Mare Peak lies just off the trail; to reach it, walk just past it and then zigzag your way up – it's a 50-metre climb. There is no marked trail so you will

Iezer Lake

have to find your own way. Retrace your steps and continue south. At Iezerul Mic Peak (2383m) the trail swings to the left (southeast). After 450 metres you'll reach a gravel road; continue on it until you reach a signpost after 150 metres. This is **Crucea Ateneului**. Iezer Refuge and Lake lie in the valley to the left and can be reached in half an hour. There is a small tarn to the right (possibly seasonal).

From Crucea Ateneului, continue straight ahead on the red stripe trail to **Căţunu Peak** (2306m), which is about 800 metres further up. The trail cuts off good chunks of the gravel road and is marked with bus stop-type signs. Some 3km after Căţunu Peak the trail bypasses **Văcarea Peak** (2068m); there are waymarks over the top as well but it doesn't look like the most exciting peak to climb.

The trail gradually swings east, which means you are now looking straight at the Piatra Craiului ridge. After another 3km pass a derelict shepherd's hut; ignore the arrow to the left. Continue down the gravel road; there are fewer waymarks here since much of the old forest has been cleared. Fortunately, reforestation is well under way. After just over 1km, enter the forest proper. The trail veers to the right (southeast) almost immediately and is well marked from here. One kilometre of steep descending brings you back to **Cabana Voina**.

ROUTE 21

From the Iezer-Păpușa to the Făgăraș

Start	Cabana Voina
Finish	Complex Turistic Sâmbăta
Distance	48.5km
Total ascent	2890m
Total descent	3110m
Grade	Moderate
Time	3 days
Maximum altitude	2470m (Roșu Peak, Stage 1)
Maps	Făgăraș, 1:75,000, Munții Noștri

The Iezer-Păpușa forms a worthy precursor to the Făgăraș. Approaching the Făgăraș from here means avoiding the rather lengthy approach walk to the ridge from busy Plaiul Foii (see Route 22, Stage 1). Few people come this way; the spur that connects the Iezer-Păpușa and the Făgăraș makes for delightful lonesome and easy walking (after you've managed to make your way down the scree slope of Roșu Peak, that is). Due to a lack of accommodation at the end of Stage 1 as described below, a tent is most likely required on this route. Happily, Curmătura Oticului makes one of the finest camping spots in all of Romania; there is a spring nearby and the path is lined with blueberries in August. As you approach the Făgăraș, you will get a sneak preview of some its main peaks, including Moldoveanu (2544m), Romania's highest summit. The waymarking on the connecting spur is poor but the trail is easy enough to follow.

Access

The Iezer-Păpușa lies snugly south of the Făgăraș, Piatra Craiului and Bucegi Mountains, which makes it a bit harder to reach. First, take a bus to the town of Câmpulung Muscel from either Brașov (2hr) or Bucharest (2hr 30min–3hr). From there, take a taxi to Cabana Voina. Your best option is to make a reservation with Rom Euro Expres; either call 0742 004 832 or contact one of the drivers, Irinel, directly at 0752 020 017, who will transport you in a comfortable BMW.

At the end of the trek, in order to reach Sibiu or Brașov, you'll have to hitchhike to Victoria (this should be easy since Complex Turistic Sâmbăta is very popular among local tourists) and from there take a minibus to Ucea railway halt (30min). The minibuses depart from Strada Victoriei, across from the Camino

Cultural; the timetable at the Camino Cultural not only lists buses but also the trains they meet. From Ucea there are eight trains daily to Sibiu (1hr 15min–2hr) and four trains daily to Braşov (1hr 40min to 2hr 20min).

Accommodation
Cabana Voina at the start of the trail; Iezer Refuge a couple of hours further on. It's possible to reach the refuge at Curmătura Brătilei in one day, although this would make for a very long stage – and at refuges a space is not guaranteed anyway. Best to bring a tent and camp at the wonderful Curmătura Oticului at the end of Stage 1, and stay at Zârna Refuge (or camp next to it) at the end of Stage 2. On the final stage there's Cabana Valea Sâmbătei, Floarea Reginei pension, Popaş Sâmbăta and numerous options in Complex Turistic Sâmbăta; see Google Maps for info.

STAGE 1
Cabana Voina–Curmătura Oticului

Start	Cabana Voina
Finish	Curmătura Oticului (Oticului Saddle)
Distance	12.5km
Total ascent	1530m
Total descent	635m
Grade	Moderate
Time	5hr 45min
Maximum altitude	2470m (Roşu Peak)
Water	Springs at Cabana Voina, Iezer Lake and Curmătura Oticului

From **Cabana Voina**, walk northwest on the DJ734 road for 750 metres, then turn left onto the combined blue circle and blue cross trail. After 2.3km the road forks at a signpost; cross the Bătrâna Stream to the left over a wobbly footbridge to stay on the blue circle trail to Iezer Lake. Walk along the stream – you might be able to pick blueberries on the way.

After 4km the blue circle trail meets the blue cross (the winter trail) again. Another 250 metres brings you to **Iezer Refuge**, refurbished in 2018. Continue to **Crucea Ateneului** on the blue circle and cross trail. When you reach the signpost at the cross after 500 metres, turn right towards Iezerul Mare and Roşu Peaks. The trail quickly veers off to the right of the gravel road. The trail bypasses

217

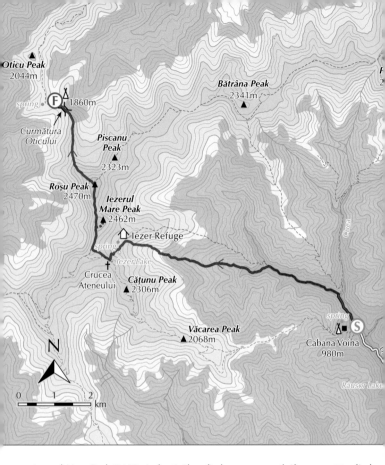

Iezerul Mare Peak (2462m) after 1.3km; find your own path if you want to climb it. Another kilometre brings you to **Roşu Peak** (2470m).

From here continue north on the red triangle trail. Descend over the boulder-strewn northern flank of Roşu Peak and through dwarf pine until you reach **Curmătura Oticului** (1860m) after 2.5km. There's a spring 200 metres down the trail from the saddle, and if you're here in August you're in for a treat: nowhere will you find more blueberry bushes on the trail than here.

STAGE 2

Curmătura Oticului–Zârna Refuge

Start	Curmătura Oticului
Finish	Zârna Refuge
Distance	16.5km
Total ascent	800m
Total descent	730m
Grade	Moderate
Time	5hr
Maximum altitude	2280m
Water	Springs at Curmătura Oticului, Curmătura Brătilei and Zârna Refuge

From **Curmătura Oticului**, continue north towards the main ridge of the Făgăraş. The path is lined with blueberry bushes for several kilometres, making it worthwhile doing this hike in August. On a clear day you can see the trapezoid shape of Moldoveanu and Viştea Mare Peaks across to the left. Often the path is no more than a sheep trail and sparsely marked if at all, and the large clumps of grass can

Looking north towards the Făgăraş from the connecting spur

ROUTE 21 – FROM THE IEZER-PĂPUŞA TO THE FĂGĂRAŞ

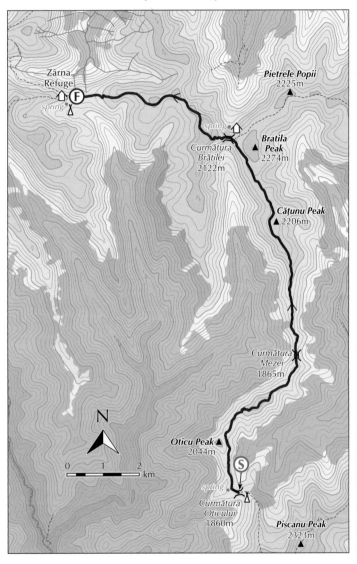

make the going a bit cumbersome. After about 5km, from **Curmătura Mezei** (saddle) onwards, the path becomes considerably easier.

Pass some tarns 1km after the saddle and continue for a further 2.5km to reach the grassy plateau below **Cățunu Peak** (2206m). Cross it north-northwest; there are no waymarks here, although there is still a clear path. Then descend for almost 3km to **Curmătura Brătilei** (2125m). From this saddle, follow the red stripe trail for 5.3km until you reach **Zârna Refuge**. (From here you could also continue west further into the Făgăraş – see Route 22, Stage 2.)

STAGE 3
Zârna Refuge–Complex Turistic Sâmbăta

Start	Zârna Refuge
Finish	Popaş Sâmbăta, Complex Turistic Sâmbăta
Distance	19.5km
Total ascent	560m
Total descent	1745m
Grade	Moderate
Time	5hr 45min
Maximum altitude	2460m (La Fundu Bândei Peak)
Water	Springs at Zârna Refuge and between Fereastra Mare and Cabana Valea Sâmbătei

From **Zârna Refuge** continue west on the red stripe trail and head up a rocky slope. At Zârna Lake the trail swings to the southwest and climbs to **Leaota Peak** (2312m). Around 1.5km later the trail swings to the northwest, around Urlea Lake and past the stage's highest point, La Fundu Bândei Peak (2454m). You can see Vişea Mare and Moldoveanu Peaks ahead of you on clear days. After a further 1km the blue circle trail departs to the right; this would take you to Urlea Lake and refuge should you need it.

Another 4km on the red stripe trail brings you to **Fereastra Mare** ('Big Window') Saddle; this is about 8km from the start of the stage. From here, descend the steep red triangle trail until you reach the **Salvamont base** and **Cabana Valea Sâmbătei** after 2.7km. Continue down the red triangle trail along the Sâmbăta Stream with its waterfalls. The path becomes a gravel road after about 3km. After another 3km you'll find the **Floarea Reginei** pension and trout restaurant on your right. **Popaş Sâmbăta** is a little bit further up.

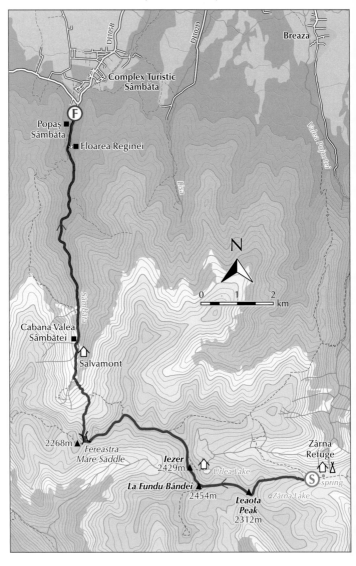

THE FĂGĂRAŞ CHAIN

ROUTE 22
Traversing the Făgăraş from east to west

Start	Cabana Plaiul Foii
Finish	Turnu Roşu
Distance	97.8km
Total ascent	6205m
Total descent	6380m
Grade	Moderate-difficult
Time	5–6 days
Maximum altitude	2544m (Moldoveanu Peak, Stage 3)
Maps	Făgăraş, 1:75,000, and Făgăraş, 1:35,000, Munţii Noştri (comes as a set)

This 98km-long trek follows the main ridge of the Făgăraş, taking you over the country's two highest peaks, Moldoveanu (2544m) and Negoiu (2535m), as well as many other peaks within the 2400–2500m bracket. For 50km, the trail hardly ever dips below 2000m. Long grassy stretches alternate with challenging ascents and notoriously difficult clambering sections such as Custura Sărăţii (Stage 4) – the most difficult and technical section of the entire ridge – and La Trei Paşi de Moarte (Stage 3; 'Three Steps to Death'). These sections can be bypassed if they seem like too much or if the weather isn't favourable. Excepting the last stage, which is mostly descending, every stage described here involves ascending, and often descending, well over 1000m.

It is possible to break this five-day trek up into smaller stages; there are plenty of springs and refuges that could function as alternative camping spots. The Făgăraş is not a national park (yet), so camping is allowed anywhere. If you would rather not make a full traverse of the main ridge, you could opt for one of the many access routes from the north – go up one spur, follow the ridge for as long as you like and descend another spur. One of these access (or exit) routes is described in Route 21 (Stage 3). Access points from the north (from west to east) are Avrig, Porumbacu de Jos, Ucea de Jos, Voila and Făgăraş, which are all on the railway line from Sibiu to Braşov. In each case, though, you will have to cover quite some distance (20–30km) before you are really at the foot of the mountains,

Ascending to the ridge from Zârna Refuge (Stage 2; photo: Dan Govareanu)

whereas you will be right at the start if you begin at the eastern or western end in Plaiul Foii or Turnu Roşu respectively.

The Custura Sărăţii scrambling section can be bypassed by descending to Cabana Negoiu (1546m) via the red cross and blue triangle route just after Călţun Lake. The next day, either return to the ridge via the blue stripe trail to Şerbota Peak or continue descending to Porumbacu de Jos railway halt (23km).

La Trei Paşi de Moarte can be bypassed by descending to Cabana Podragu via the red triangle from Podragu Saddle, from where you can go back up the ridge via the blue cross trail, bringing you to Fereastra Zmeilor. This should take about two hours.

The first two stages of Route 21 make a good alternative to Stage 1 of this route, combining a quick exploration of the Iezer-Păpuşa with a more scenic approach walk to the Făgăraş via a connecting spur.

Access
Take a bus or train to Zărneşti from Braşov (1hr). Buses depart from Autogara 2, Strada Avram Iancu 114. Trains are operated by Regio Călători, not CFR. From Zărneşti, take a taxi to Cabana Plaiul Foii (13km). Ideally, take it all the way up to Canton Rudăriţa; this will save you 9km of walking along an uninteresting access road. Not all drivers are willing to do this though. Sorin Rusu, the owner of Coronensis Apartment in Braşov, will drive you to Plaiul Foii for a very reasonable fee; see Appendix B for his contact details. See also Route 18, Stage 5 (in reverse) and its alternative finish for a walking route – most likely in two days – from Zărneşti to Cabana Plaiul Foii via Cabana Curmatura.

From Turnu Roşu there are seven direct trains a day to Sibiu; the journey takes between 30min and 1hr. You can also travel south to Râmnicu Vâlcea for access to the Cozia and/or Buila-Vânturariţa (Routes 24 and 25). The journey takes between 1hr 45min and 2hr 30min; it's about half an hour less if getting off at Mănăstirea Turnu (for the Cozia).

Accommodation

This trail goes over the ridge and the assumption is that you are entirely self-sufficient. The Făgăraş is not a national park (yet), so camping is allowed anywhere.

The cabanas listed here are on the trail, or at a short distance from it: Cabana Plaiul Foii (beginning of Stage 1), Cabana Bâlea Lac (off-route, end of Stage 3), Cabana Podragu (off-route, midway on Stage 3). Sadly, Scara Refuge (end of Stage 4) was destroyed in the autumn of 2018. The tiny old refuge has been cleaned up and funds are being raised for a new one, but in the meantime don't count on finding a berth here. There are several other cabanas but these are always far down from the ridge, and easily involve an extra 700–800m of descent/ascent. Refuges are mentioned in the description of each stage. There are multiple other options around Cabana Plaiul Foii; see Google Maps. This area is notorious for pickpockets though, so if you decide to camp make sure there is always someone near the tent, and take your valuables with you.

STAGE 1

Cabana Plaiul Foii– Curmătura Brătilei

Start	Cabana Plaiul Foii
Finish	Curmătura Brătilei (Brătilei Saddle)
Distance	26km
Total ascent	1730m
Total descent	485m
Grade	Moderate
Time	7hr 30min (minus 2hr if starting from Canton Rudăriţa)
Maximum altitude	2197m (near Berevoescu Refuge)
Water	Springs after 20km, at Berevoescu Refuge and Curmătura Brătilei

From **Cabana Plaiul Foii**, walk northwest on the road, marked red stripe, along the Bârsa River until you reach **Canton Rudăriţa** after 9km. Here the road forks;

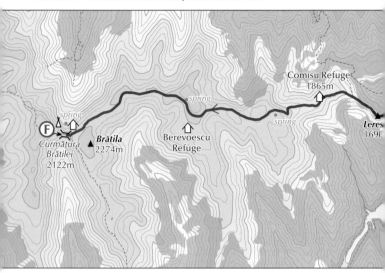

take the path to the left (west) and continue walking along the Bârsa. After 400 metres the path continues to the left of the road. There is an arrow on a tree and an old signpost. Cross a tributary stream after about 30 metres and continue south, up into the forest.

When you hit a path after about 1km, turn right towards Curmătura Brătilei, signed 5hr. After another kilometre you come to a crossing – this is **Curmătura Lerescului** (1396m). Head northwest (310°) on an inconspicuous grassy trail in between the two tracks. After 1km stay with the trail as it veers to the right, off the track.

When you exit the forest after about 1.2km you get your first view of the ridge. Comisu Refuge can be seen to the right, and Pecineagu Lake to the left. After 900 metres you'll reach **Comisu Refuge** (1865m); the red stripe trail is crossed by the blue triangle. Continue on the red stripe trail towards Berevoescu Refuge, signed 2hr. After 400 metres turn left (southwest) off the track, onto a grassy trail; there are waymarks on rocks. After 2.8km you'll find a **spring** just to the left of the trail.

After a further 1.5km you'll see several tarns in the valley to the left. Another 300 metres brings you to the old **Berevoescu Refuge**. There's a spring 600 metres further up, and another one within 150 metres of it. Near the first spring the red stripe meets the red circle, which departs to the right. Looking to the left, you can see the Iezer-Păpuşa Mountains. It is around here that you find your highest

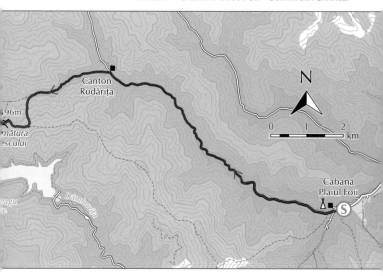

point of the day (2197m). From here, follow the red stripe trail as it descends gently towards the saddle of **Curmătura Brătilei** (2122m) and its shelter, which you'll reach after 3.7km.

Easy trail towards Curmătura Brătilei

227

STAGE 2
Curmătura Brătilei–Viștea Mare Refuge

Start	Curmătura Brătilei
Finish	Viștea Mare Refuge
Distance	19.3km
Total ascent	1230m
Total descent	1040m
Grade	Moderate
Time	6hr 20min
Maximum altitude	2470m (Gălășescu Mare Peak)
Water	Several springs before Zârna Refuge; one near Zârna Refuge and one in a cleft in the valley to the left after Leaota Peak. There's a trickle on the path in Viștișoara Saddle if you're lucky, and there's a spring 15–20min south of Viștea Mare Refuge.

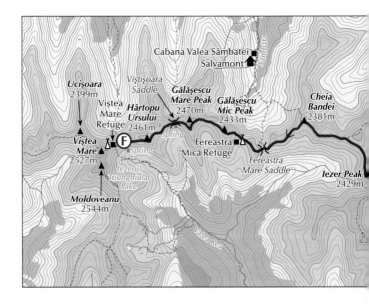

From **Curmătura Brătilei** head west on the red stripe trail and quickly ascend to an altitude of 2300m, then descend back to 1900m. This is a very green, uneventful and easy stretch of the route. When you reach **Curmătura Zârnei** you can see many tarns ahead of you. Head into this valley and walk past the tarns until you reach **Zârna Refuge**, almost 6km from the start.

Continue west and head up a rocky slope. At Zârna Lake the trail swings to the southwest and climbs to **Leaota Peak** (2312m). Around 1.5km later the trail swings to the northwest, around **Urlea Lake**. You can see Viștea Mare and Moldoveanu Peaks ahead of you on clear days. After a further 1km the blue circle trail departs to the right; this would take you to Urlea Lake and refuge should you need it. Continuing on the red stripe trail over **Iezer Peak** (2429m), another 4km brings you to **Fereastra Mare Saddle** ('Big Window') – from here the red triangle descends into the Sâmbăta Valley (see Route 21, Stage 3) and Cabana Valea Sâmbătei can be reached in under 2hr.

Moldoveanu Peak is signed 5hr from Fereastra Mare Saddle. Continue briefly southwest, then northwest on the red stripe trail. If you'd like to make this stage shorter, you can pitch your tent at **Fereastra Mica Refuge**, 500 metres from the saddle. (The refuge itself is in a bad state.) To reach to the end of the stage, continue up **Gălășescu Mic Peak** (2433m) – the trail bypasses the summit. After

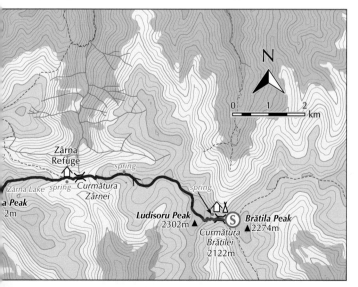

Lakes in the Zârna Valley

bypassing **Gălăşescu Mare Peak** (2470m) about 45min later, the splendid Valea Rea glacial valley with its lake and streams lies to the left. There's a small spring on the path in **Viştişoara Saddle**; ideally fill up your bottles here so you don't have to look for water later. Make a final push to just under **Hârtopu Ursului** (2461m) – this should take about 1hr – then descend to **Viştea Mare Refuge** (1933m).

STAGE 3
Viştea Mare Refuge–Capra Lake

Start	Viştea Mare Refuge
Finish	Capra Lake
Distance	13.5km
Total ascent	1085m
Total descent	1140m
Grade	Moderate-difficult
Time	6hr 30min
Maximum altitude	2544m (Moldoveanu Peak)
Water	Spring at Podul Giurgiului Lake; many springs after Fereastra Zmeilor; at Capra Lake
Note	La Trei Paşi de Moarte is a difficult section that involves scrambling over very smooth and steep slabs of rock. It is equipped with chains and cables but requires great care.

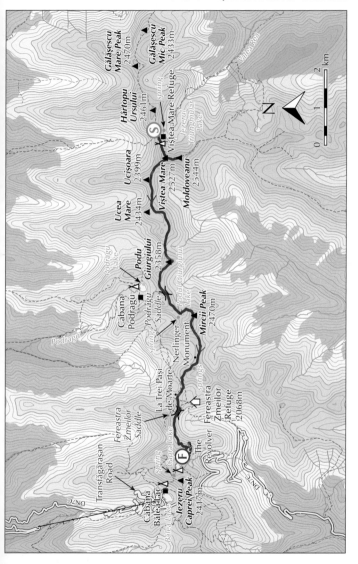

La Trei Paşi de Moarte:
'Three Steps to Death'

From **Viştea Mare Refuge** head west on the red stripe trail and up the steep slope of **Viştea Mare** (2527m), Romania's third highest peak. Leave your pack on the peak and head south on the red circle trail towards **Moldoveanu Peak** (2544m), Romania's highest peak. This is a challenging 400-metre section that involves some cables and clambering. Retrace your steps to Viştea Mare Peak and descend west, back onto the red stripe trail.

The path is fairly level for a good while. After 3.5km, at **Podu Giurgiului Peak** (2358m), it swings to the northwest. After another kilometre, at **Podragu Saddle**, you have the option to descend the red triangle trail to Cabana Podragu (take this if you want to avoid the Trei Paşi de Moarte). Less than 1km after this intersection you reach **Podul Giurgiului Lake**; there's a spring on the other side of the lake.

Climb to **Mircii Peak** (2470m), pass **Nerlinger's Monument** after 1.5km, then brace yourself for **La Trei Paşi de Moarte**, 'Three Steps to Death'. This is a tricky (but very short) section with lots of chains and cables; you will need to clamber over very smooth and steep slabs of rock. Proceed with care – it's best tackled backwards on all fours. After you've conquered this passage, you're rewarded with a view of the famous Transfăgărăşan Road to the left.

Another 400 metres on the trail brings you to the saddle of **Fereastra Zmeilor**, 'Dragon's Window'. There are a great many springs on the next section. Climb to 'The Revolver', an evocative rock below Capra Peak, then descend to **Capra Lake**, where you stand a good chance of seeing chamois and marmots.

STAGE 4
Capra Lake–Scara Refuge

Start	Capra Lake
Finish	Scara Refuge
Distance	14km
Total ascent	1570m
Total descent	1415m
Grade	Difficult
Time	7hr 45min
Maximum altitude	2535m (Negoiu Peak)
Water	At Capra Lake and Călţun Lake, just after Turnu Paltinului, just before Negoiu Peak and at Scara Refuge
Note	Sadly, Scara Refuge was destroyed in the autumn of 2018. Funds are being raised for a new refuge, but in the meantime don't count on it for shelter.

This stage contains the most difficult and technical section of the entire ridge – Custura Sărăţii, just after the ascent of Romania's second highest peak, the Negoiu. It's best to tackle this on a dry day, since the rocks can get very slippery. The scramble is equipped with chains but is nonetheless a serious challenge – especially if you're carrying a full pack.

From **Capra Lake**, walk northwest up the red stripe trail to Capra Saddle, from where you can see the Transfăgărăşan Road and Bâlea Lake. From here, head west and up **Iezeru Caprei Peak** (2417m). Continue for 1.5km until you reach **Turnul Paltinului**, an impressive rock tower – there are two parallel trails; one over the ridge and one just to the left of it. It doesn't matter which one you take.

To reach Bâlea Lake
If you're craving a good meal you might want to make a pit stop at Bâlea Lake. To reach it, descend for 300 metres on the blue triangle trail from Capra Saddle; it takes about 30min to reach the cabana. You could also camp here instead of at Capra Lake, but it gets horrendously busy with tourists who reach it over the Transfăgărăşan Road, so it's not the most peaceful spot.

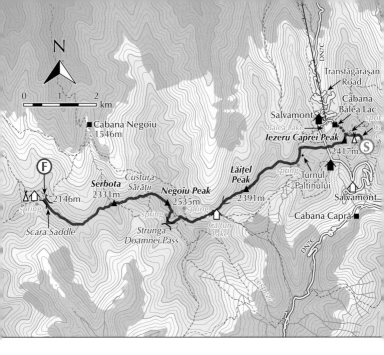

From Turnul Paltinului descend and walk past a tarn and spring, then continue up a rocky section with chains. Climb to **Lăițel Peak** (2391m), then descend to **Călțun Lake** with its refuge in 30min. At the intersection 1km after the lake (where there is the option of descending to Cabana Negoiu and thus avoiding Custura Sărății), turn left onto the red and yellow stripe trail for Negoiu Peak via **Strunga Doamnei Pass**; Strunga Dracului Pass to the right is closed to the public because falling rocks have caused too many accidents. Climb a chimney and then continue up the rock-strewn slope of **Negoiu Peak** (2535m).

From the peak, descend the steep western scree slope of the Negoiu, and brace yourself for Custura Sărății, a seemingly endless succession of chains and clambering – although in reality it stretches for less than a kilometre. It is well marked but you need to be sure of your grip, and you are going to need your hands a lot. Do not attempt this in bad weather. At the end of it you reach **Șerbota Peak** (2331m), your last peak for the day. From here descend a grassy, marked trail for the best part of 3km until you reach **Scara Saddle** and refuge (2146m). There's a spring about 10min down the blue cross route to the south.

STAGE 5
Scara Refuge–Turnu Roşu

Start	Scara Refuge
Finish	Turnu Roşu Station
Distance	25km
Total ascent	590m
Total descent	2300m
Grade	Moderate
Time	7hr
Maximum altitude	2324m (below Budislavu Peak)
Water	At Scara Refuge and Avrig Lake; several springs after Budislavu Peak and Suru Saddle

From **Scara Refuge** head southwest on the red stripe trail and ascend **Scara Peak** (2306m), then descend to **Gârbova Saddle**, where the red stripe is joined by a red cross. Continue descending to **Avrig Lake** (2011m) and then climb to the saddle of **Portiţa Avrigului**. From here head west-northwest; the signpost points in the wrong direction (although this may have been remedied). The terrain gradually changes: rocks make way for shrubs, rhododendrons and blueberries.

About 2.5km after bypassing **Budislavu Peak** (2343m) the trail veers to the right (west), over a grassy plain and to a signpost in **Curmătura Surului**. Turnu Roşu is signed 6hr from here but this is generous to say the least; you are in fact halfway in terms of time. There's an exit route to Cabana Suru via the red triangle, signed 1hr 30min. However, to continue on the main route, from the signpost gently descend for 7km, still on the red stripe trail, until you come to **Corbului Saddle** (1568m). Here turn right (northwest) onto the red cross trail for Turnu.

To continue to the end of the ridge

If you're bent on walking to the very end of the ridge, from Corbului Saddle continue on the red stripe trail all the way to the Olt River (10km, 100m ascent, 1230m descent). The disadvantage of this is that you don't end anywhere near a station; you'll either have to walk 3km south to Valea Fratelui halt or 4km north to Valea Mărului halt, and the last train departs around 6.30pm; whereas in Turnu Roşu you have until 10.30pm should you need it – with the added benefit that you end in a village with some shops and bars.

Around 1km after Corbului Saddle turn right onto a forest road; after another 2.8km turn right again at a signpost. After a further 1km cross a stream and turn left onto a gravel road, past the **monastery**. Continue for 5km until you reach the village and cross it to reach **Turnu Station**.

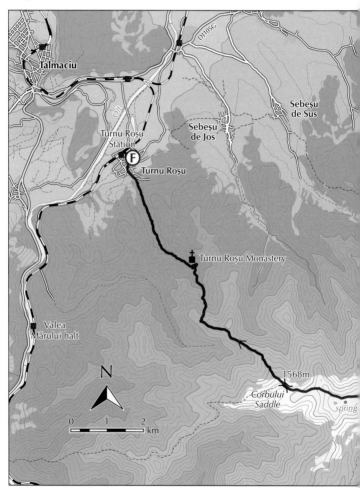

On Scara Peak

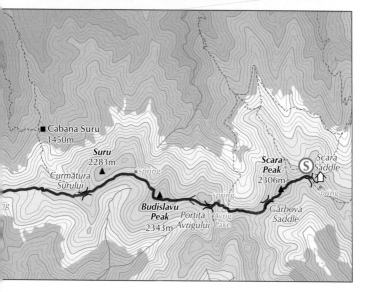

FROM THE OLT TO THE JIU

*Keep an eye out for chamois on Stogșoare Rock
in the Buila-Vânturarița (Route 25, Stage 1)*

Although the Cindrel and the Parâng are separate mountain ranges with very different characters, they form an excellent marriage (Route 23). The Cindrel stretches from just southwest of Sibiu to Oașa Lake on the wonderful Transalpina Road; the Transfăgărășan's lesser-known, but no less beautiful, sister road. Hitchhiking 23km down the Transalpina from Oașa Lake brings you to the village of Obârșia Lotrului, which is an excellent starting point for exploring the western half of the Parâng.

The main ridge of the **Cindrel**, also known as the Cibin, stretches from northeast to southwest, with a length of approximately 35km. It lies to the southeast of the charming medieval town of Sibiu, which has its own airport and is worth spending a few days in. Consider renting a bike at Casa Luxemburg on Piața Mică to explore the surrounding villages with their fortified churches; climb the tower of the Lutheran church in the centre and try local, Saxon-inspired cuisine at Hermania restaurant. The Cindrel is probably one of Romania's most pastoral mountain ranges; it is mostly grassy with rich vegetation and is home to countless sheepfolds – which, as usual, are accompanied by guardian dogs. Rhododendrons

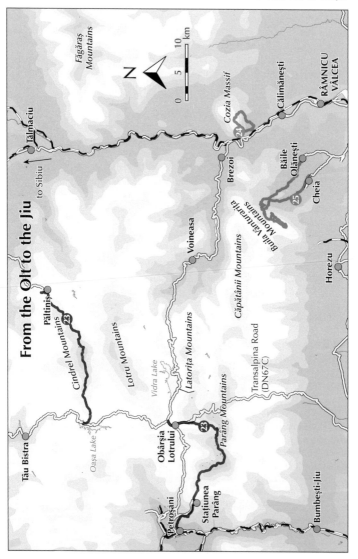

can be found higher up while the lower slopes are covered in blueberries and cranberries in season. Its beech, birch and coniferous forests are home to large wildlife populations, including wild boar, deer, brown bears, wolves, lynxes and wildcats. Walking along the main ridge does not present any challenges; the trail mostly goes over a cart track, is mostly well marked and involves relatively little ascending and descending. It is also very suitable for mountain biking – MTB routes are marked on the Bel Alpin map. Since the Cindrel is not a national park you can camp anywhere you like, although staying away from sheepfolds is recommended.

The **Parâng** is the second highest mountain range in the Southern Carpathians, after the Făgăraş – its highest peak, the Parângul Mare, stands 2519m tall, which makes it the fourth highest peak in the country. The Parâng is lesser known than its popular northern neighbour, the Retezat, but it certainly is no less alluring. The landscape is decidedly alpine; most of the ridge, consisting of igneous rocks, is well over 2000m. There are plenty of lakes and tarns and, since this is also not a national park, you can camp wherever you like. Its western half stretches from the Transalpina in the east to the mining town of Petroşani in the west. East of the Transalpina – the highest national road in the country, reaching 2145m – the Parâng is much gentler and forms a continuation of the Căpăţânii ridge. Note that the Transalpina is open during summer months only.

The much lower **Cozia** Massif (Route 24) is densely forested but cliffs offer great views over the mountains and valleys. This is also possibly one of the most religious corners of Romania; the monastery density is certainly high. The 14th-century Cozia Monastery in Călimăneşti is an important representative of Byzantine architecture in Romania. Although technically the eastern part of the Cozia – where the main walking routes are – lies east of the Olt River, the Cozia has been filed in this chapter rather than under the Făgăraş; its western half does lie across the Olt and it really belongs to the mountains of 'Oltenia de sub Munte' in Vâlcea County. The Cozia is a national park; camping is allowed in designated areas only.

The **Buila-Vânturariţa** (Route 25) is both the youngest and the smallest national park in Romania. More importantly, it is one of the most stunning too. It is often referred to as the little sister of the Piatra Craiului; its limestone ridge is certainly reminiscent of the King's Rocks, but less jagged and saw-like, and quite a bit lower. It offers plenty of challenging hiking and, if you wish, climbing too. The park is very isolated, to such an extent that few Romanians seem to have heard of it. This makes it a uniquely quiet and unspoilt corner of Romania. Camping is allowed next to Cabana Cheia but not anywhere else since the Buila-Vânturariţa is a national park.

THE CINDREL AND THE PARÂNG

ROUTE 23
From Păltiniş to Petroşani

Start	Păltiniş
Finish	Petroşani
Distance	67.5km
Total ascent	3225m
Total descent	3965m
Grade	Easy-moderate
Time	4–5 days
Maximum altitude	2519m (Parângul Mare, Stage 4)
Maps	The Cindrel Mountains, 1:60,000, Bel Alpin, and Parâng, 1:50,000, Munţii Noştri; or Parâng Mountains, 1:50,000, Erfatur-Dimap
Note	It's necessary to hitchhike 25km on the Transalpina Road from Cabana Oaşa (end of Stage 2) to Cabana Obârşia (start of Stage 3). This road is open during summer months only – precise dates vary from year to year, but generally it should be open June–September; see www.transalpina.biz (click 'Program' in the top menu) for opening and closing dates (including an overview of the last few years' dates).

The Cindrel is a small mountain range that lies just southwest of the charming medieval town of Sibiu. Its highest peak is the Cindrel (2244m); most of the ridge is grassy with rich vegetation – carpets of rhododendrons adorn the higher slopes whereas at lower altitudes you will find plenty of cranberries and blueberries during summer. The starting point, Păltiniş, is Romania's oldest and highest (1450m) mountain resort. Its altitude means this route involves relatively little ascending and that you will quickly rise above the tree line. Apart from the climb of Cindrel Peak, much of the ridge makes for rather easy walking, with views to the Lotru Mountains to the south, the Sureanu to the west and the Parâng to the southwest. It is also possible to start in either Cisnădie or Cisnădioara, two charming villages just south of Sibiu. It's approximately 25km from Cisnădie over the red cross and red stripe trail; the distance is about the same from Cisnădioara except you start on the blue cross trail. There is a refuge on each of the routes. The Cindrel, a national park, is also very suitable for mountain biking.

Crossing over into the Parâng Mountains requires hitching down the Transalpina Road, the Transfăgărăşan's lesser-known but no less beautiful sister road, reaching its highest altitude at Urdele Pass (2145m). The Transalpina is open during summer months only. This section of the route explores the western and highest half of the Parâng, starting in the village of Obârşia Lotrului. The Parâng lies south of the more popular and hence busier Retezat. Most of the ridge is well over 2000m; its highest summit, Parângul Mare, reaches 2519m, making it Romania's fourth highest peak. The central Parâng mostly consists of granite and other igneous rocks; ascents to the higher peaks, many of which reach over 2400m, are short and steep. There are a good many lakes and plenty of springs. Trail maintenance has been slightly neglected here and there, so good navigational skills and/or a GPS device are required.

Access
Take the 22 TurSib bus to Păltiniş from Sibiu Station. It leaves at 7am, 11am and 4pm – do check https://online.tursib.ro before you leave. Click 'Trasee' in the top menu, then Route 22 at the bottom of the page, then click on 'Gara' to see what times the bus leaves from the station. The journey takes around one hour. Get off at the last-but-one stop; this gets you right to the start of the trail.

The best way to get away from Petroşani at the end of the trek, despite the fact that it has a train station, is to take a bus – to Haţeg (1hr), Deva (2hr), Râmnicu Vâlcea (4hr) or Alba Iulia (3hr). The fastest train connection is the one to Deva (2hr). From any of the aforementioned places you can easily continue towards Sibiu, although you may want to make an overnight stop since there are no fast connections. From Petroşani you can also continue into the Vâlcan and Retezat (Route 28).

Accommodation
Although there are some refuges in the Parâng, you will need to bring a tent – there is no shelter at the end of Stage 3. It is OK to wild camp in the Parâng and you might well find other attractive spots to do so than suggested in the itinerary below.

Although there are a few (pricey) hotels in the Păltiniş resort (see Google Maps), you might as well spend the night in Sibiu, which is one of the best-preserved Saxon cities and deserves exploring. If you take the 11am bus you will have ample time to arrive at Cânaia Refuge before dusk. If you do want to start in Păltiniş, try Cabana Nora. Cânaia Refuge is more a cabana than a refuge; you're supposed to make a reservation. It's run by Mr Doru Podia (tel 0765 659 218) and only open when he's there. If you can't reach him, send him a text – reception is quite poor in the area. Bring your own meals (although he might prepare you something). If it isn't open, you could try the unmanned Cindrel Refuge, which is on the other side of Cindrel Saddle, 30min down the blue triangle trail.

At the end of Stage 2, Cabana Oaşa on the DN67C (Transalpina) is more like a hotel and serves good food. Cabana Obârşia Lotrului (start of Stage 3) has rooms and a restaurant, and camping territory with small wooden huts for rent. There's plenty of accommodation available in Staţiunea Parâng, although not everything will be open in (late) summer (it's mostly a skiing resort). Try Vila Iulian, just down from the Salvamont base. There are also plenty of options in Petroşani. Essentially, a tent is only required at the end of Stage 3, although it is very much worthwhile to camp every night – glorious camping spots are abundant.

There's a small shop at the parking lot near Cabana Obârşia Lotrului (Stage 3), selling bananas, some vegetables, bread and other basics. It is open until November, presumably from the point at which the Transalpina Road opens – ie June.

STAGE 1
Păltiniş–Cânaia Refuge

Start	Chairlift station, Păltiniş
Finish	Cânaia Refuge
Distance	11.5km
Total ascent	620m
Total descent	275m
Grade	Easy
Time	3hr 30min
Maximum altitude	1954m (Rozdeşti Peak)
Water	Several streams cross the path before Poiana Găujoara and after Bătrâna Saddle; at the latter you will also find a spring. Spring at Cânaia Refuge.

The red cross trail starts at the **Păltiniş** chairlift station. Follow the signpost to Poiana Găujoara, passing underneath the viaduct, past Cabana Nora. The asphalt road soon deteriorates into a gravel road. After 200 metres, turn right (south) and descend a narrow path into the forest, signed 2hr to Bătrâna Saddle. After 1.3km, cross a stream; the path widens and veers southwest, gently ascending to **Poiana Găujoara**. Here the blue circle trail departs to the left; stay on the red cross trail until you reach **Bătrâna Saddle** after 2.5km.

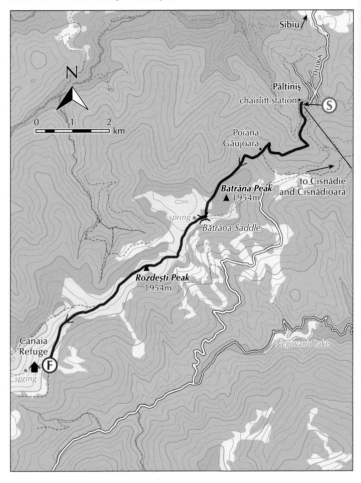

From the saddle, turn right (west) onto a cart track marked red stripe, signed 2hr–2hr 30min to Cânaia Refuge. The Lotru Ridge can be seen to the left. Climb to **Rozdeşti Peak** (1954m). From here you'll be descending mostly. Continue for 4km until you reach **Cânaia Refuge**. There's a stream just before you get to the refuge, and a spring behind it.

Descending to Cânaia Refuge

STAGE 2
Cânaia Refuge–Cabana Oaşa

Start	Cânaia Refuge
Finish	Cabana Oaşa
Distance	20km
Total ascent	725m
Total descent	1185m
Grade	Mostly easy; moderate towards Cindrel Peak
Time	5hr 45min
Maximum altitude	2244m (Cindrel Peak)
Water	At Cânaia Refuge; trickles of water cross the trail after about 8km and 11km

From **Cânaia Refuge**, walk northwest up the blue triangle trail, towards Cindrel Saddle (also known as Cânaia Saddle). When you reach it after 1.6km, turn left onto the red stripe route, signed 5hr–5hr 30min to Cabana Oaşa. From here it's a 30min climb to Cindrel Peak. After 400 metres follow the markings as they depart to the right (northwest), off the obvious path (a cart track). At the first bus stop-type sign, the trail swings southwest again. There's a fork in the route up the peak; either way will get you there, but the left one is shorter, and marked.

From **Cindrel Peak** (2244m) with its many crosses, continue west on the red stripe trail. It is briefly joined by the blue stripe trail to Jina Village. (If you want to

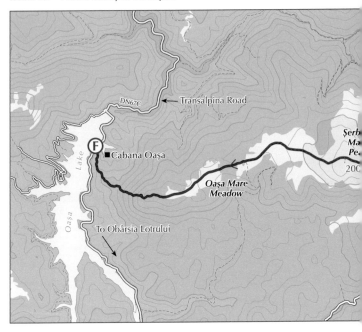

head straight to the Parâng, you can cut a corner here by following the red cross trail southwest, signed 6–9hr to Obârşia Lotrului. From there see Stage 3.)

Confusingly, after Cindrel Peak some of the waymarks are red cross, painted over to look like red stripe. There are also bus stop-type signs to the left and right of the trail, presumably for winter use – stick to the path on the ridge.

From Cindrel Peak it's mostly descending; whatever little ascending you have to do is very gentle. After 1km there are info panels about the Iezerele Cindrelului Reserve on the right; the blue stripe trail departs north here. Continue on the red stripe trail as it passes over **Frumoasa** (2168m) and **Şerbota Mare** (2007m) peaks; there's about 3.5km in between them, but the peaks are not readily identifiable since the terrain is very smooth. About 2km after Şerbota Mare Peak the path forks; bear left. There's a trickle of (drinkable) water flowing through a big pipe under the track after about 500 metres, and another 3km on from here. About 1km after the second trickle, there's a house on the left, just off the trail.

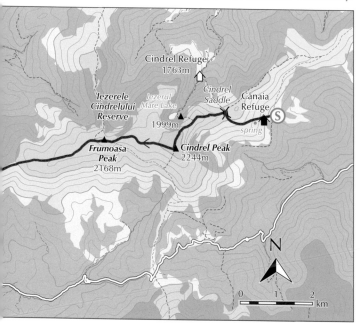

After a further 1.5km, enter the forest – there's a picnic table here. After just 700 metres in the forest you'll arrive at **Oaşa Mare Meadow** – navigation gets a bit tricky here since much of the waymarking has disappeared. Walk up to a signpost on the left (southwest), off the path; cross the meadow to the southwest; staying in between the corral and the barn (about 225°). Head for the open space in between the forested flanks of the hill you're heading towards. When you hit a grassy cart track (marked red stripe occasionally), continue west-southwest on it.

When you enter the forest again after about 3km you can see the enormous Oaşa Lake shimmering through the trees in front of you. Cross a forest road and a clearing by going down a narrow trail (northwest) which is marked with red 'pencils'. As you enter the forest again, take care: there's a very treacherous little path down to the southwest here; however, the waymarks lead north-northwest. There's a T-fork in the road as you close in on the lake; turn right (north). After 300 metres you'll reach the Transalpina Road (DN67C); **Cabana Oaşa** is just a few steps to the right.

STAGE 3

Obârşia Lotrului–Zănoaga Mare Lake

Start	Cabana Obârşia Lotrului (hitchhike 25km over the Transalpina Road to get there)
Finish	Zănoaga Mare Lake
Distance	11.5km
Total ascent	770m
Total descent	120m
Grade	Moderate
Time	4hr 20min
Maximum altitude	2055m (Zănoaga Mare Lake)
Water	At Cabana Obârşia Lotrului, Gâlcescu Lake and Zănoaga Mare Lake; there's a spring at the start of the forest road, and plenty of streams cross the path

From Cabana Oaşa you'll need to hitchhike 25km south along the glorious Transalpina Road to reach the start of this stage. It's a popular road so it shouldn't be difficult to find a ride.

From **Cabana Obârşia Lotrului**, head southwest towards Rânca over the DN7A road. It's marked red cross and triangle; the Lotru River runs parallel to it. After 1.5km, the road forks; go left to continue on the **Transalpina** (DN67C). After almost 3km on this road, turn right (south) onto a forest road marked red cross; the Transalpina departs to the left here and the Lotru River joins the forest road. There's a spring after 500 metres.

Walk past **Cabana Aviatorilor** (not open to tourists, it seems). After 750 metres the forest road forks; turn left (east), crossing a stream. When the road forks again after about 1.4km, keep left again to stay on the forest road. There are no way-marks for the next 600 metres, until you reach a bridge over the Lotru River.

Just after the bridge there's a signpost up a tree on the left; Gâlcescu Lake (spelled Calcescu here) is signed 2hr 30min. After 300 metres the road forks; turn left (southwest) and walk up along a stream, off the forest road. About 400 metres on you'll reach a modest waterfall at the confluence of two tributary streams. Don't follow the road, which bends to the left; instead, cross the stream and walk up alongside the waterfall. After perhaps 50 metres you'll see a forest road leading

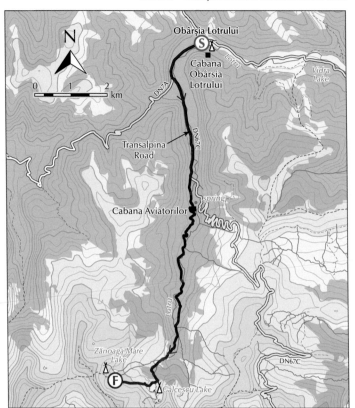

west (right) and a path to the left (southeast), and in between them, a stream coming from the south, straight ahead. Follow the stream. After about 200 metres you'll see a waymark on a tree; then another one plus an arrow after perhaps another 200 metres (keep right).

Cross another tributary to the Lotru, then turn left (southeast) immediately. When you see a giant arrow to the right, make just a few steps to the right, then head south again. There's lots of dead wood here, which makes the going a bit more difficult. You'll soon see an old signpost to Gâlcescu Lake, signed 1hr 15min. The forest opens up to an unnamed meadow from where you have excellent views of the main ridge of the Parâng.

A grassy trail leads to a lively stream; cross it and continue on the other side. You'll have to cross it twice more in the next 500 metres. Continue southwest; the grassy trail becomes a rocky path which goes up steeply through dwarf pine, and brings you to a stream with a small waterfall. Continue along the right bank, then cross it when you see a waymark on the other side. Cross a very soggy meadow south, then southwest to reach **Gâlcescu Lake**, which makes an excellent camping spot if you want to call it a day.

To continue to Zănoaga Mare Lake, walk along the western shore of Gâlcescu Lake and turn right (west) at a big boulder. Waymarks are scarce in between both lakes, but the trail is easy to follow and marked with cairns. Climb past a tarn and keep heading west, crossing a grassy valley strewn with boulders until you see **Zănoaga Mare Lake** on your right after 1.3km. Turn northwest to reach the lakeshore, or stop at the stream that flows into it.

STAGE 4
Zănoaga Mare Lake–Petroșani via Stațiunea Parâng

Start	Zănoaga Mare Lake
Finish	Petroșani
Distance	24.5km (14km to Stațiunea Parâng)
Total ascent	1110m (960m to Stațiunea Parâng)
Total descent	2385m (1305m to Stațiunea Parâng)
Grade	Moderate
Time	8hr 20min (5hr 20min to Stațiunea Parâng)
Maximum altitude	2519m (Parângul Mare Peak)
Water	Stream near Zănoaga Mare Lake; beyond that, nothing until Stațiunea Parâng. There's a stream along the final section to Petroșani (water needs filtering).

Done in one day, this makes for a long but doable stage. It can be broken up by overnighting at Stațiunea Parâng – but bear in mind that this is mostly a ski resort and accommodation may be closed in late summer. If you don't want to walk the somewhat uninteresting final section from Stațiunea Parâng to Petroșani you should be able to hitchhike it.

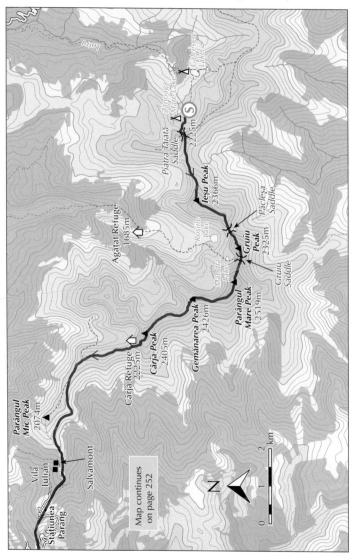

251

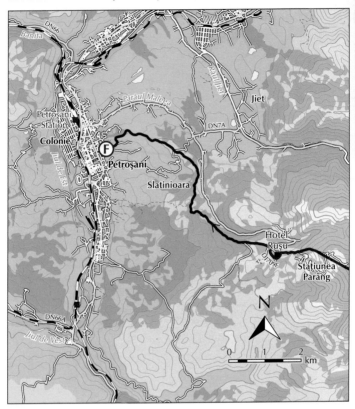

From **Zănoaga Mare Lake**, return to the path. There's a rock with a cairn on top to help you navigate. Head northwest towards Piatra Tăiată Saddle; the signpost can be seen from below. As on the previous stage, you will hardly find any waymarks, except for some faded marks higher up. However, there are cairns and the trail is easy to follow. It winds past Piatra Tăiată ('Cut-Off Rock'). Some 1km of ascending brings you to **Piatra Tăiată Saddle** (2225m).

From here, head west and down towards Parângul Mare Peak, following the red stripe waymarks – the waymarking is excellent from this point onwards. After about 2km you'll reach **Ieşu Peak** (2366m). From Ieşu Peak (spelled Leşu on the Dimap map), head southwest. You can see the Transalpina in the valley to the

Looking back down to Zănoaga Mare Lake from Piatra Tăiată Saddle

south. An easy section follows: an almost level paths leads you over Ieşu and **Pâcleşa** Saddles; you can see Roşiile Lake in the valley to the right in the latter. A short and steep ascent to **Gruiu Peak** (2325m) follows. Catch your breath in the subsequent saddle before the ascent of the highest summit of the Parâng, **Parângul Mare Peak** (2519m), about 30min climbing from the signpost in the saddle.

The red circle trail departs north from **Gruiul Saddle**; it leads past a few lakes and to Agăţat Refuge (1685m), should you need it – it can be reached in 1hr 45min.

To stay on the main route, after Parângul Mare Peak continue west on the red stripe trail; you will soon see the city of Petroşani to the northwest. The trail passes beneath **Gemănarea Peak** (2426m); when you see arrows follow them to the left, cross a gully, then turn right again (northwest), either over the rocky ridge or to the right of it. There are plenty of camping opportunities here; lots of grassy spots and some stone rings to offer shelter (but no water).

After passing beneath **Cârja Peak** (2405m) with its 'walking cane' on top, you'll rapidly descend to **Cârja Refuge** (2225m). At the second signpost, 2km from here, bear left (west) to continue towards Staţiunea Parâng – unless you want to go for the small detour over **Parângul Mic Peak** (2074m). Another 2km brings you to the gravel road that leads down into **Staţiunea Parâng**; after 800 metres you'll see the Salvamont base on your right. Vila Iulian is just a little further down and to the left.

To continue to Petroşani, take the gravel road down from the Salvamont base/Vila Iulian. Follow the yellow and blue pillars down. When another road comes in from the right after about 1.3km, continue following the pillars down northwest – there's a waymark on a concrete shed. About 500 metres from here, turn left (west); there's a yellow circle waymark on an old beech tree, and bus stop-type signs further down. Continue down a gravel road; after 200 metres on it you'll see a signpost (2hr 30min–3hr to Petroşani). Another 200 metres brings you to Hotel Ruşu. A further 600 metres down the road, the red stripe trail departs to the left; either follow this all the way to **Petroşani** (6km, 1hr 30min) or hitchhike from here.

THE COZIA

ROUTE 24
Cozia circuit

Start/finish	Mănăstirea Turnu
Distance	12.5km
Total ascent/descent	1400m
Grade	Moderate
Time	1–2 days
Maximum altitude	1572m (Cabana Cozia, Stage 1) or 1667m (Cozia Peak, Stage 1)
Maps	Cozia, 1:35,000, Munții Noştri

Geographically, the Cozia is part of the Făgăraş group, but culturally and historically it seems to be more a part of the 'Oltenia de sub Munte' mountains in Vâlcea County. Tucked away to the south of the forbidding Făgăraş, this remote mountain range and its surroundings has been home to many monasteries for centuries. It is possible to spend the night at Turnu Monastery, the start and finish of this circular trail, and get a glimpse of monastic life. The monks will host you for free and even share their meal with you. Although Cozia Peak – also known as Ciuha Mare Peak – only reaches a modest altitude of 1667m, you will have plenty of ascending to do since you're starting from the Olt Valley. Most of the massif is densely forested, but there are quite a few vantage points en route and around the peak that offer magnificent views over the Olt Valley and towards the neighbouring Buila-Vânturariţa Massif. The easy second stage takes you back down to Turnu Monastery via the western flank of the Cozia Massif. It's possible to do the whole circuit in one day if you leave early.

Access
Take a bus to Călimăneşti (under 2hr from Sibiu, under 3hr from Bucharest) and ask the driver to drop you off at the dam (*barajul*) in Căciulata. Cross the dam and turn left to reach the monastery. There are two direct trains from Sibiu to Mănăstirea Turnu halt as well, but this takes considerably longer than the bus and they leave very early. However, if you're coming from Bucharest it's worth taking

an IR train to Râmnicu Vâlcea (under 3hr) and from there change to the R train to Mănăstirea Turnu (35min). This brings you right to the start of the trail.

Accommodation and food

The monks at Turnu Monastery will happily host you and quite possibly feed you too. No need to make a reservation. A good alternative is Camping Mănăstirea Turnu, in between the dam and the monastery, which has little cottages for rent. You can also pitch your tent here. It belongs to the monastery, so phone them to check for availability. Cabana Cozia just below Cozia Peak is popular so do make a reservation. Camping is allowed here too although there's not much space for tents and it gets infamously windy at times. The cabana serves hot meals, drinks and snacks; there are outdoor toilets.

Restaurant Dada just before the dam (next to the petrol station) offers excellent meals, mostly traditional Romanian food.

STAGE 1

Mănăstirea Turnu–Cabana Cozia

Start	Turnu Monastery
Finish	Cabana Cozia
Distance	7km
Total ascent	1340m (another 80m to reach Cozia Peak)
Total descent	155m
Grade	Moderate
Time	3hr 30min
Maximum altitude	1572m (Cabana Cozia) or 1667m (Cozia Peak)
Water	At Turnu Monastery, Stânişoara Monastery and Cabana Cozia

From **Turnu Monastery**, head up the dirt track in front of the monastery, just east of due north. Pass a small wooden chapel after 630 metres and a derelict wooden shelter after another 750 metres. Some 300 metres later you'll reach **La Troiţă Saddle**, with another small chapel. Continue north on the blue and red striped route towards Stânişoara Monastery. After 750 metres the red stripe trail departs to the left; continue straight ahead (north) on the blue stripe trail, signed 30min–1hr to the monastery. The path is almost level for a while. After 350 metres an arrow with the words *Admiraţi peisajul* ('admire the landscape')

The imposing cliffs of the Cozia

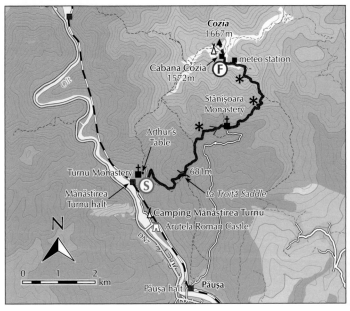

points you to a great vantage point, a few steps off the trail. From here you can see Cozia Peak and the adjacent meteo station.

After crossing a stream the path begins to climb. Walk along the stream, then when the path forks after 200 metres keep right (east) and climb to a meadow. Continue east to the grounds of **Stânişoara Monastery**. Walk up the paved road for about 100 metres, then bear left and walk along the fence of the monastery gardens. After about 300 metres turn left (north-northwest) onto a narrow trail, up into the forest. When you see a shelter to your right after 50 metres, turn left (northwest); the gradient becomes steeper here. After 750 metres there's another vantage point, just off the trail to the left. From here you can see the Buila-Vânturariţa ridge.

Continuing on the main trail, after 1km ascend along a stream with the help of a cable. There are more cables a bit further up. After 300 metres you'll arrive at another viewpoint, looking south this time. Exit the forest after 300 metres; walk past the **meteo station**. Now that you're out in the open you can see the beautiful Olt Valley and the Buila-Vânturariţa to the left. After 400 metres you'll arrive at **Cabana Cozia** (1572m). From here it's a short hike up to **Cozia Peak** (1667m) and back (15min total).

STAGE 2
Cabana Cozia–Mănăstirea Turnu

Start	Cabana Cozia
Finish	Turnu Monastery
Distance	5.5km
Total ascent	55m
Total descent	1245m
Grade	Moderate
Time	2hr 30min
Maximum altitude	1572m (Cabana Cozia)
Water	At Cabana Cozia and Turnu Monastery

From **Cabana Cozia**, head northwest on the red triangle trail, also marked red and blue stripe. After 1.2km the blue stripe departs left; stay on the red triangle/stripe trail. After a further 500 metres or so descend to **Turneanu Refuge**. At a derelict shelter 800 metres further up, the red stripe departs to the left; keep right to stay on the red triangle. Descend steeply for 2.7km until you reach Arthur's Table, then descend the last few metres to the back of **Turnu Monastery**.

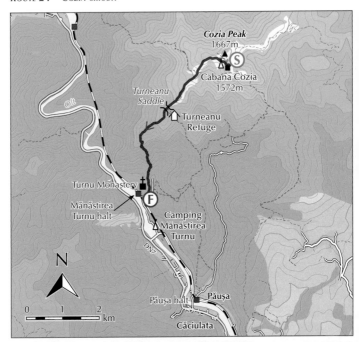

Looking towards the Buila-Vânturariţa

THE BUILA-VÂNTURARIȚA

ROUTE 25
Cheia Village–Buila-Vânturarița ridge–Băile Olănești

Start	Cheia Village
Finish	Băile Olănești
Distance	53.7km
Total ascent	2770m
Total descent	2795m
Grade	Moderate-difficult
Time	3 days
Maximum altitude	1885m (Vânturarița Peak, Stage 2)
Maps	A map issued by the park can be found here: www.buila.ro/harta_turistica_ro. Another, interactive, map can be found by googling 'Harta Masivului Buila Vanturarita'. No maps commercially available.

The Buila-Vânturarița is Romania's youngest and smallest national park. It isn't very easy to access, and thanks to that its natural treasures are well preserved. The Buila-Vânturarița ridge, essentially a southern spur of the larger Căpățânii Mountains, is reminiscent of the Piatra Craiului, although lower: its highest peak reaches 1885m. Its jagged limestone ridge offers challenging clambering sections alternating with grassy plateaus where you can catch your breath. Floral variety is incredibly rich, resulting in a wide range of butterfly species; the Cheia River is full of trout. The route ends in the spa town of Băile Olănești, with its numerous sulphurous springs.

Cabana Cheia, the base for the stages described below, is possibly the most wonderful cabana in all of Romania, with its jolly host, cosy bedrooms, fireplace, trampoline and hammock. There's even a bath! The cabana isn't always manned but you can still stay there; just check with the hut warden in advance. From the cabana you can see chamois frolicking around on the Stogu Rock right in front of it. Camping is allowed on the cabana grounds but not beyond, as the Buila-Vânturarița is a national park.

Access
The city of Râmnicu Vâlcea is the best access point for the Buila-Vânturarița. There are a great many buses and trains between Bucharest and Râmnicu

Vâlcea; the journey takes under 3hr. It can also be reached by bus from Sibiu (2hr). From Râmnicu Vâlcea, take an Antares bus to Cheia (45min). These leave from Autogara 1 Mai, Strada George Coşbuc 4. Alternatively, take a bus to Băile Olăneşti and get off at the junction to Cheia in Valea Cheii (30min). Either walk or hitchhike the remaining 6km to the start of the trail.

At the end of the trail, frequent buses to Râmnicu Vâlcea depart from the bus stop across from Hotel Central in Băile Olăneşti. These are operated by Antares and they go more frequently than the schedule on https://autogari.ro suggests (every half-hour in fact). The journey takes around 45min.

Access to the park costs 5RON per person for seven days; however, it is unclear to whom this should be paid.

Accommodation

If you want to start from Cheia in the morning, consider staying at Buila Basecamp cottage, where you can also pitch your tent. Cabana Cheia is an excellent base for exploring the ridge and you can camp there too. Plenty of accommodation in Băile Olăneşti – see Google Maps and www.booking.com.

STAGE 1
Cheia Village–Cabana Cheia via Brâna Caprelor

Start	Cheia Village
Finish	Cabana Cheia
Distance	15.7km
Total ascent	620m
Total descent	200m
Grade	Moderate
Time	4hr 20min
Maximum altitude	945m
Water	Several springs on the forest road; spring at Cabana Cheia

Follow the DJ654 road through the village of **Cheia** until you reach a signpost. Continue on the gravel road, following the blue triangle waymarks for Cabana Cheia, signed 4–5hr, with the Cheia River to your right. Pass the beautifully decorated **Iezer Hermitage** after 3.5km. Continue gently ascending on the gravel road; after a further 4.5km the red cross trail to Pahomie Monastery bends off to the left, signed 45min.

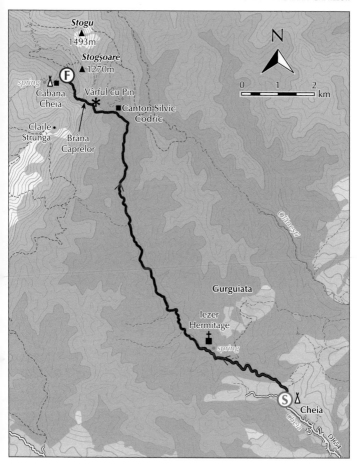

Continue straight ahead on the forest road for another 3.7km, then turn left, off the road and up into the forest, still following the blue triangle trail. Walk past the privately owned **Canton Silvic Codric**. The section that follows is called Brâna Caprelor ('Goat's Path') and is a much shorter and much more exciting way to reach Cabana Cheia than the winding forest road. After 450 metres you come to a fork; take the blue triangle trail which is the narrow path leading west

in between the two prongs of the fork. Another 650 metres brings you to the start of Brâna Caprelor, marked by an amazing and vertigo-inducing vantage point called **Vârful cu Pin** ('Pine Peak').

The path continues through the Cheile Cheii gorge, in between the steep rock walls of Stogşoare to the right and Claile Strunga to the left. There's a splendid waterfall after 1.5km. After another kilometre you'll reach **Cabana Cheia** (910m), at the foot of the Stogşoare, after having crossed two tributaries of the Cheia River. Do keep an eye on the Stogşoare because it's possible, not to say likely, that you'll see chamois frolicking around on the impossibly steep cliffs.

STAGE 2
Vânturarița and Buila Peaks circuit from Cabana Cheia

Start/finish	Cabana Cheia
Distance	19km
Total ascent/descent	1450m
Grade	Difficult
Time	7hr 15min
Maximum altitude	1885m (Vânturarița Peak)
Water	At Cabana Cheia; springs at Curmătura Oale, below Curmătura Builei and about halfway back on the red triangle trail

This challenging hike covers the central portion of the ridge including the two main peaks, then lets you catch your breath on the return journey below the ridge. Prepare for lots of clambering.

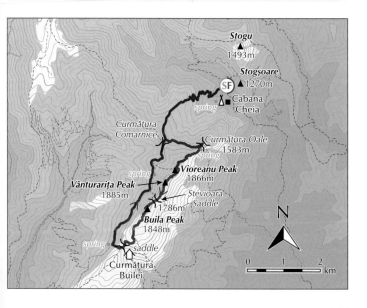

Looking towards Buila Peak, where the going becomes easier

From **Cabana Cheia** head west up the combined red triangle, red stripe and blue stripe trail. It winds up through the forest for about 4km. Turn left (southeast) at a signpost to continue on the red stripe trail to Curmătura Oale. When you reach the saddle at **Curmătura Oale** (1583m) after 1.3km, make a sharp right (southwest) onto the red stripe and yellow circle trail towards Vânturarița Peak. The waymarks are a bit hard to spot; there's an old unmarked trail just to the right of the ridge but it's best to stay as high up as you can.

What follows is a short section of ridge scrambling, leading to a beautiful craggy peak. Looking north, you can see the Căpățânii Ridge. The trail now briefly descends to the right, then quickly climbs to the ridge again. Soon you will come to a gigantic boulder field; this is known as the Bomba Atomica. At the end of it stands a conical rock. Walk past it and turn left; then scramble up to **Vioreanu Peak** (1866m) via a very steep and narrow 'goat's path'. Continue on the rocky trail to **Vânturarița Peak** (1885m) for 750 metres then descend to **Stevioara Saddle** (1786m).

Confusingly, what is shown as **Vioreanu Peak** on the map used to be called **Vânturarița Peak**, to which the writing on the rock on Vioreanu Peak testifies. Conversely, what is now Vânturarița Peak used to be called Vioreanu Peak. The park staff wanted to close the section between Curmătura Oale and Vânturarița Peak to the public and has decided to rename Vioreanu as Vânturarița – presumably so that tourists could still reach a peak with that name. However, the trail is still open and the name changing has only caused confusion. The names used in this description are the names as shown on the map.

Walk up the grassy slope to **Buila Peak** (1848m). The ridge is no longer a spine but turns into something more like a plateau, with steep limestone cliffs to the right. Descend for about 2km to the shelter at **Curmătura Builei** (1561m). You may encounter a flock of sheep and the accompanying dogs here.

To return to Cabana Cheia, turn right after the signpost, just before the corral. You are now on the yellow circle trail, although marks are hard to spot. After 300 metres turn right (north-northeast) towards a **spring**, where you'll find a signpost. Continue on the red triangle trail towards Cabana Cheia. Initially the waymarks are hard to spot because they're old and faded. After about 650 metres stay with the trail as it veers off to the right, away from the obvious path.

About 4km of easy walking brings you to the signposted **Curmătura Comarnice**. Turn right (east) to Cabana Cheia. After 200 metres you'll reach the signpost where you started off towards Curmătura Oale; turn left and descend to **Cabana Cheia** the way you came to arrive there in an hour or so.

STAGE 3
Cabana Cheia–Băile Olăneşti

Start	Cabana Cheia
Finish	Băile Olăneşti
Distance	19km
Total ascent	700m
Total descent	1145m
Grade	Moderate
Time	5hr 15min
Maximum altitude	1102m (Curmatura Stogşoare)
Water	At Cabana Cheia; spring in the forest near Gurguiata

This walk takes you out of the Buila-Vânturariţa to the spa town of Băile Olăneşti, from where you can take a bus back to Râmnicu Vâlcea.

From **Cabana Cheia**, walk south on the blue triangle trail for about 100 metres until you reach the river, then cross it over two beams and a fallen tree and turn left to continue north on the other side of the stream. Alternatively, walk north

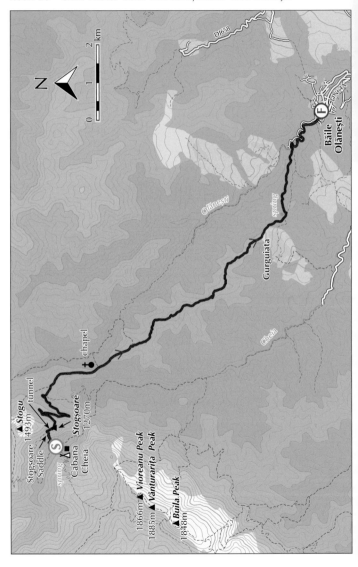

The trail to Băile Olănești

from the cabana, following the road briefly until you see a signpost and wade through the stream there.

When you see an old signpost after about 800 metres, turn right (east) and head into the forest, up a steep trail. When you reach a gravel road after 750 metres turn right onto it, towards Prislopel Saddle. Follow the gravel road through the tunnel (Curmatura Stogșoare) in between **Stogșoare** and Stogu Peaks.

To approach the Căpățânii Mountains

After 3km on this road there's an option to head into the Căpățânii Mountains via the blue cross trail (signed 6–7hr to Gera Peak). A traverse of the Căpățânii and the eastern Parâng, ending at the Transalpina Road, can be completed in four days. A full description of the Căpățânii is beyond the scope of this book.

After just over 3km – 100 metres after the blue cross trail to the Căpățânii – turn left for Băile Olănești. The signpost suggests the waymarks are red cross; in reality they're red stripe. After 2km you'll arrive at a small **chapel**; the yellow stripe trail departs left. Continue straight ahead on the combined blue and red stripe trail. After about 100 metres the trail forks; keep left to stay on what is now, all of a sudden, the red and blue cross trail.

After almost 8km of easy descending through the forest, turn right onto a signed cart track. Follow it for 100 metres – you are now in the hamlet of **Gurguiata** – then turn left into the forest again (there is a spring here). The trail is marked red and blue cross as well as red circle. After 700 metres, follow the red and blue cross trail to the right (southeast) and up. After about a kilometre the trail is almost completely overgrown; struggle through the young beech trees to find it again. When you meet the road after 1km, turn right, then almost immediately left over a bridge. Continue on the paved road along the Olănești River for 2km, heading past the famed springs of **Băile Olănești** and into the spa town.

THE RETEZAT MOUNTAINS

In between Pleşa and Piule Peaks in the Retezatul Mic (Route 28, Stage 2)

The Retezat Mountains are part of the Southern Carpathians, and rise up between the Haţeg and Petroşani Depressions. The massif is bordered by the Râul Mare River in the west and the Jiul de Vest River in the east. It lies in the heart of Hunedoara County, which according to local legend is the cradle of Romanian civilisation. The Retezat has a lot to offer: it is compact yet versatile. Its block shape makes it relatively easy to hike straight to its heart. It boasts more than 20 peaks over 2000m and has 58 permanent glacial lakes (lovingly referred to as *ochi albastri*, 'blue eyes'). Over one-third of all the flora in Romania can be found in the Retezat Mountains, and it has over 90 endemic plant species. The animal kingdom is represented by chamois, lynxes, bears, wolves, deer, otters and marmots, as well as the golden eagle, lesser spotted eagle and several other birds of prey. You will most likely encounter several flocks of sheep – and therefore guard dogs. Watch out for vipers sunbathing on the rocks, especially in the Retezatul Mic.

Geologically, it is characterised by igneous rock, with lots of glistening mica and quartz. The main ridge runs from west to east and includes the two highest peaks, Peleaga (2509m) and Păpuşa (2508m); several longer and higher spurs

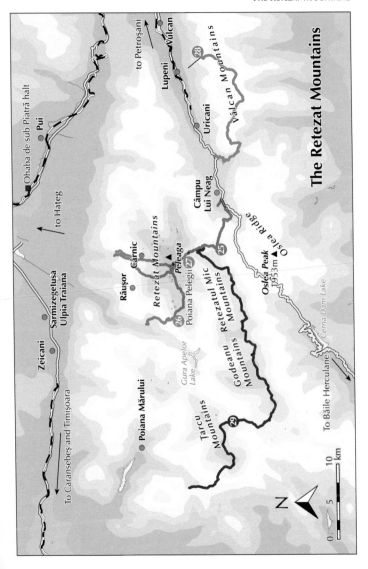

depart to the north of it and some lower and shorter ones to the south. A second, lower ridge, mostly consisting of limestone, runs to the south of the main ridge; this is known as the Retezatul Mic, or the Lesser Retezat. The Retezat owes its name to its most characteristic peak: the flattened top of Retezat Peak (2482m) is a landmark that can be recognised from afar – Retezat means 'cut off'. According to legend, a giant chopped off its top in the distant past, resulting in its present flattened appearance.

June and July are the wettest months here; the first half of August is best weather-wise if you want to hike in the summer. If you prefer quieter months then September and October are good options.

The **Retezat** National Park covers an area of 38,000ha and is the oldest national park in Romania; it was established in 1935 by botanist Alexandru Borza. To access the park you will have to buy a ticket, valid for seven days. These are cheap and are usually sold by park rangers at the various entry points; otherwise, ask at the first cabana you hit. Camping is allowed in designated areas only.

The national park lies just south of the ancient capital of the Roman province of Dacia, Sarmizegetusa – often referred to with its Roman name behind it, Ulpia Traiana, so as not to confuse it with Sarmizegetusa Regia, the Dacian capital, which lies 70km further east in the Sureanu Mountains. Both are worth visiting because of their impressive ruins. The nearest airports are Timişoara and Sibiu (See 'The Banat Mountains' in this book for more on Timişoara).

Two routes in the Retezat National Park (Routes 26 and 27) are described below; however, you will find that you can pick and mix from these since all the major trails depart from Bucura Lake – so essentially you will have to decide which entry and exit routes please you most and how many circular hikes you want to do from the lake. Once you've reached Bucura Lake, the largest glacial lake in Romania, you can pitch your tent and make excursions from there. Although the area around Bucura Lake is popular and can get very busy during the summer months, it's easy enough to find a challenging trail away from the tents, into the wilderness. It's fairly easy to spot marmots and at Bucura Lake you might even spot a local celebrity, Bella the fox, who is not at all shy.

To the south of the Retezatul Mic and the Jiu de Vest Valley with its mining towns lies another, lower and grassier ridge: the **Vâlcan** (Route 28). A day in the Vâlcan can easily be extended with a hike in the Retezatul Mic. A walk on the ridge offers fine views north towards the Tulişa Mountains and the Retezat and east towards the Parâng. It is also suitable for mountain biking and has a popular skiing resort south of Straja Peak (1868m). It is possible to do a complete traverse of the ridge, starting at Motel Gambrinus in Petroşani, but it is very difficult to navigate your way to the ridge through the forest east of Straja because of deforestation and a general lack of maintenance. You can camp anywhere you like in this area.

The **Ţarcu Mountains** lie west of the Râul Mare River, which separates them from the Retezat; a north–south ridge connects it with the **Godeanu**. The Ţarcu and Godeanu Mountains (Route 29) are rarely visited so offer some fine lonesome walking. It is also a great approach to the Retezatul Mic ridge, which in turn offers great views towards the central Retezat. This area is known for its strong winds and the weather can be very changeable, so make sure you bring wind- and rainproof clothing. There are no restrictions on camping in the Ţarcu and Godeanu; however, the Retezatul Mic falls within the bounds of the Retezat National Park so camping is restricted to designated areas there. Since no good maps are commercially available for the Ţarcu, Godeanu and Vâlcan, you might want to bring a GPS to make sure you stay on the trail – navigation isn't always straightforward.

THE RETEZAT

ROUTE 26
Cârnic to Cabana Gura Zlata via Bucura Lake

Start	Cârnic
Finish	Cabana Gura Zlata
Distance	33km
Total ascent	2880m
Total descent	3140m
Grade	Moderate-difficult
Time	3–4 days
Maximum altitude	2509m (Peleaga Peak, Excursion)
Maps	One of the following: Retezat National Park, Retezat National Park Administration, 1:50,000; Dimap, Retezat Mountains, 1:50,000; Retezat Mountains, Munţii Noştri

The Retezat National Park is a firm favourite with Romanian and foreign hikers alike, and for good reason. Its compact size makes it relatively easy to hike straight to its heart. It is home to some of Romania's highest peaks – including Peleaga (2509m) and Păpuşa (2508m) – and has a great many glimmering lakes, connected by a dense network of streams and springs. Its many granite boulder fields and steep slopes present plenty of challenge to those seeking it, but there is something for everyone: there are easier routes as well (see Route 27).

This challenging route leads from one of the most popular and easiest access points, Cârnic, to Bucura Lake – Romania's biggest glacial lake, which lies right in the centre of the massif and is a great base for day hikes. Stage 2 takes you over the massif's name-giving peak, the Retezat (2482m); its characteristic flattened top is visible from afar (Retezat means 'cut off'). The long exit route to Gura Zlata crosses through lesser-known territory, past Zănoaga Lake, Romania's deepest glacial lake; the final descent takes you through magical old-growth beech forests. At the end of it, Cabana Gura Zlata awaits to restore hungry hikers.

Self-sufficiency is required on this trek; at Bucura Lake there is no accommodation (except in emergencies) so you will need to camp. The area around the lake is known for its strong winds, so make sure you and your tent are wind-proof.

Looking towards Bucura Peak after the descent from Peleaga Peak (Stage 3)

Bears are known to come up here occasionally, so do not store meat or other bear delicacies in your tent – ask if you can store food at the Salvamont base. The Salvamont crew usually scares them away with flares at night.

Hiking in the Retezat can be combined with a visit to nearby Sarmizegetusa Ulpia Traiana, where you can admire the ruins of the former capital of the Roman province of Dacia.

Access

There are two options to reach Ohaba de sub Piatra: take a train from Deva or travel via Haţeg. There is one direct train to Ohaba de sub Piatra from Deva (1hr 20min) while the others go via Simeria. Deva itself is a 3hr 30min train ride away from Timişoara and 3hr from Sibiu. Alternatively, make your way to Haţeg – again from Timişoara (180km) or Sibiu (140km), where the nearest airports are. No buses stop at Ohaba de sub Piatra, so from Haţeg you will have to hitch-hike or hail a cab to get to the foot of the Retezat Mountains (24km). The best place to do this is Autogara Haţeg on Strada Progresului 51. If hitchhiking, ask the driver if they can drop you off at Ohaba de sub Piatra – unless they're going to Cârnic themselves, of course. If travelling by taxi, head straight for Cârnic. You could make a stop at Mălăieşti Castle on the way.

Once in Ohaba de sub Piatra, call Mr Victor Farcaş, tel 0724 560403. He runs a minivan service between Ohaba and Cârnic. (He doesn't speak English though.) If you're unlucky, you might have to walk all the way up to Cârnic via Nucşoara Village (17km). In short, your best bet is a taxi. If you have a car, you can park it in Cârnic for a fee.

To leave the area at the end of the trek you'll have to either walk or hitchhike 20km north along the DJ685 road until you get to the DN6B again, from where it's another 2km west to Sarmizegetusa. Timişoara and Sibiu (both about 160km away) can be accessed from Sarmizegetusa. Hitchhiking shouldn't be too difficult since people coming from Poiana Pelegii, another entry point to the Retezat (see Route 27), have to pass this way.

Accommodation
Cabana Codrin, Cabana Lolaia, Cabana Pietrele, Cabana Gura Zlata. Camping spots at Cârnic (Cabana Codrin), Cabana Pietrele, Bucura Lake, Zănoaga Lake and near Cabana Gura Zlata. There's a Salvamont refuge at Bucura Lake and another one at Zănoaga Lake but you can sleep here only in case of emergency, so you will need to camp. Cabana Pietrele is especially busy during the summer months; you're advised to make your reservation well in advance if you want to stay there. Both Cabana Codrin and Cabana Pietrele serve decent meals.

STAGE 1
Cârnic–Cabana Pietrele

Start	Cabana Codrin, Cârnic
Finish	Cabana Pietrele
Distance	3.5km
Total ascent	450m
Total descent	Negligible
Grade	Easy
Time	1hr 45min
Maximum altitude	1480m (Cabana Pietrele)
Water	You can buy drinks at one of the huts in Cârnic; there's a spring at Cabana Pietrele

Starting from Cârnic is the easiest option if you don't have a car; it also offers a gentle approach to the heart of the Retezat, Bucura Lake, because there's a cabana right at the start and one after just 4km. Expect things to get tougher after that though! Essentially you'll be following the gravel road almost all the way up to Cabana Pietrele, but there are a few shortcuts and a waterfall just off the trail.

If you arrive in Cârnic early enough you have the option of following the route described below as far as the Cabana Genţiana turn-off and then taking the blue stripe route to Bucura Lake. This is an easier option than the 'main' Stage 2 and will take you to Bucura Lake a good deal faster (about 4hr 30min from Cârnic). It is Route 27, Stage 2 in reverse.

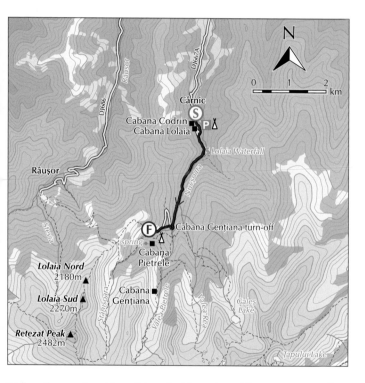

Walk up the gravel road from **Cabana Codrin**, and turn left onto a narrow trail up into the forest after about 300 metres; this is marked blue stripe and blue triangle. After 100 metres take the shortcut back to the road. After another 400 metres or so you have the option to turn left to **Lolaila Waterfall**; it takes just 5min to get down there. After visiting the waterfall, walk back up to the road and continue south; when it forks, keep right towards Cabana Genţiana.

After about 2km you have the option to turn left to Cabana Gențiana; follow this blue stripe trail if you want to head straight for Bucura Lake (see note above). However, to reach Cabana Pietrele, keep going straight ahead on the blue stripe trail. Less than 100 metres after the fork, turn left (northwest) for Cabana Pietrele, signed 15min. After about 300 metres you'll see a sign to the camping spot (*loc de campare*) on the right. To arrive at **Cabana Pietrele** (1480m), continue for another 300 metres.

STAGE 2
Cabana Pietrele–Bucura Lake via Retezat Peak

Start	Cabana Pietrele
Finish	Bucura Lake
Distance	9km
Total ascent	1200m
Total descent	670m
Grade	Difficult
Time	6hr 30min
Maximum altitude	2482m (Retezat Peak)
Water	Fill bottles at the spring at Cabana Pietrele; there is no water on the trail until Tău Porții Lake (which you would have to filter). Spring at Bucura Lake.

This is an unusual trail: although the Retezat is known for its multitude of lakes and springs, there is no water on this trail. Most of it leads south over the westernmost ridge of the Retezat, Culmea Lolaia, from where you will have beautiful views of the various spurs that lie to the east of it; a vision of what is to come if you decide to do some circular hikes from Bucura Lake. To the east lies the Land of Hațeg (Țara Hațegului) and, after you've climbed Retezat Peak, the Gemenele Reserve with its beautiful lakes. This is a tough hike but well worth it, and not frequented as much as the easier blue triangle and blue stripe trails.

From **Cabana Pietrele**, cross the bridge towards the spring and set off on the yellow stripe trail (northwest), up into the forest. After 500 metres, turn left onto

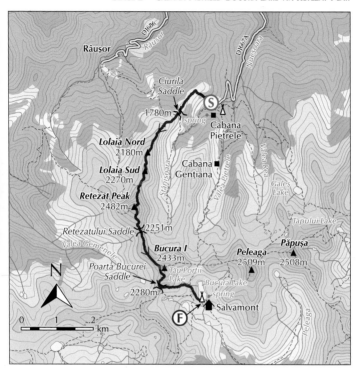

a rocky slope. Another 300 metres brings you to the start of the ridge, Culmea Lolaia, which is lavishly strewn with boulders. At **Ciurila Saddle** (1780m) the yellow stripe trail is crossed by the blue cross trail; Retezat Peak is signed 3hr 30min from here. Continue southeast on the yellow stripe trail. The yellow lichen on the boulders can make the waymarks a bit harder to spot. Fields of boulders are replaced by dwarf pine and blueberry bushes after a while.

After about 2km of ridge walking, the trail goes over **Lolaia Nord Peak** (2180m), soon followed by **Lolaia Sud Peak** (2270m). After Lolaia Sud Peak, follow an arrow to the right and head down a rocky path with sparse and faded waymarks. Walk south along the flank of the Lolaia Sud and descend to about 2200m; you are now approaching Retezat Peak. Although its top is flattened, it is challenging enough to climb; expect a difficult and steep ascent (about 300m over a distance of about 700 metres) with lots of boulders.

After you've reached **Retezat Peak** (2482m), retrace your steps for a bit and descend east for 45min, following the blue triangle and yellow stripe waymarks. From **Retezatului Saddle** (2251m), where the blue triangle trail comes in from the east, continue south towards Bucura Peak via the combined yellow and red stripe trail.

Bypass **Bucura Peak** (2433m) over a tricky path to arrive at **Poarta Bucurei Saddle**, meaning 'Gate of Joy'; an apt name because from here you can see the promised land: Tău Porții and various other lakes – although not Bucura Lake yet, even though you're close now – and have brilliant views over the lakes of the Gemenele Reserve to the right.

Descend towards **Tău Porții Lake**, then continue east for 1.2km to reach **Bucura Lake** (2041m). Walk southeast along the shore until you reach the **camping spot** and Salvamont base. The spring is two minutes north of the latter.

Bucura Lake (left) and its neighbouring lakes make for a stunning setting

EXCURSION

Peleaga and Bucura Peaks circuit from Bucura Lake

Start/finish	Bucura Lake
Distance	6.5km
Total ascent/descent	730m
Grade	Moderate
Time	3hr 30min
Maximum altitude	2509m (Peleaga Peak)
Water	Spring at Bucura Lake. Stream along the first section of the trail, but no water on the ridge.

This is a pleasant circuit from Bucura Lake that gives you stunning views over much of the Retezat from its highest peak, the Peleaga, without being overly long – which makes it an excellent route if you want to take it relatively easy for a day. It does involve some scrambling around Bucura Peak.

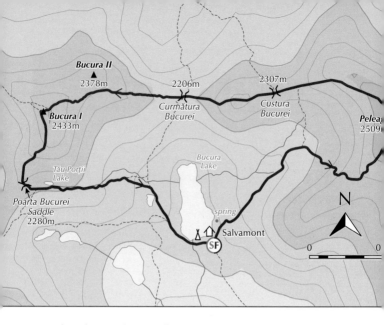

From the Salvamont base, walk north along the eastern shore of **Bucura Lake** until you reach the spring. From there, head up the yellow cross trail towards Peleaga Peak (northeast). After 750 metres the trail swings to the right and makes a curve to the south. Another 500 metres brings you to an unnamed saddle (2343m); turn left (east) here and begin the ascent of **Peleaga Peak** (2509m), which you will reach after 500 metres. To the west, you can see Păpuşa Peak (2508m) and a great many lakes.

Continue north-northwest on the yellow cross trail for a bit; after less than 50 metres the yellow cross trail departs to the right. Continue straight ahead on what is now the red stripe trail. A gentle descent to about 2300m follows; after a kilometre or so, ascend to the saddle of **Custura Bucurei** (2370m), which involves a bit of scrambling. From there, descend for 650 metres to **Curmătura Bucurei** (2206m).

At this point it's possible cut the circuit short and descend to Bucura Lake via the blue stripe trail in 30min. Otherwise, continue on the red stripe trail to the Bucura peaks; the trail bypasses **Bucura II** (2378m). The 30min ascent to Bucura I involves more scrambling and crossing of boulder fields. From **Bucura I** (2433m), 1km from Curmătura Bucurei, descend southwest (beware: lots of scree) until you meet the yellow stripe trail again. Return to Bucura Lake via **Poarta Bucurei Saddle** (2280m) as described in Stage 2.

STAGE 3
Bucura Lake–Cabana Gura Zlata

Start	Bucura Lake
Finish	Cabana Gura Zlata or the nearby camping spot
Distance	14km
Total ascent	500m
Total descent	1740m
Grade	Moderate
Time	6hr 15min
Maximum altitude	2370m (Judele Saddle)
Water	Springs at Bucura Lake and Zănoaga Lake

This is another hike that takes you off the most frequented routes in the Retezat. It is fairly long and involves a lot of descending so can be heavy on the knees, but it is possible to break it in two if you need to – there's another Salvamont base you can camp next to at Zănoaga Lake. The route offers a fun climb to Judele Saddle, views of the Țarcu Mountains to the east and a descent through truly magical virgin forest.

Walk north along the western shore of **Bucura Lake** and follow the red triangle and circle waymarks. After 300 metres, turn left (west); head for the signpost. Make sure you follow red circle and triangle, not yellow circle and red triangle!

Continue west and up; the ascent is gentle at first. After you've passed the three lakes to your left (named Ana, Viorica and Florica), climb the steep rocky section to Judele Saddle (2370m). This will involve some hands on rock. If you like you can climb the unnamed peak to the left of the saddle (2388m) or Judele Peak (2398m) to the right of it.

From the saddle, descend west towards Zănoaga Lake. The trail leads over the ridge for a while, then you descend quite rapidly over a fairly easy path through shrubbery. Eventually cross a meadow to arrive at **Zănoaga Lake** (1997m) and the Salvamont base.

With a depth of 29m, **Zănoaga Lake** is the deepest glacial lake in Romania. To find the spring, walk along the shore; the spring is located just off the trail. You should see a huge red dot pointing you towards it. Retrace your steps along the shore to get back on the trail.

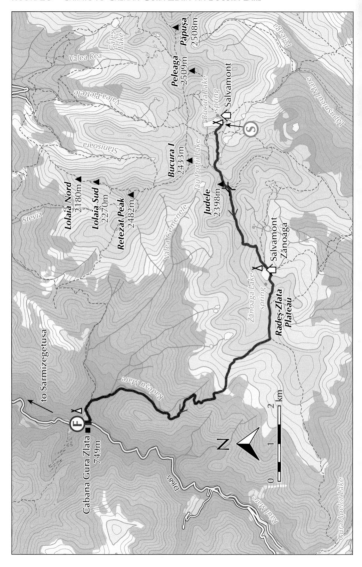

A shepherd and his flock near Judele Saddle

Climb to the next, unnamed pass (2142m). This brings you to the **Radeş-Zlata Plateau** in 30min or so. From here the going is easy for a while; you can see the Ţarcu Mountains ahead of you. After just over a kilometre on the plateau, there's a fork: keep right towards Gura Zlata (northwest) to stay on the red triangle trail. The waymarks are a bit hard to find initially, but things improve once you descend into the beautiful forest – dwarf pine until an altitude of about 1800m, but a fully-fledged shade-providing forest as you descend further.

The Radeşu Mare Stream runs parallel to the path in the valley below, and forms the natural border of the Gemenele Reserve. Cross it over a bridge after some 5km in the forest; by now the coniferous forest has made way for a gorgeous ancient beech forest. After 200 metres, cross the bridge over the Zlata River. Continue down the gravel road. When you come to the bridge over the Râul Mare River, turn right to reach the camping spot, which you'll find on your left after 500 metres. If you want to stay (or just eat) at the 120-year-old **Cabana Gura Zlata**, cross the bridge and turn left; you'll find it on your right after 250 metres.

ROUTE 27
Poiana Pelegii to Cârnic via Bucura Lake

Start	Poiana Pelegii
Finish	Cârnic
Distance	23km
Total ascent	1960m
Total descent	2535m
Grade	Moderate-difficult
Time	3 days
Maximum altitude	2509m (Peleaga Peak, Excursion)
Maps	One of the following: Retezat National Park, Retezat National Park Administration, 1:50,000; Dimap, Retezat Mountains, 1:50,000; Retezat Mountains, Munţii Noştri

This is the shortest and easiest route through the Retezat National Park, cutting right through its heart at Bucura Lake, Romania's biggest glacial lake. It can be done in reverse as well (see Route 26 for access to Cârnic). The circular excursion to Galeş Lake is among the best day hikes in the Retezat, if not in the country. This route can be easily extended with one or more of the excursions from Bucura Lake proposed in Route 26. While you're in the area, do visit the ruins of Sarmizegetusa Ulpia Traiana, the former capital of the Roman province of Dacia.

Self-sufficiency is required on this trek; at Bucura Lake there is no accommodation (except in emergencies) so you will need to camp. The area around the lake is known for its strong winds, so make sure you and your tent are wind-proof. Bears are known to come up here, so store your food wisely.

Access
Unless you have a car yourself, access to the start of this route this will involve hitchhiking from the DN68 road junction near Sarmizegetusa. Sarmizegetusa (Ulpia Traiana, not to be confused with Sarmizegetusa Regia) itself can be reached by bus from Timişoara or Sibiu (both about 160km away) – but check that the driver is willing to stop at Sarmizegetusa. From the DN68 junction it's then a 50km ride to Poiana Pelegii and especially the last section is very bumpy. During the summer there should be quite a few people heading that way though.

To get away from Cârnic at the end of the trek, either hitchhike the 17km down to Ohaba de sub Piatra (there should be plenty of people making the journey) or call Mr Victor Farcaş, tel 0724 560403. He runs a minivan service between Cârnic and Ohaba – but he doesn't speak English, so you may have to ask somebody to make the call for you. From Ohaba you can take a train to Deva (journey takes 2–3hr), and from Deva you can continue towards Sibiu and other hubs. If you want to hitchhike beyond Ohaba from Cârnic, try to make your way to Haţeg from where there are many buses in all directions, including Timişoara, Deva and Alba Iulia.

Accommodation

All of the cabanas are on the final stage, near the end of the trek: Cabana Pietrele, Cabana Genţiana, Cabana Lolaia, Cabana Codrin. There are camping spots at Poiana Pelegii near the start, then near Bucura Lake, at Cabana Pietrele and at Cârnic. There's a Salvamont refuge at Bucura Lake, but you can sleep here only in case of emergency so you will need to camp. (Since the Retezat is a national park you are only allowed to camp in designated areas.) Cabana Pietrele is especially busy during the summer months; you're advised to make your reservation well in advance if you want to stay there.

STAGE 1

Poiana Pelegii–Bucura Lake

Start	Poiana Pelegii
Finish	Bucura Lake
Distance	2.5km
Total ascent	400m
Total descent	25m
Grade	Moderate
Time	1hr 30min
Maximum altitude	2054m (just before Bucura Lake)
Water	Spring at Bucura Lake

The road to Poiana Pelegii isn't exactly comfortable and it's fairly long (50km), but this starting point does offer the shortest approach to Bucura Lake. This route can also be treated as an extension of Route 28.

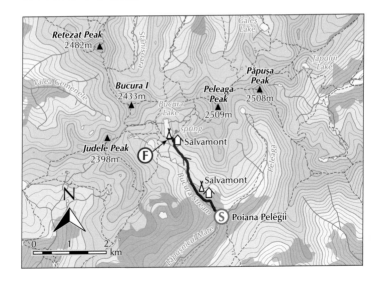

From the end of the road at **Poiana Pelegii**, cross the bridge over the Peleaga Stream and head north onto the combined red cross and blue stripe trail towards Bucura Lake. After 5min, you'll see Poiana Pelegii meadow with the **Salvamont base** (1633m) on your right. Walk along the Bucura Stream, which is to your left, as are the spikes of the Slăveiu spur. After 1.3km from the start the forest opens up and you'll be able to see Bucura and Peleaga Peaks ahead. The path is joined by a stream. Another kilometre or so brings you to the southern shore of **Bucura Lake** and another Salvamont base. The spring is a couple of minutes north of the base.

EXCURSION

Porțile Închise and Galeș Lake circuit from Bucura Lake

Start/finish	Bucura Lake
Distance	10.5km
Total ascent/descent	1350m
Grade	Difficult
Time	6hr 15min
Maximum altitude	2509m (Peleaga)
Water	Spring at Bucura Lake and at lakes after Galeș Lake

This is quite possibly the most satisfying hike in the entire Retezat. It takes you over its two highest peaks (Peleaga and Păpușa), offers some fine scrambling in the Porțile Închise ('Closed Gates') section, a fine break at Galeș Lake and many excellent vantage points over other lakes and glacial cirques. It is possible to continue directly to Cabana Pietrele and Cârnic from Galeș Lake, but this would mean carrying your full pack which is not recommended on this route.

From the Salvamont base, walk north along the eastern shore of **Bucura Lake** until you reach the spring. From there, head up the yellow cross trail towards Peleaga Peak (northeast). After 750 metres the trail swings to the right and makes a curve to the south. Another 500 metres brings you to an unnamed saddle (2343m); turn left (east) here and begin the ascent of **Peleaga Peak** (2509m), which you will reach after 500 metres. It will take you around 1hr 10min from the start to get to this point. From here, continue on the yellow cross trail for 150 metres, then turn right (east) to Păpușa Peak via **Pelegii Saddle** – this should take another hour or so.

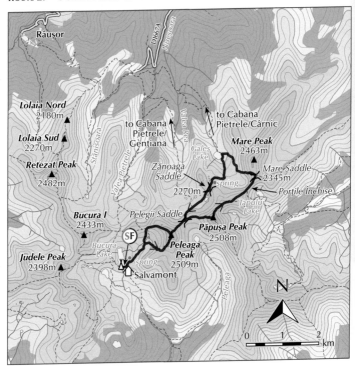

From **Păpușa Peak** (2508m), retrace your steps just slightly and descend north-east on the red stripe trail (not marked as such on the Dimap map). To the right you can see Adânc Lake, also known as Tău Răsucit, or 'Wrung-Out Lake', because it looks much like a wrung-out tea towel – as does, in fact, this entire trail on the map.

After about 300 metres there's a steep section with cables, after which there's a window to the left through which you can see the many lakes in the Rea Valley, which you will traverse on the return journey. A bit further up you can see Tău Tapului on the right, with its skull-shaped island, and Galeș Lake to the left. The trail is easier for a kilometre or so, leading over a grassy plateau, allowing you to catch your breath before you reach **Porțile Închise** ('Closed Gates').

The 'gates' are not as closed as the name suggests, but passing through them does involve a lot of hefty clambering – just for a few hundred metres though. Ahead of you is Mare Peak (2463m). When you reach **Mare Saddle** (2345m), turn

Heading towards Porțile Închise, with Mare Peak in the background

left (west) onto the red triangle trail. The descent is fairly steep and leads over lots of rubble – trekking poles are helpful here. After 1.5km you'll reach **Galeș Lake** (1990m). There's the option of heading directly to Pietrele (1hr 40min, 5km) and Cârnic (3hr, 9km) by continuing northwest on the red triangle trail from here.

However, to complete the circuit and return to Bucura Lake, from the Galeș Lake shore make a sharp left turn (southeast), signed 2hr–2hr 30min to Pelegii Saddle and 1hr to Zănoaga Saddle. The trail is marked red cross, not red stripe as the Dimap map suggests. It takes you past the three little lakes above Galeș Lake; there's a wonderful spring to the left.

After 1km you'll reach **Zănoaga Saddle** (2270m) – this can be done in 45min rather than 1hr. The last bit of climbing towards the saddle is a bit steep but none too difficult. From the saddle you have stunning views over the Rea Valley with its many lakes. Descend south into the valley; then ascend again and make your way back to **Pelegii Saddle** via the yellow cross trail, the same way you came.

To avoid having to climb Peleaga Peak again and to make a quick descent to Bucura Lake, turn right at Pelegii Saddle onto the red stripe trail towards Custura Bucurei. After about 400 metres, turn left (southwest) and go down an unmarked trail towards the lake. Cross a stream after 300 metres, then turn right onto the familiar yellow cross trail which brings you back to **Bucura Lake**.

STAGE 2

Bucura Lake–Cârnic via Pietrele Valley

Start	Bucura Lake
Finish	Cârnic
Distance	10km
Total ascent	210m
Total descent	1160m
Grade	Easy-moderate
Time	3hr 30min
Maximum altitude	2206m (Curmătura Bucurei)
Water	Springs at Bucura Lake and Cabana Pietrele

From the camping spot at **Bucura Lake**, walk north along the western shore on the blue stripe trail. Climb to **Curmătura Bucurei** (2206m) – this should take just over half an hour. From the saddle, continue north, down a rocky gully initially, quickly descending into the Pietrele Valley. Once in the valley, simply continue walking north along the Pietrele Stream. After about 2.5km in the valley, cross a suspension bridge to the left, as you descend into spruce forest. After 300 metres you'll reach **Cabana Genţiana** (1670m).

From here, descend through the forest to **Cabana Pietrele** (1480m) in about 45min. (If you want to head straight for Cârnic there's a shortcut that bypasses Pietrele: take the blue triangle route to Poiana Cârnic shortly after Cabana Genţiana.)

Lakes in the Rea Valley

From Cabana Pietrele, cross the stream over a bridge and walk east past the wooden huts and the camping spot until you reach the gravel road. Continue down the road for about 4km (there's one shortcut through the forest, clearly signed) until you reach **Cârnic** – it's possible to visit the Lolaia Waterfall on the way.

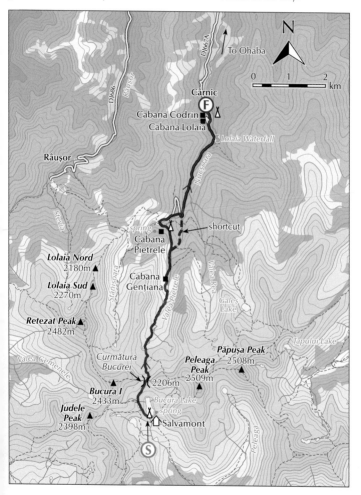

THE VÂLCAN MASSIF

ROUTE 28
From the Vâlcan to the Retezat

Start	Stațiunea Straja
Finish	Poiana Pelegii
Distance	42km
Total ascent	2660m
Total descent	2500m
Grade	Moderate
Time	2–3 days
Maximum altitude	2081m (Piule Peak, Stage 2)
Maps	No good maps of the Vâlcan are available – you might find it reassuring to take a GPS device. There's a printable map on www.carpati.org (select 'Ghid', then 'Hărți' and 'Harta Muntii Valcan') but it's outdated and hardly legible. Part of the ridge is visible on the digital map of the Retezat in the Muntii Nostri app.

This route combines a fine day of lonesome walking in the Vâlcan – a lower and grassier ridge south of the Retezat – with an exploration of the Retezatul Mic (the Lesser Retezat), with the option to continue into the central Retezat (see Route 27). The Vâlcan is very suitable for mountain biking too. In between, it's possible to visit beautiful waterfalls near Cabana Cheile Butii. Stage 2 takes you over the westernmost spur of the Retezatul Mic, the Piule–Pleşa ridge. You'll meet very few other walkers, if any, and the walk offers splendid views of the central Retezat and some pleasant ridge walking, and quite possibly encounters with shepherds and their flocks – accompanied, of course, by guard dogs. Unlike the central Retezat, the Retezatul Mic mainly consists of limestone, resulting in a very different appearance – a narrow limestone ridge and impressive rock formations such as Gurganu Rock.

Note that Stage 1 ends on the DN66A road about 7km east of Cabana Cheile Butii. From here you'll have to walk or hitchhike along the road to the cabana – or to Pensiunea Retezat 2km before it. This should be factored in to what is already quite a long day. The road is busy enough though, so it shouldn't be difficult to get a ride.

Gurganu Rock looms impressively over the trail on Stage 2

From near the end of the trek it's possible to continue further west, towards Oslea Peak (1946m). This slim limestone ridge is popular with trail runners (see http://oslea.nightridge.ro (in Romanian)) and offers grand views towards the Retezat to the north and the Cernei-Mehedinți Mountains to the south. This extension would take another day and you would need to bring camping equipment.

Access

There are minibuses between Petroșani and Uricani; see www.zmk.ro (Romanian website). Take one to Lupeni (30min) and then a taxi up to Stațiunea Straja (20min), or take a taxi all the way from Petroșani (40min). Alternatively, you could take a taxi to the cable car to Straja about 7km up the road (running year-round 9am–4.30pm but closed on Tuesdays for maintenance – see www.skistraja.ro for the schedule (Romanian only)).

At the end of the trek, the only way out is to hitchhike 50km along the sometimes very bumpy road from Poiana Pelegii to the DN68 near Sarmizegetusa, from where you can travel west towards Timișoara (160km) or east to Sibiu (same distance). However, during the summer there should be quite a few cars making this journey.

Accommodation

Although not everything will be open in summer – it is mainly a ski resort – there should be plenty of choice in Staţiunea Straja; see https://cazarestraja.info (English-language option available). Vila La Moşu is good; go to Vila Alpin for your meals. At the end of Stage 1, you can either stay at Cabana Cheile Butii or Pensiunea Retezat; then at Cabana Buta at the end of the next stage unless you decide to combine this short stage with the first stage of Route 27, in which case you can stay at Bucura Lake (you would need a tent though). You can camp anywhere on the Vâlcan ridge although there are no water sources. You can also pitch your tent at Cabana Buta or the nearby Salvamont base, as well as at the Salvamont base at Poiana Pelegii.

STAGE 1
Staţiunea Straja–Cabana Cheile Butii

Start	Vila La Moşu, Staţiunea Straja
Finish	DN66A road, about 7km east of Cabana Cheile Butii
Distance	27km
Total ascent	950m
Total descent	1475m
Grade	Moderate
Time	7hr 30min
Maximum altitude	1617m (Piscu Verde Peak)
Water	Spring after about 12.5km
Note	From the end of the described stage it's necessary to hitchhike or walk west along the DN66A road to either Pensiunea Retezat (5km) or Cabana Cheile Butii (7km). This is not included in the stage statistics given above. A GPS device may well come in handy on this stage since navigation is far from straightforward and the trail is unmarked most of the time.

From Vila La Moşu, walk up the main road through **Staţiunea Straja** and take the first right towards Platoul Soarelui, the beginner ski slope, past Hotel Alpin, then turn left onto the slope. After about 300 metres turn right onto Muţu slope. After ascending the slope for about 400 metres, veer off it to the southwest, towards the trail which is now visible in the distance. Head for a line of wooden pallets that

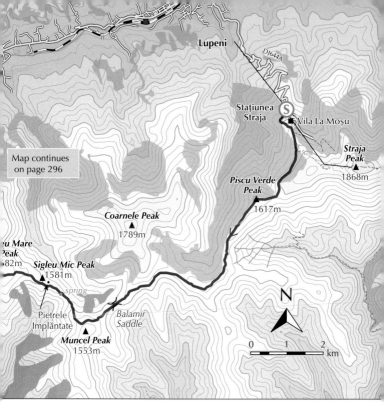

Map continues
on page 296

marks the border of the slope and cross it; then look for two black and white poles
on the trail. About 3km from the start, turn right (southwest) towards **Piscu Verde
Peak** (1617m), which you will reach after another 700 metres or so. You can now
see the trail leading back to Straja Peak (1868m) behind you.

After about three unmarked kilometres on the ridge, the trail swings west
to Coarnele Peak (1789m). Before you get to the peak, get off the track and find
the well-used sheep trail that takes you west, then southwest to bypass the peak.
From here, you will finally see red stripe waymarks appearing. Another 3km
brings you to **Balamir Saddle**.

Two trails depart from the saddle; one that leads over Muncel Peak (1553m),
to the left, and a lower one to the right (west) – take the latter. After a kilometre,
enter the beech forest (with marked trees!). After a further 500 metres, turn right
(northwest), exiting the forest again. Head down an unmarked gravel road. After

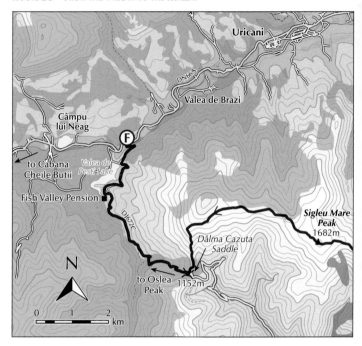

2km there's a spring on the right. Continue straight ahead, over a plateau, towards Sigleu Mic Peak and Mare Peak; less than a kilometre from the spring the landscape is disrupted by **Pietrele Implăntate**, 'Implanted Rocks'. Get off the track (which leads to Uricani); walk past the northern side of the rocks, then continue west on an unmarked grassy trail.

After 2.5km veer off the trail, to the left, just before **Sigleu Mare Peak** (1682m); head southwest towards the rocks to the left of the peak on another unmarked grassy trail. After about 1km on this trail you'll reach a sheepfold. Cross the track and walk past a wooden hut. Walk southeast, to the left, along the edge of the forest, then follow the unmarked trail south when you find it. Descend until you reach **Dâlma Cazuta Saddle** on the forest road.

To continue towards Oslea Peak

It is possible to continue further west, towards Oslea Peak (1946m), from here; to do so, follow the trail southwest signed 10km to Arcanu. From Oslea Peak you can descend to Cabana Buta and from there continue to Poiana Pelegii. This would take another two days (or one very long day) though, so you would need camping equipment (Dâlma Cazuta Saddle–Oslea Peak, 6–7hr; Oslea Peak–Cabana Buta, 4–5hr).

From the saddle, descend the left path. Exit the forest and walk past a forester's hut after about 1.5km; when you reach the paved DJ672C road (essentially a continuation of the path you were already on) turn right onto it; ignore the red stripe and blue circle marks on a shed. Walk along the Arcanu Stream, past a cottage (good shelter if you need it), the **Fish Valley Pension** and the **Valea de Peşti Reservoir** until you reach the **DN66A road** just east of Câmpu lui Neag after about 6km.

To get to the rather luxurious Cabana Cheile Butii you'll have to walk or hitchhike 7km west up the DN66A; a short walk from the main road brings you to the cabana. Alternatively, you can stay at Pensiunea Retezat, 2km earlier on the DN66A.

To visit the waterfalls
There are two beautiful waterfalls close to Cabana Cheile Butii; Cascada Valea Mării and Cascada Lazăru. To reach them, walk back to the DN66A road, turn left, follow the road for about 200 metres and turn left again. After about 2km you'll see signposting towards both of them. If you visit both it's a 9km round trip.

Cascada Lazăru

STAGE 2

Cabana Cheile Butii–Cabana Buta

Start	Cabana Cheile Butii
Finish	Cabana Buta
Distance	12km
Total ascent	1380m
Total descent	750m
Grade	Moderate
Time	5hr 15min
Maximum altitude	2081m (Piule Peak)
Water	At both cabanas, and a spring halfway

This walk takes you over the westernmost spur of the Retezatul Mic, the Piule–Pleşa ridge. You will meet very few other walkers, if any, and the route offers splendid views of the central Retezat and some pleasant ridge walking. If you're strapped for time there's a much quicker route to Cabana Buta (2hr 30min): the red cross route, departing from the back of Cabana Cheile Butii. This 9km route mostly goes over a gravel road and is much lower (maximum altitude 1547m) than the described route.

From **Cabana Cheile Butii**, walk back down to the DN66A road. Turn right onto it and follow it for the best part of a kilometre. Cross the Jiu de Vest River over a green iron bridge; there's a faded yellow stripe waymark on the bridge and a sign up a tree on the right. Follow the path to the left (southwest), which soon turns into a forest road up along the Pleşa Stream. After 1.5km the path forks: keep right. When you see a tiny chapel (there are lots of these along this path), turn right again (west). After 50 metres there's another fork: keep right again. After a few hundred metres you'll arrive at **Schitul Dâlma Mare Monastery**. (It's possible to visit the monastery provided you're not wearing what's described on the gate as 'indecent apparel' – this includes leggings and shorts.)

From here the trail swings to the right (northwest), back into the forest. After just under a kilometre you'll reach a meadow with a **spring**. The path swings to the left and up and becomes a grassy trail; waymarks are scarce for a while. The central Retezat is now ahead of you. Cross another meadow to the southwest; waymarks and the trail reappear. Walk past the last few trees and head west up the ridge. The

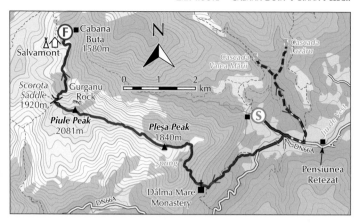

first peak you'll reach is **Pleşa Peak** (1840m). Continue over a plateau, then over the rocky Piule–Pleşa ridge for 3km until you reach **Piule Peak** (2081m).

Continue west until you see a bus stop-type sign down to the right; this is one of two possible ways down but it's the hardest. Best to descend the next path, perhaps 150 metres on. This brings you to **Scorota Saddle** (1920m). From the signpost in the saddle, descend north. The path winds steadily down, underneath the impressive Gurganu Rock. After almost 2km you'll reach a sheepfold; walk along the fence, turn right and cross the stream to arrive at **Cabana Buta** (1580m).

EXIT ROUTE

Cabana Buta–Poiana Pelegii

Start	Cabana Buta
Finish	Poiana Pelegii
Distance	2.5km
Total ascent	330m
Total descent	275m
Grade	Easy
Time	1hr 15min
Maximum altitude	1879m (Plaiul Mic Saddle)
Water	At Cabana Buta

This is a very short stage which takes you to Poiana Pelegii, from where you can either enter the central Retezat (see Route 27) or hitchhike back towards Sarmizegetusa.

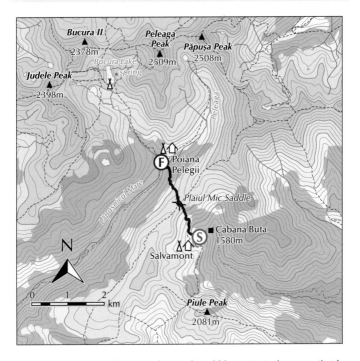

From **Cabana Buta**, head west up the combined blue stripe/red cross trail. After 350 metres there's a signpost to the Salvamont base and camping spot to the left. Continue walking up to **Plaiul Mic Saddle** (1879m), where the trail from the Retezatul Mic comes in from the left (see Route 29, Stage 4). It should take about 45min to reach this point. You can see the Retezat Peak ahead of you. Cross the plateau to the north and descend to **Poiana Pelegii** through the forest in about 30min.

THE ȚARCU, GODEANU AND RETEZATUL MIC

ROUTE 29
Jigora Saddle to Cabana Buta

Start	Jigora Saddle
Finish	Cabana Buta
Distance	57km
Total ascent	3545m
Total descent	3350m
Grade	Moderate
Time	4 days
Maximum altitude	2229m (Godeanu Peak, Stage 3)
Maps	No decent maps of the Țarcu and Godeanu are available. There's a fairly rudimentary downloadable map on www.carpati.org (go to 'Ghid', then 'Hărți' and 'Harta Muntii Tarcu–Muntele Mic'). You may want to bring a GPS device to help you navigate. The Retezatul Mic is visible on the Retezat maps (see Route 26).

This route leads through three massifs: the Țarcu, Godeanu and Retezatul Mic. It can be extended by continuing into the central Retezat (Route 27). The Țarcu and Godeanu are rarely visited and make for a fine approach walk to the Retezatul Mic. Both massifs mostly consist of gentle grassy slopes, although the ascent and descent of Godeanu Peak itself are a bit more challenging. It is mainly the navigation and at times treacherous weather that can turn this into a challenging hike – but it is a rewarding one if you really want to get off the beaten track and meet no-one except the occasional shepherd. Stage 4 is a long but not a difficult day; it leads you over the main ridge of the limestone Retezatul Mic, past or over the legendary Piatra Iorgovanului ('Iorgovan's Rock') and offers great views to the central Retezat, and ends at Cabana Buta with its friendly owners. Note that from Cabana Buta it is necessary to walk onward to either Poiana Pelegii or Cabana Cheile Butii (both on Route 28) in order to leave the area. See below.

Access

First, make your way to Caransebeş (served by buses (2hr) as well as trains (1hr 30min) from Timişoara). Then find a taxi to take you towards the Muntele Mic mountain resort over the DJ608A road, but get off at Jigora Saddle (45min), some 6km before the resort (best to show the driver on the map; it can be found on Google Maps as 'Şaua Jigoria').

To leave the area at the end of the trek, from Cabana Buta either walk north to Poiana Pelegii (2.5km) and hitchhike towards Sarmizegetusa from there, or walk southeast to Cabana Cheile Butii (12km). From Cheile Butii you can take a minibus to Petroşani (see www.zmk.ro for a schedule, in Romanian), from where you can easily make your way to hubs like Timişoara and Sibiu by bus. A quicker but less scenic route from Cabana Buta to Cabana Cheile Butii would be the blue stripe trail (13km, 3hr 30min–4hr). See Route 28 for further information.

Accommodation

Ţarcu meteo station has a fair few spare beds and is always manned; they are happy to let you stay the night and use their kitchen. If you don't make it that far on the first day, the meteorologist at Cuntu station probably won't send you away. Other than that, there is no accommodation until Cabana Buta at the end of Stage 4, so you do need to bring a tent and prepare to be self-sufficient. You can wild camp anywhere in the Ţarcu and Godeanu, but in the Retezatul Mic camping is restricted to designated areas since it is part of the Retezat National Park.

STAGE 1

Jigora Saddle–Ţarcu meteo station

Start	Jigora Saddle
Finish	Ţarcu meteo station
Distance	9.5km
Total ascent	1025m
Total descent	100m
Grade	Moderate
Time	3hr 30min
Maximum altitude	2186m (Ţarcu meteo station)
Water	There's a spring just after Cuntu meteo station; the tap water at Ţarcu meteo station needs filtering

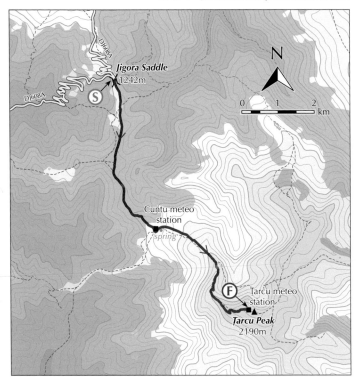

From **Jigora Saddle**, walk south following the red stripe route, signed 2hr–2hr 30min towards Cuntu. When the path forks after 700 metres, keep left (south) to stay on the red stripe route. The trail is straightforward and mostly leads over a gravel road, all the way to **Cuntu meteo station**.

Continue on the red stripe trail signed 3hr to Țarcu Peak; the trail goes past the meteo station and leads northeast. Sometimes it leads over a road, sometimes there isn't even a path; stone cairns point the way. Waymarks reappear as you close in on **Țarcu meteo station**. It is quite large so you may have to knock and shout a fair few times to make your presence known to the meteorologist.

STAGE 2

Țarcu meteo station–Șes River

Start	Țarcu meteo station
Finish	Șes River
Distance	13km
Total ascent	350m
Total descent	1080m
Grade	Moderate
Time	4hr
Maximum altitude	2190m (Țarcu Peak)
Water	Two springs on the trail within the first 3km, and the Șes River at the end

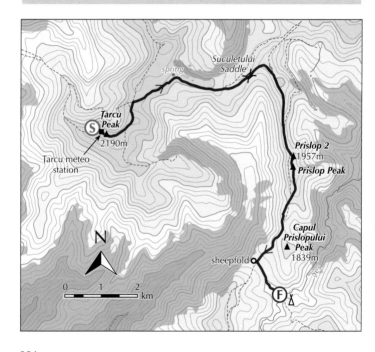

The gentle slopes of the Țarcu Mountains

From **Țarcu meteo station**, head north on the red stripe trail, which then swings east to **Țarcu Peak** (2190m). After 1.6km on a wide track, turn right (northeast) towards Prislop over a grassy trail. The red stripe trail merges with another red stripe here; there's a signpost to the left. After 1.4km the trail swings to the right (east) again. After a further 1.5km you'll reach a meadow; cross it to the northeast towards a large rock with a red stripe waymark on it. This is **Suculetului Saddle**; it marks the start of the corridor that connects the Țarcu to the Godeanu Mountains.

The red stripe trail continues northeast towards the Baicu Mountains; instead follow the red circle waymarks from here. They are hard to find initially, but essentially you have to make your way up the ridge that leads to the right seen from the rock in the saddle. The rock isn't exactly on the trail even though it's marked; the trail is a little to the left, then goes up to the northeast before it bends to the southeast.

Once you're on the ridge, all you have to do is walk south over a gentle grassy trail for about 4km. Walk over the Prislop 2 peak (1957m) after 2.75km; the slightly lower Prislop Peak follows after 500 metres. The Retezat Peak can be seen to the left. After 4km the trail continues to the left, up **Capul Prislopului Peak** (1839m) – however, bypass it to the right. There is no obvious trail here; keep heading southeast on an unmarked grassy track for about 1.3km, pass a **sheepfold** and then turn left immediately. Again there is no obvious trail, just a sheep trail – but the stream should guide you. Walk along the stream until it meets the bigger and livelier **Șes River**, which streams from south to north. There's an excellent camping spot here and the bend in the river makes a fine bath.

STAGE 3

Şes River–Scărişoara Lake via Godeanu Peak

Start	Şes River
Finish	Scărişoara Lake
Distance	12km
Total ascent	1160m
Total descent	680m
Grade	Moderate; some sections difficult
Time	5hr
Maximum altitude	2229m (Godeanu Peak)
Water	Şes River and Scărişoara Lake

Cross the **Şes River** and begin your ascent to Godeanu Peak (about 650m over 5km). There are no waymarks but the path is clearly visible. There are some forks; generally, the trail goes southeast so keep left. After 2km you'll arrive at a plateau. Cross it to the southeast over a cart track. After a further 1km, bypass the rocky **Tucila Mic Peak** (1975m) to the left, over a narrower trail. After 1km it's joined by the cart track again.

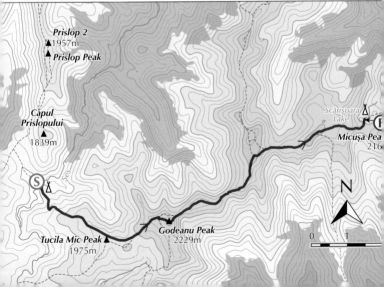

The trail now veers to the left (northeast); as you close in on Godeanu Peak you should see red stripe waymarks appearing. Follow them to the southeast for a bit to reach **Godeanu Peak** (2229m).

Things get a bit tricky here; the red stripe waymarks lead south, but you'll want to descend from the Godeanu to the northeast. Either walk some 20 metres on from the peak and then descend to the left for 250 metres on a scree slope without a trail, or retrace your steps for 400 metres and find the path that winds down the side of the Godeanu a bit more gently – northeast initially, then southeast. There's a balloon-shaped lake on the right. Continue on this path, which fortunately is marked (red stripe); it takes you to Scărişoara Lake over a mostly grassy, sometimes rocky ridge – there's a quite a lot of ascending and descending but nothing major. **Scărişoara Lake** is to your left after about 6km on the ridge; there's no obvious trail so find your own way down to it.

STAGE 4
Scărişoara Lake–Cabana Buta

Start	Scărişoara Lake
Finish	Cabana Buta
Distance	22km
Total ascent	1010m
Total descent	1485m
Grade	Moderate
Time	7hr 30min
Maximum altitude	2225m
Water	At Scărişoara Lake and Cabana Buta

From **Scărişoara Lake**, walk back up to the ridge, towards the southeast. Aim for the pole towards the left side of the saddle; from there, turn left (east) and climb to **Micuşa Peak** (2162m) to continue on the red stripe trail. Descend east, then cross a saddle to the northeast; then climb towards **Galbenă Peak** (2201m). The path passes beneath this peak, 4km from the last one.

Cross a plateau, following red stripe waymarks. After 1km, descend into the Galbenă Valley – there's a signpost here; then ascend towards the rocky mass of Piatra Sturului and Paltina Peak (2149m), signed 1hr (the sign reads 'Vârful Sturu'). Cross the plateau, bypassing Piatra Sturului to the left and then going over **Paltina Peak**.

Orientating on the approach to Galbenă Peak

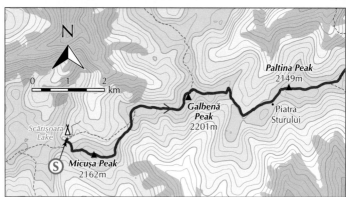

Descend for about 2.5km to the next signpost just below **Stănuleţii Mari Peak** (2025m); from here it's 1hr to the iconic Piatra Iorgovanului ('Iorgovan's Rock'). The trail gets a bit confusing as you close in on **Piatra Iorgovanului** (2014m); when the trail forks just below its rocky mass, keep right. You can climb the peak if you wish – a short path leads up to it.

According to **legend**, a young man called Iorgovan decided to live on this rock after his true love had been kidnapped by a dragon. He ended up lopping the dragon's head off with a mace.

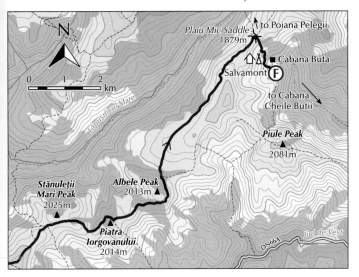

The red triangle trail, which has briefly joined the red stripe trail, departs south here; continue east on the red stripe trail over a grassy plain. Shortly after Piatra Iorgovanului the trail hugs the flank of **Albele Peak** (2013m) and swings to the north. Descend a rocky gully; ahead of you, a big reddish cleft in a grassy plain appears. The trail continues to the left of, and alongside, this crack. Continue north over the plain and eventually through dwarf pine towards the central Retezat for about 5km, until you reach **Plaiul Mic Saddle** (1879m). Descend to the southeast down the red cross trail; you'll arrive at **Cabana Buta** in about 35min.

Exit routes
From Cabana Buta you can either walk 2.5km north to Poiana Pelegii and then hitchhike to the DN68 road near Sarmizegetusa, or follow the red cross waymarks southeast to Cabana Cheile Butii, an easy trail that mostly goes over a gravel road (it should take no longer than 3hr). To reach Poiana Pelegii head west from Cabana Buta up the combined blue stripe/red cross trail. After 350 metres there's a signpost to the Salvamont base and camping spot to the left. Continue walking up to **Plaiul Mic Saddle** (1879m), where the trail from the Retezatul Mic comes in from the left. It should take about 45min to reach this point. You can see the Retezat Peak ahead of you. Cross the plateau to the north and descend to **Poiana Pelegii** through the forest in about 30min.

THE BANAT MOUNTAINS

The town of Băile Herculane, seen from Route 31

The Banat Mountains are the extreme western part of the Southern Carpathians. The Banat is a historical region that since 1918 is divided up between Serbia, Romania and Hungary. Its historical capital was Timişoara, which is the best base to explore the region from. Today, Timişoara is a vibrant and colourful city with clear Austro-Hungarian influences and many wonderful parks, including the Botanical Gardens just outside the city centre. Three impressive squares lined with elegant baroque buildings dominate the pedestrian-friendly old town; from north to south, these are Piaţa Unirii, Piaţa Libertăţii and Piaţa Victoriei. The latter is of especial interest because it was the scene of the 1989 uprising against the communist regime, which was brutally repressed – many lost their lives. To gain insight into the complex history of the 1989 revolution, visit the Memorial Museum of the 1989 Revolution, just off Unirii Square (Strada Oituz 2B). Timişoara also was the first city in Europe to light the streets with electricity, and the second worldwide after New York.

To the south, the Banat is bordered by the Danube. In Orşova, where the Cerna River meets the Danube, a giant sculpture of the head of Decebalus (the last king of Dacia) has been hewn out in the rocks. Various ethnic minorities

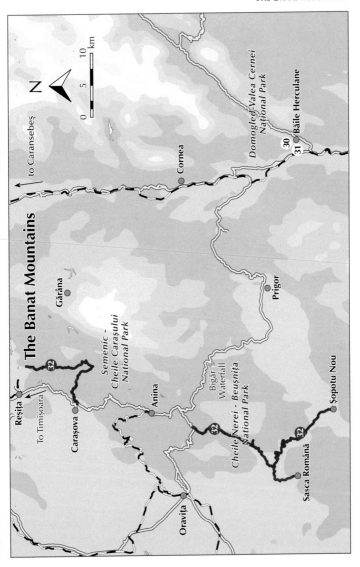

can be found in the region, including Serbs, Croats, Hungarians, Bulgarians and Ukrainians, making this the most 'Balkanic' region in Romania. Belgrade in Serbia is only a 3hr bus ride away from Timişoara.

Although part of the Pannonian Basin, the Romanian part of the Banat is quite mountainous. The easternmost range is the Mehedinţi, which lies south of the Retezat and is home to the **Domogled-Valea Cernei** National Park (Routes 30 and 31).

The town of Băile Herculane, just 20km north of Orşova, has been a spa resort since the time of the Romans and is a good access point for the Domogled-Valea Cernei. Unfortunately, the stately buildings dating back to Austro-Hungarian times have been severely neglected, only hinting at former glory. New spa hotels have risen up in their stead; the town remains a popular destination with local tourists, who you can see bathing in the river where the often sulphur-rich spring water streams into it.

Slightly further to the west is the **Semenic**, characterised by its many gorges cut out in limestone (Route 32) – the Nera Gorge being the largest and best-known. The Semenic is also the base of the very popular Gărâna Jazz Festival, held annually in July: see www.garana-jazz.ro/en.

THE DOMOGLED-VALEA CERNEI NATIONAL PARK

ROUTE 30

Domogled Peak circuit from Băile Herculane

Start/finish	Hotel Trandafirul Galben
Distance	11km
Total ascent/descent	1040m
Grade	Moderate
Time	4hr 40min
Maximum altitude	1105m (Domogled Peak)
Maps	Cernei-Mehedinți, Munții Noştri, 1:60,000
Access	Băile Herculane is served by several trains from Caransebeş; the fastest trains take just under 1hr 30min. There's also a direct train from Timişoara (3hr). There are many buses too; see https://autogari.ro
Accommodation	Since Băile Herculane is a spa resort there are many options. Hotel Trandafirul Galben is central and affordable. Pensiunea Soimul is another affordable option. See www.cazare.baileherculane.ro for an overview of hotels and pensions; the website is in Romanian but is easy to navigate. Please be aware that outside the summer season not everything may be open.
Water	In Băile Herculane; a spring towards the end of the trail

Băile Herculane has been a spa town since the days of the Romans, and although its old stately buildings have crumbled, it is still popular with local tourists. The Cerna River runs right through the town; the mountains of the Domogled-Valea Cernei park rise up on both sides of it. Considering that these mountains do not rise above the tree line, they are especially glorious to explore in autumn. The ridge is exposed so you will get to look down into the Cerna Valley and further afield once you're on top. This hike takes you to the massif's highest point, Domogled Peak (1105m) and through the splendid Feregari Gorge. A day or two in the Domogled-Valea Cernei is easily combined with a hike in the Semenic (Route 32) or the Retezat and surroundings (Routes 26–29).

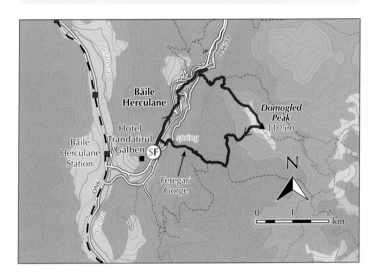

From **Hotel Trandafirul Galben**, walk up Strada Trandafirilor and Strada Castanilor for 3.3km, then make a sharp right onto the DN67D road. After 400 metres on this, turn left onto the yellow stripe and blue cross route, signed 2hr 30min–3hr to Domogled Peak. There are a couple of forks in the path – ignore these. After about 1km there's a section with a cable; after this the path forks. Keep right (southeast) towards Domogled Peak, and follow yellow stripe and red triangle. After another kilometre a short scrambling section brings you to the ridge; follow it southeast. The trail is initially rocky, but the closer you get to Domogled Peak the grassier it becomes.

From **Domogled Peak** (1105m), descend west down the yellow stripe trail to Valea Feregari, through beech forest. After 1.5km, turn right (west) towards Băile Herculane. Another 500 metres brings you to the splendid **Feregari Gorge**. Continue through the gypsy quarters of Băile Herculane, then turn left onto the DN67D road; make a sharp right onto Strada Fabrica de Var, then turn left twice and cross the bridge – if returning to **Hotel Trandafirul Galben** turn left again and continue for 600 metres.

ROUTE 31

Poiana cu Peri circuit from Băile Herculane

Start/finish	Hotel Trandafirul Galben, Băile Herculane
Distance	14.5km
Total ascent/descent	740m
Grade	Easy
Time	5hr 30min
Maximum altitude	779m (Poiana cu Peri)
Maps	Cernei-Mehedinți, Munții Noștri, 1:60,000
Access	Băile Herculane is served by several trains from Caransebeș; the fastest trains take just under 1hr 30min. There is also a direct train from Timișoara (3hr). There are many buses too; see https://autogari.ro
Accommodation	Since Băile Herculane is a spa resort there are many options. Hotel Trandafirul Galben is central and affordable. Pensiunea Soimul is another affordable option. See www.cazare.baileherculane.ro for an overview of hotels and pensions; the website is in Romanian but is easy to navigate. Please be aware that outside the summer season not everything may be open.
Water	In Băile Herculane

This easy walk explores the mountains to the west of the Cerna River. It offers great views over Băile Herculane and leads past the enigmatic Grota cu Aburi ('Steam Cave') and the remains of the Roman baths.

From **Hotel Trandafirilor Galben**, walk north up Strada Trandafirilor and Strada Castanilor. After 2.5km, cross the Cerna River over a red footbridge to the left. Turn left onto Strada Zavoiului, then right onto Strada Coronini, where you will see blue and yellow circle and red triangle waymarks appearing. After almost 2km the asphalt road ends and you enter an open area with a signpost; this is Platoul Coronini. Follow the red triangle trail north-northwest towards Poiana cu Peri ('Meadow with Pear Trees'), signed 5hr.

Walk up to a cross, passing by a solar farm. Just before you reach the cross, turn left through a wooden gate onto a narrow path marked yellow circle. When

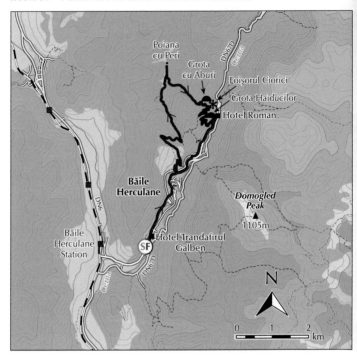

you see a parallel road, walk down to it and continue northwest on a narrow path into the forest. After 400 metres the trail swings to the right (east). After another 500 metres you reach a picnic bench; there's an arrow to Arendasu on a tree to the left (north); follow this, not the continuation of the path you're on.

The path climbs steadily through the forest and is marked red triangle, sometimes yellow circle. After 1.3km it's joined by the red stripe trail; the red triangles disappear for a while. Follow the trail north towards **Poiana cu Peri**, which you will reach after a further kilometre or so. The meadow itself is slightly off the trail, but makes a worthy lunch spot.

Retrace your steps for 250 metres until you are back on the trail, at the point where it forks. Make a sharp left turn and head south on the red triangle trail back towards Băile Herculane. The imposing cliffs above the Cerna Valley shimmer through the trees. After about 1.5km you'll reach the first lookout, Foişorul

View across the Cerna Valley from one of the lookouts

Elisabeth/Roşu; just 400 metres on is **Foişorul Ciorici**. From here you can make a 10min detour to Grota cu Aburi ('Steam Cave').

Continue southwest on the red and blue triangle trail. After 700 metres the path forks; continue left (north) towards Grota Haiducilor and Băile Herculane. Things get slightly confusing after a further 300 metres: two marked paths depart to the right; take the second. There are lots of paths here, and many of them probably lead in the right direction. **Grota Haiducilor** ('Cave of the Outlaws') is to the left, just off the trail and just before you get down to the DJ608D road.

Turn right onto Strada Română and pass beneath **Hotel Roman** and go past the Roman baths and sulphurous springs. Continue on this road until you get to the centre of **Băile Herculane** again, crossing a bridge over the Cerna River early on. It's a 4.5km walk back to **Hotel Trandafirul Galben**.

THE SEMENIC

ROUTE 32
The gorges of the Semenic

Start	Şopotu Nou village
Finish	Reşiţa
Distance	80km
Total ascent	2055m
Total descent	1580m
Grade	Easy-moderate
Time	3 days
Maximum altitude	709m (Poiana lui Marcu, Stage 2)
Maps	Cheile Nerei, 1:25,000, Discover Eco-Romania (only covers Stage 1 and the first half of Stage 2)

Two national parks make up the core of the Semenic – the Cheile Nerei-Beuşniţa Park and the Semenic-Cheile Caraşului Park. This route consists of three stages that are loosely strung together; you will have to bridge the gaps by hitchhiking and/or busing. In one case, you can even make an excursion by narrow-gauge railway, although this is optional (but highly recommended). A hike through the 22km Nera Gorge (Stage 1) means crossing through spectacular karst scenery, over paths and through tunnels carved out by the river. The middle stage leads past the mesmerising Beuşniţa Waterfall and Ochiul Bei Lake; if you don't feel like doing the entire (long) walk you could just walk to the waterfall and back to Sasca Română and move on from there. Stage 3 leads through the lesser-known Caraş Gorge with its many caves, starting from the colourful village of Caraşova, inhabited by a Croat minority.

Access
Hitchhike the 80km to Şopotu Nou from Băile Herculane (which is served by trains from both Caransebeş and Timişoara); get dropped off at the bridge over the Nera River just before you enter the village from the north. If you just want to do the Nera Gorge you might want to do Stage 1 in reverse; in that case take a bus from Reşiţa to Oraviţa (1hr 15min) and then another one to Sasca Montană (1hr). Whichever way you look at it, without a car access is not going to be easy.

To leave Reşiţa at the end of the trek, take a train from Reşiţa Nord to Caransebeş (six trains daily, under 1hr), from where you can continue towards Timişoara or Haţeg/Deva. Since there are no direct trains to Timişoara and some stopovers are rather long, you may prefer to take a bus; there are three that leave early in the morning and take less than 3hr. See https://autogari.ro for the schedule. A bus to Deva via Haţeg takes just over 3hr; there's one bus at 2.30pm.

Accommodation

Stage 1: Pensiunea Cheile Nerei in Sasca Română or Pensiunea Agathos in Sasca Montană, or one of the numerous other pensions in one of those two adjacent villages. There's a camping spot 5km before the end of the Nera Gorge. **Stage 2:** Pensiunea Anina, among others, in Anina (11km north along the DN57B from the end of the yellow stripe trail; hitchhiking is both necessary and usually easy). Camping on this stage would only be possible near Păstrăvarie La Bei early on. **Stage 3:** Pensiunea Perla Caraşului in Caraşova; Casa Bănăţeană and Hotel Dusan şi Fiul in Reşiţa.

STAGE 1
The Nera Gorge

Start	Şopotu Nou
Finish	Sasca Română
Distance	24.5km
Total ascent	610m
Total descent	590m
Grade	Moderate
Time	6hr 45min
Maximum altitude	367m (just before Dracului Lake)
Water	Springs after 3.5 and 8km, and the Nera River
Note	This stage involves hiking alongside (and at one point wading across) the Nera River on a path that is at times narrow and requires good balance. Do not attempt this hike during or after heavy rain.

From just north of **Şopotu Nou**, cross the bridge over the Nera River at the red stripe signpost to Sasca Română and continue north. After 2.3km the road forks at another signpost; bear left (west) and walk through a wooden gate over private property. Pass through another gate and continue towards Dracului Lake ('Devil's

Lake'). Pass several farmsteads in the hamlet of **Drişţie** to arrive at **Poiana lui Trifu** after 3.2km. Do not follow the signpost straight ahead to Lacul Dracului; instead, walk around the enclosure and cross the green suspension bridge over the Nera River and continue on the other side.

After a few hundred metres pass **Moara lui Untan**, a dysfunctional water mill. Cross a tributary stream and head up left (northwest) into the forest. After 1km of ascending you have the option to turn right to Dracului Lake; it takes about 10min to get there and slightly longer to get back up.

Continue west on the red stripe trail towards Canton Damian. Descend to the riverbank, where you'll find a **spring** to the right, then head back up into the forest. Continue straight ahead, passing a trail on the left to Sasca Română. About 1.3km further up you'll find yourself at the start of the path carved out in the rocks by the Nera River. The path is often narrow and it can be difficult to keep your balance. There are several tunnels too.

After 3km you'll need to wade through the river; a kind soul has placed towels and slippers on both sides. On the other side you immediately face a tricky section with cables called **La Cârlige**. There's a spring here. About 1.5km later you arrive at **Canton Damian**. The building is in tatters but it makes a good camping spot. If you have a tent and don't need to go to Sasca Română you might want to stay here.

Following the winding river for 4km more brings you to **Podul Bei** at the end of the gorge, and to the start of the DJ571K road. To get to Sasca Română, follow the wooden signpost west and continue along the Nera River. Walk through a series of low and narrow rock tunnels; when the path forks, keep left. After 300 metres cross a bridge to the left, then turn right and keep right to head into **Sasca Română**. (To get to Sasca Montană, 2km further on, keep left at the crossroads and continue south over a narrow road until you reach the DJ571 road, on which all the pensions are.)

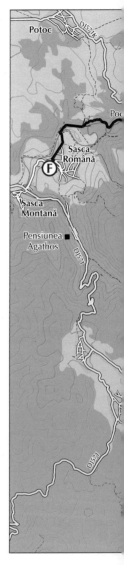

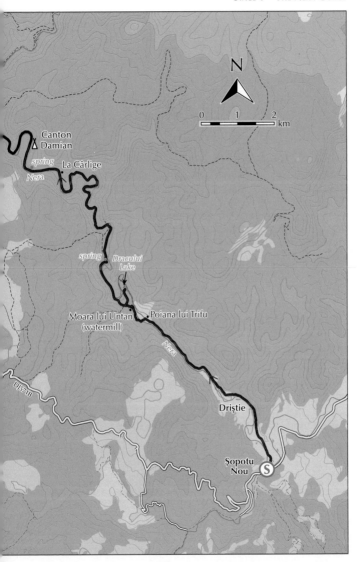

STAGE 2

Sasca Română–Anina

Start	Sasca Română
Finish	Anina
Distance	28.5km to the DN57B road, then 11km (hitchhiking) to Anina
Total ascent	760m
Total descent	375m
Grade	Easy
Time	7hr to the DN57B road
Maximum altitude	709m (Poiana lui Marcu)
Water	No springs, but water can be taken from the Bei Stream
Note	From the end of the yellow stripe trail near Canton Crivina it's an 11km hitchhike along the DN57B road to Anina. This should be straightforward enough since it's a well-travelled road.

One of the tunnels out of Sasca Română

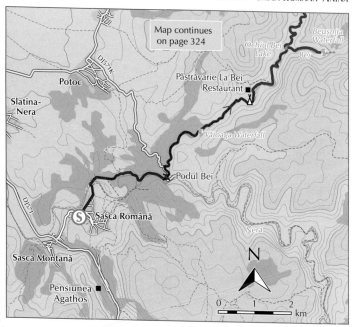

From **Sasca Română**, return towards Podul Bei via the tunnels described in Stage 1 above. After 3.5km, cross the Podul Bei bridge to the left (northeast) and continue onto the yellow stripe trail to Cascada Beuşniţa (Beuşniţa Waterfall). Walk along the Beiu Stream over a pleasant, wide path. After 2.6km you'll find the charming **Văioaga Waterfall** down to the right. Continue straight ahead to **Păstrăvarie La Bei** – a trout restaurant – preceded by a camping spot. Cross the grounds of the restaurant and turn left, before the green gate. After 800 metres the red cross trail departs to the left; you can use this as an exit route if you prefer a shorter route and want to reach nearby Potoc (3hr 30min), from where you can take the 7am bus to Reşiţa (2hr).

Continue straight ahead on the yellow stripe trail until you reach the azure **Ochiul Bei Lake** after 1.5km. Cross the bridge to the right and follow the red cross trail along the Beuşniţa Stream to the fairylike **Beuşniţa Waterfall** – this takes about 20min. Please be aware that the waterfall dries up in autumn.

Retrace your steps and continue northeast through the forest on the yellow stripe trail towards Canton Crivina, gradually ascending to an altitude of 700m over the next 12km; the trail changes into a dirt road. After 10km (from the waterfall) the

323

trail swings northwest and traverses **Poiana lui Marcu** meadow, after which it leads northeast again. Descend past **Canton Crivina** to the DN57B. It's a busy road and it should be easy enough to find a ride to Anina, 11km further north.

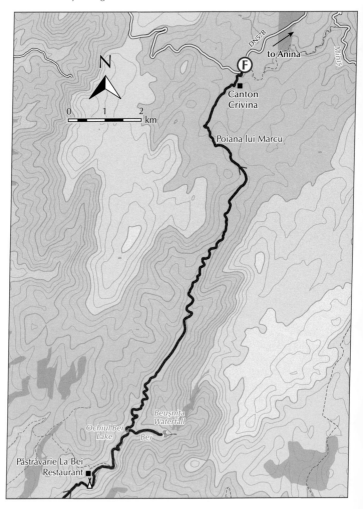

STAGE 3
The Caraş Gorge

Start	Pensiunea Perla Caraşului, Caraşova; for access see below
Finish	Casa Bănăţeană, Reşiţa
Distance	27km
Total ascent	685m
Total descent	615m
Grade	Moderate
Time	6hr 30min
Maximum altitude	665m (on the DJ582C road, about 5km north of Peştera Comarnic)
Water	Spring water can be obtained 70 metres from the start of the blue triangle trail; to reach the water you have to climb down a manhole. You're walking along the Caraş River most of the time.
Note	This hike involves wading across the Caraş River, and although it isn't usually deep you might want to avoid this stage after heavy rain.

Colourful Caraşova itself is worth wandering into; it is one of a handful of villages inhabited by Croatians (Krashovani) strewn around this corner of the Banat. There are also several karstic caves on or near the trail; to visit the spectacular Peştera Comarnic cave you'll have to book a guided tour in advance – see www.pnscc.ro (Romanian website). The minimum group size is five. In Reşiţa you can also visit the open-air steam locomotive museum; see www.mlaresita.org (Romanian website).

GETTING TO CARAŞOVA BY BUS OR RAIL

The most straightforward way to bridge the gap from Anina to Caraşova is to take a bus towards Reşiţa (20–40min). There are several in the morning; see https://autogari.ro. Enter Caraşova as well as Reşiţa as your destination to see all available options. Ask the driver to drop you off at Pensiunea Perla Caraşului; this is located on the main road, not in the village itself.

However, an interesting detour can be made at this point by taking the narrow-gauge train from Anina to Oraviţa, and then taking the 5pm BusTrans bus to Reşiţa and changing there for Caraşova. It will cost you a day but it's worth it. Nicknamed 'the Semmering of the Banat', the railway is the fifth ever built in Romania and the first traversing the mountains. It was completed in 1863 and takes almost two hours to cover a distance of 33km, conquering an altitude difference of 340m. It goes through 14 tunnels hewn out of the calcareous rocks and over 10 viaducts, offering breathtaking views over the valleys of the Semenic. The doors remain open (or can be opened) during the journey, adding to the sense of adventure. There is one train a day in each direction; see www.cfrcalatori.ro/en for the schedule. Tickets can be bought on board.

The spectacular narrow-gauge line from Anina to Oraviţa

From Pensiunea Perla Caraşului on the outskirts of **Caraşova**, descend to the river from behind the pension. The signpost is on the other side of the river and there is no bridge, but there is no need to ford the river – the signpost is simply on the wrong side. Start following the blue triangle trail to Comarnic along the Caraş

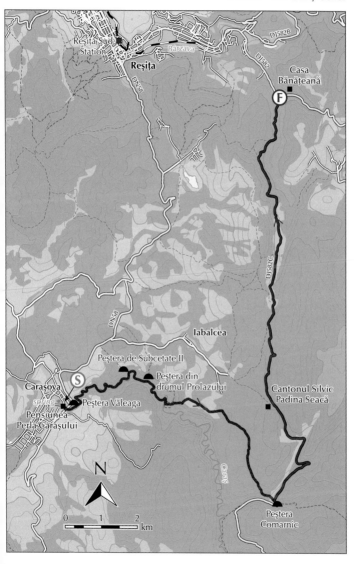

River. This gorge is characterised by its many caves; you reach the first one, **Peştera Văleaga**, after a few hundred metres. Around 3km further up you have the option to cross the river and explore **Peştera de Subcetate II**, signed 10–15min away.

Continue along the river past **Peştera din drumul Prolazului**. After about 1.5km you're supposed to cross the river over a very rickety bridge, but it's in such a state that it's unsafe to do so. Instead, walk back along the riverbank until you see two cables hanging above each other. Cross the river using these or wade to the other side – the river isn't deep or wide.

Walk south along the river until you're almost opposite the bridge again; then turn left and follow a grassy, unmarked trail uphill. There's a mark on a shed and, a bit further up, a signpost to Peştera Comarnic. Follow it up into the woods; ignore the arrow to the right. For the next kilometre or so, the ascent is steep and difficult. The trail is marked with faded blue stripes now. After another kilometre or so the blue triangle reappears. When you come to a clearing continue for 300 metres until you see no more waymarks, then turn right (southeast) onto a grassy trail, descending to a marked trail. Look out for an arrow; the path continues southeast through a ditch, past a couple of houses.

There are two signposts within 350 metres of each other; at the first, head southeast, and at the second keep left to continue on a rather inconspicuous but marked trail. Follow it northeast. When you get to a clearing, turn right and continue southeast until you come to a marked path again. Cross a meadow with apple trees and some sheds, then descend through forest, down towards Poiana Comarnic. Cross a stream and walk up to the road. To visit **Peştera Comarnic**, turn right, cross the bridge (with a great many signposts on it) and walk up the stairs. Access is by pre-booked guided tour only.

You have now reached the end of the gorge but are essentially in the middle of nowhere. To get to Reşiţa, walk north on the DJ582C forest road. After 3.7km, at **Cantonul Silvic Padina Seacă**, there's a fork; you have the option here of turning left and following the trail to the village of Iabalcea – it takes less than an hour. From Iabalcea you can take a bus back to Caraşova or onwards to Reşiţa. Do not count on finding accommodation in Iabalcea though. However, to continue walking to Reşiţa, bear right at the fork and stay on the DJ582C forest road for 11.3km, heading north. The road goes steadily up for the first 4km or so, then gently descends among the hills and wooded areas. When you reach the DJ582, **Casa Bănăţeană** is right at the corner; if you prefer to stay in the centre of Reşiţa it's best to call a taxi.

THE APUSENI MOUNTAINS

Looking back towards Gârda de Sus from a meadow below Scărişoara (Route 37, Stage 1)

The Apuseni Mountains, in the very west of Romania, are part of the Bihor Mountains. They are perhaps best known for the **Padiş Region** (Routes 36 and 37); a karstic plateau north of the Arieş River that harbours a dense network of tunnels, caves and gorges. Unlike most mountainous areas in Romania, the Padiş Region is inhabited; the small villages you will find en route are inhabited by the Moţi people. Their traditional houses have steep thatched roofs that reach all the way to the ground.

The central Apuseni is characterised by green rolling hills, and does not rise above 1500m. South of the Arieş lie a few higher peaks, the tallest being Cucurbăta Mare Peak (1849m). To the north of the Padiş Region lie the Vlădeasa Mountains, which offer a lengthy exit route towards Tranişu Village, where you can pitch your tent or rent a cabin at the Casa Careel Estate. From here you can walk onwards to Bologa, the nearest railway station, and take a train to Cluj.

East of the central Apuseni lies the **Trascău** (Routes 33–35); essentially the foothills of the Apuseni. It makes for delightful walking that combines visiting hidden villages with traversing gorges. The most exciting one has got to be the Râmet Gorge (Route 33), which you need to wade through for two kilometres.

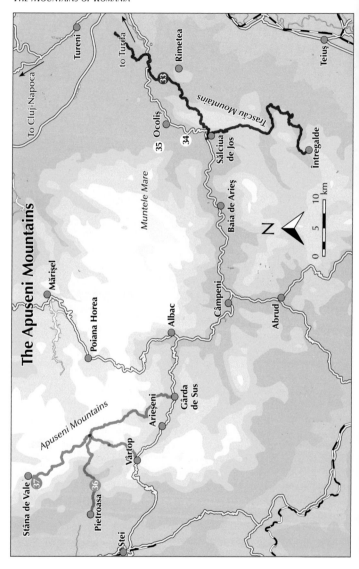

The Apuseni Mountains

To Cluj-Napoca
Tureni
to Turda
Rimetea
33
Teiuş
Ocoliş
35
34
Trascău Mountains
Sălciua de Jos
Întregalde
Muntele Mare
Baia de Arieş
N
0 5 10
km
Mărişel
Poiana Horea
Albac
Câmpeni
Abrud
Arieşeni
Gârda de Sus
Apuseni Mountains
Vârtop
Stâna de Vale
37
36
Pietroasa
Ştei

The atmospheric ruins of Colţeşti Castle are glimpsed on Route 33, Stage 2

The proximity of the cities of Cluj-Napoca, Oradea and Alba Iulia adds extra charm to the Apuseni. All three cities are very very much worth visiting. Cluj has an airport and is a buzzing student city – and the second largest city in Romania, although it only has 325,000 inhabitants. It hosts two major festivals every summer – Untold and Electric Castle, during which the city is to be avoided (unless, of course, you're planning to visit one of the festivals). Oradea is smaller and the Austro-Hungarian influence is more clearly felt here. Alba Iulia's Roman citadel centre is incredibly well preserved. All in all, the Apuseni and surrounding massifs are perfect for those who want to combine some easy hiking with discovering the authentic Romanian countryside and vibrant Transylvanian cities.

Mysterious round rock on the Pleşa side of Râmet Gorge (Route 33, Stage 4)

THE TRASCĂU AND MUNTELE MARE

ROUTE 33
The gorges of the Trascău

Start	Turda Gorge
Finish	Întregalde
Distance	84km
Total ascent	3945m
Total descent	3870m
Grade	Moderate
Time	4 days
Maximum altitude	1233m (Piatra Cetii plateau, Stage 4)
Maps	For Stages 1 and 2: Munții Trascăului, partea nordică cu Cheile Turzii, 1:50,000, Erfatur-Dimap; or Munții Trascău, 1:55,000, Munții Noștri. For Stage 1, take a picture of the map on the wall of Cabana Cheile Turzii; it is much more detailed than either of the above. For Stages 3 and 4: Munții Trascăului, partea de sud, 1:50,000, Erfatur-Dimap.

The Trascău Mountains, just south of the city of Cluj-Napoca, is characterised by its many gorges. This route leads through the most spectacular ones, including Turda Gorge and Râmet Gorge. They can be threaded together by doing all stages of this route, but each stage can also be tackled on its own. Each one of these walks ends in a charming village or hamlet; in between the gorges the trail winds through the pastoral hills of Alba County.

It is possible to go paragliding, rock climbing, rafting or mountain biking around Rimetea; see www.a-tat.ro for all four activities and http://pgtandem.com for tandem paragliding flights. There's a Hungarian folk music festival in Rimetea in late June/early July called Double Sunrise: see http://doublerisefestival.ro (Hungarian website). There are also several walking routes from the village to Piatra Secuiului or Szekler's Rock; Colțești Castle in the next village is also worth visiting.

Access
Take a bus from the centre of Cluj to Turda (30km). Buses depart every 20 or 30 minutes from Piața Mihai Viteazu. Check with the driver whether he's going to

Traditional Moți house in Valea Poieni (Stage 3)

'Turda centru'; some buses go to 'Micro trei' which is not where you want to end up. All of these also stop at Tureni, where you will find another interesting gorge (route not included in this guide). The best way to reach Turda Gorge is to take a taxi from the centre of Turda (15km). There are a few buses (see https://autogari.ro) but they go no further than the village of Cheia, about 3km from the entrance to the gorge. Taxis depart from the square at Strada Horea; or call Mr Corneliu Meret at 0744 878 797. Give Cabana Cheile Turzii as your destination.

Leaving the area on foot at the end of the trek means another long hike – your best option is to take a minibus to the city of Alba Iulia, which is worth a visit in itself with its impeccably restored citadel, Roman roots and its historical importance as the former Principality of Transylvania. There are direct buses from Întregalde at 12.45pm and 5.30pm; the journey takes 1hr 30min. See https://autogari.ro.

Accommodation

Casa Rodisa in Turda; Cabana Cheile Turzii; Pensiunea Torockó and Camping Gyopár near Rimetea; plenty of other accommodation in Rimetea (see Appendix B) – make sure you book well in advance though, because Rimetea is a very popular place. There's a popular camping spot just out of Rimetea, on the trail. Pensiunea Codru in Sălciua de Jos (among other options); Cabana Râmeț. There's a camping spot near Cheia, about 16km along the trail on Stage 3; if you prefer you can split the stage in two and stay here overnight – although it is perfectly doable to tackle the whole stage in one day. Cabana Râmeţ does not serve meals (except for large groups, in which case you may be able to obtain a portion); there's a bar 300 metres down the road that serves fries and sausages and the like. The exquisite Raven's Nest, consisting of three refurbished 18th- and 19th-century houses, is en route in the hamlet of Sub Piatră (Stage 3) – slightly pricier than most options though. Wild camping should be OK on this route although be aware that you are in inhabited territory – you may want to ask the villagers if it's OK to stay in your chosen spot before you pitch your tent. Note that there are no accommodation options in Întregalde, but the villagers are hospitable so asking around could very well lead to finding a roof over your head.

STAGE 1

Turda Gorge–Rimetea

Start	Cabana Cheile Turzii, Turda Gorge
Finish	Village square, Rimetea
Distance	12km to Buru Cabana (which is closed); another 3km to Buru intersection on road; after that, 8km to Rimetea on road (easily hitchhiked)
Total ascent	540m
Total descent	605m
Grade	Easy in terms of effort and technique; difficult when it comes to navigating – a GPS device will come in handy.
Time	3–4hr to Buru Cabana, 2hr 30min (if walking) to Rimetea
Maximum altitude	732m (near Muncelu monastery)
Water	Bar at Cabana Cheile Turzii; no water on route

From **Cabana Cheile Turzii**, go down the steps and keep right. Cross the suspension bridge; the signpost to Buru Cabana is hidden behind a larger sign. Go straight ahead, up into the very sumptuous oak and beech forest, following the red triangle waymarks. After 1.2km you have the choice to turn right onto the circuit trail. However, keep following the red triangle if you want to continue to Buru Cabana.

After a further 1.3km you'll see another signpost; it's rusty and hardly legible – turn left here onto a very overgrown path. Waymarks are sparse and sometimes the path seems to disappear altogether. Keep going – things will improve

Turda
Gorge

Cabana Cheile
Turzii

DJ103G

S

Borzeşti

Muncelu Monastery

Cheia

DN75

to Turda

Hăsdate

Arieş

Buru Cabana

Buru

nsiunea
Crockó
Gyopár

DJ107M

Rimetea

Piatra Secuiului
▲ 1129m

Rimetea

eşti

N

0   1   2
└────┴────┴────┘ km

The Turda Gorge

after 500 metres or so. After another 500 metres turn left (south) and cross a clearing – it can get soggy here. Red triangle and yellow stripe waymarks will reappear after the clearing. Soon the path forks; turn right to stay on the red triangle trail to Buru Cabana.

When the path joins a cart track, turn right onto it. Turn left after about 200 metres on this track. When the path forks, keep right. After about 1km, the path forks twice: take the middle path, marked red stripe; the rightmost path, marked red triangle, leads to Muncelu Monastery. It isn't very far off the trail and is quite pretty so you can visit and then retrace your steps if you want a break. There are two forks in the path again; keep left in both cases. After 1km or so on this very overgrown path, red triangle and red stripe waymarks will reappear again. Keep heading south/southwest until you reach a gravel road. Cross it and continue onto the grassy trail that takes you northwest through a meadow. This may feel counterintuitive, but it will lead to a path that heads south soon, and allows you to cut off a corner. When the path forks, turn left; then right when it forks again.

When you get to a gorgeous hillside, make your way down to the gravel road. There is no path so you will have to wade through knee-high grass, flowers and herbs. Turn left (southeast) onto the gravel road – the Borzeşti Stream runs next to it. From here, the waymarks will reappear with reassuring regularity. When the road forks, turn left and keep left. After 1.5km on this path you will see an info panel about the Borzeşti Gorge. When you reach the DN75 road, **Buru Cabana** is on your right hand (it is closed, however).

Turn right onto the DN75 road and walk 3km towards Buru; you can try to hitchhike but it is a narrow road with fast traffic so this may not be easy. Take care while walking on this section. When you arrive at the intersection, turn left onto the DJ107M road to Rimetea. Hitchhiking the scenic last 8km should be easy since **Rimetea**, a Hungarian enclave (called Torockó in Hungarian) at the foot of Piatra Secuiului ('Szekler's Rock'), is a popular tourist destination. If you prefer to stay at Pensiunea Torockó or Camping Gyopár rather than in the busier and more expensive centre of the village, hike just 5.5km down the road; you will find both the campsite and the pension on your right.

STAGE 2
Rimetea–Sălciua de Jos

Start	Village square, Rimetea
Finish	Pensiunea Codru, Sălciua de Jos
Distance	18.5km
Total ascent	1190m
Total descent	1280m
Grade	Moderate
Time	6hr
Maximum altitude	1162m (just before Poarta Zmeilor)
Water	Spring in the central square in Rimetea; another one after about 2.5km on the trail
Note	The trail goes through a couple of patches of nettles on this stage; long trousers may be useful!

The red stripe trail departs from the central square in **Rimetea**, just before the school and the church (coming from Buru). As you follow it, you will see yellow triangle, yellow cross and red stripe waymarks on a concrete electricity pole to the right. At Spirit Bistro the road forks; turn left to continue on the red stripe trail. After about 800 metres the trail splits into three. Turn left (south) onto a grassy trail, past what seems to be a popular **camping spot**; there's a waymark and an arrow on a tree. From here, the path leads steadily up into the woods.

After almost 2km, turn left. The path is level for a while; shortly you'll descend for a bit. When you get to a meadow, head south-southwest (210°) to a marked tree. From there, head southeast for about 20 metres, then southwest again. You'll get treated to one splendid view after another (including a glimpse of the ruins of Colțeşti Castle to the left), and the floral variety is just incredible.

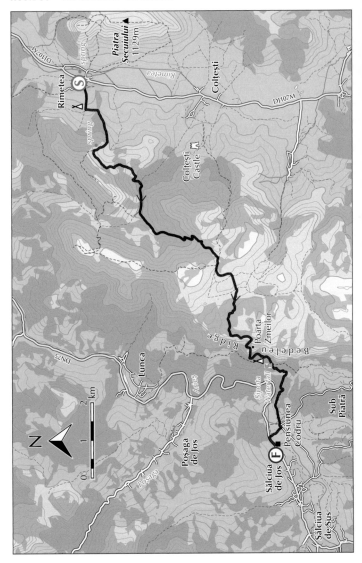

The path now steadily descends to 750m, until you get to a stream. Cross it and turn right onto the forest road, which runs parallel to a stream. The red stripe trail is joined by the blue cross trail coming from Colțești here. After about 800 metres on this road, it splits into three. Take the leftmost path (southwest). After just over 2km, the path forks; veer to the left (south).

When you get to a grassy valley, stay on the path that veers to the right. The red stripe trail is joined by the blue stripe trail here. After 2km, stay on the trail as it inconspicuously veers to the left (southwest), off the cart track; there are blue and red arrows on a stone and waymarks on trees a bit further up. Follow the narrow trail through the birch trees (not the lower cart track); it goes unmarked for the first 300 metres. When you meet a cart track, turn left onto it, then right (southwest) when you see a shepherd's caravan and a signpost. Bison and horses roam here.

From the signpost, follow the red cross waymarks northwest towards Sălciua de Jos and Peștera la Poarta Zmeilor. Initially the grassy trail is unmarked, but you'll soon see a rather large red cross on a rock. After passing a black and white pole, turn left almost immediately. If you're wearing shorts, you may want to change into longer trousers here; for the next 500 metres or so the trail leads through a field of nettles (and there are more of them later). The path veers to the left and descends through beech forest to the karstic **Poarta Zmeilor** ('Dragon's Gate'); then it goes steeply up again. Watch out for a sign that says 'balcon' – it leads to a balcony with great views over the Arieș Valley.

Continue walking along the **Bedeleu Ridge** for a short while; then turn right and start the steep descent into the valley. After about 2km you'll reach a good camping spot and a stream. Shortly afterwards you have the option to turn right and visit Cascada Șipota (**Șipota Waterfall**), which is just a short distance off the main trail and worth seeing. From here, the descent is easy.

When you get to a stream, cross the makeshift bridge and continue onto the road. When you meet the junction with the blue cross trail leading to a monastery and Huda lui Papara Cave, turn right onto a grassy trail and cross the suspension bridge over the Arieș River. Turn left onto the DN75 road and follow it for 750 metres; turn left to arrive at Pensiunea Codru on the outskirts of **Sălciua de Jos** – or continue on the DN75 if you prefer to stay elsewhere in the village.

Onward from Sălciua de Jos

From here you have two options: either continue towards Râmet Gorge (Stage 3) or, if you want to visit Scărița Belioara Nature Reserve (also highly recommended), switch to Route 34. That route starts in Poșaga de Jos and is a continuation of the red stripe trail that took you to Sălciua. However, you would first have to bridge the gap between the two places; you can either hitchhike or bus the short distance down the DN75 road (there should be a bus around 12.15pm). Alternatively you could do that walk in reverse, starting from the hamlet of Runc (take a bus or hitchhike 17km north to Ocoliş on the DN75, then walk 4km to Runc), so that you end up in Sălciua again and can continue on Route 33.

STAGE 3
Sălciua de Jos–Cabana Râmeţ via Râmet Gorge

Start	Pensiunea Codru, Sălciua de Jos
Finish	Cabana Râmeţ
Distance	21.5km
Total ascent	865m
Total descent	805m
Grade	Moderate
Time	7hr 20min
Maximum altitude	982m (Brădeşti)
Water	In Sălciua de Jos, at Brădeşti, and spring at Cabana Râmeţ. There's a spring on the trail after almost 3km, and another one between Brădeşti and Cheia.
Note	This stage includes a number of stream crossings, and the main route through the Râmet Gorge involves wading through the stream for some distance, with the only alternative being a challenging (waymarked) route over the Brâna Caprei cliffs. This stage therefore requires surefootedness and should not be attempted after heavy rain or in bad weather. Bring a torch if you want to visit Huda lui Papara Cave.

From **Sălciua de Jos**, return along the DN75 to the suspension bridge over the Arieş River and cross it. When you reach the road after 450 metres, head northeast onto the blue cross route towards Huda lui Papara and the monastery, along the Morilor Valley. After 2.5km you'll see the first houses of **Sub Piatră** ('Under the Rock'); 300 metres beyond these, turn right towards Huda lui Papara Cave. There's a tourist information point here, and a monastery up to the left.

After 300 metres, cross the suspension bridge. **Huda lui Papara Cave** is just off the trail; to reach it, turn left just after you've crossed the stream. It is possible to enter the cave, but not without getting your feet wet – leave your luggage

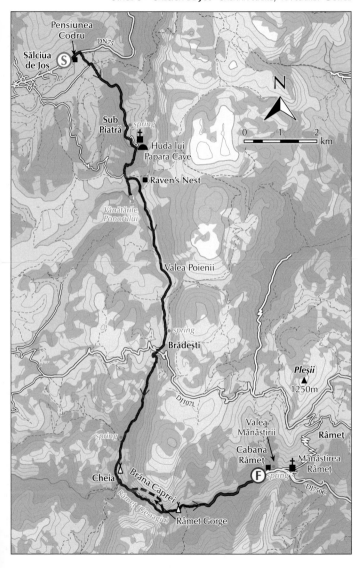

behind if you want to explore it, and only do so if you feel confident wading through water over slippery stones; and bring a torch.

To continue towards Râmeţ Gorge, walk up to the info panel at the end of the suspension bridge, then turn left immediately onto a grassy trail that leads south along a fence, and head up into the forest. Climb the hill until you get to a forest road. From here, you will have beautiful views of the Trascău and Muntele Mare Mountains behind you. Turn left (southeast) onto the forest road to Râmeţ Gorge. You will soon see an info panel; you have the option to make a short detour to **Vânătările Ponorului** here; essentially this is a big, 80m-deep pit into which three streams disappear with much roaring. You can also admire the Dâlbina Waterfall here. To reach it, turn right onto the blue stripe route, then return to the forest road to continue towards Râmeţ Gorge.

After 3.5km through flowery fields – passing the pricey but wonderful lodgings of **Raven's Nest** early on, and past the scattered Moţi houses of **Valea Poienii** – you'll reach the hamlet of **Brădeşti**. Only eight families live in the village today. Turn right past the shop, towards Cheia. Almost immediately, turn right again (west-southwest). When you see a traditional hut with a thatched roof with a waymark painted on the wall, walk around it and head down a narrow trail and subsequently an earthen staircase. Initially it takes you northeast, then southwest, as you descend a grassy trail which soon delves into the forest, where the trail runs next to a lively little stream. When the trail forks; keep going straight ahead. You'll pass a **spring** soon; the path is lined with mint. When you see a signpost (15min to Râmeţ Gorge, 3hr 15min to Cabana Râmeţ), cross the stream; at the marked wooden hut continue south (bear left), which means you need to cross the stream again.

After 1km or so, cross a dry streambed over a wooden beam (assisted by a cable) and continue south. You'll pass a camping spot; just a little further down, as you meet the Geoagiu Stream just north of the hamlet of **Cheia**, turn left (east) at a signpost towards Cabana Râmeţ. Cross the stream when you see a blue triangle on a pole, then turn right onto a narrow trail along the stream; it's marked blue cross and blue triangle, but the marks are sparse.

After 300 metres or so the blue triangle trail departs to the left (east). If you want to avoid the next section, which involves wading through the stream, you can opt for the blue triangle trail here – although this 1.2km-long route takes you over the challenging and serrated cliffs of Brâna Caprei and you will still have to ford the stream where the blue triangle trail joins the blue cross again at the end of the gorge.

However, to enter the gorge, continue straight ahead (south) on the blue cross trail. After 100 metres the fun begins: to follow the trail, you will have to descend into the stream. There are some sections with cables and footholds, but only use these when absolutely necessary – wading is probably the safer option. The water is likely to be knee-deep during the summer months. There is an amazing rock

arch halfway through the gorge; the water is chest-deep here, so you might want to bypass it by using the path to the right.

After about 2km you can climb back onto dry land, following waymarks; the trail continues to the right of the stream. Continue down the gravel road past a number of houses until you see **Cabana Râmeţ** on the left. Do visit the monastery down the road if you have time.

STAGE 4

Cabana Râmeţ–Întregalde via Piatra Cetii and the Întregalde Gorge

Start	Cabana Râmeţ
Finish	Întregalde
Distance	21km
Total ascent	1350m
Total descent	1180m
Grade	Moderate
Time	6hr 30min
Maximum altitude	1233m (Piatra Cetii)
Water	Spring at Cabana Râmeţ; another after about 4km on the trail
Note	A GPS device might come in useful on navigationally tricky sections. There are some nettles on the trail; long trousers may be a wise choice for this stage.

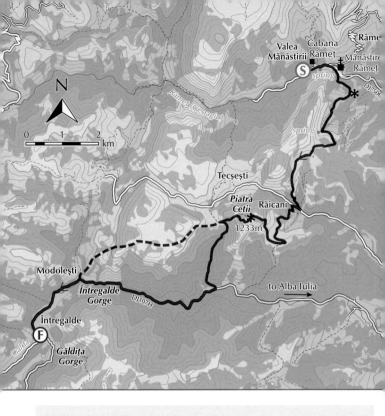

This long hike takes you through friendly hills with small farms and over the more challenging cliffs of Piatra Cetii, and ultimately to the village of Întregalde through the Întregalde Gorge.

From **Cabana Râmeţ**, turn left onto the road. There's a spring on the right after 100 metres. After 750 metres, with the steep cliffs of the eastern half of Mănăstirii Gorge to your left, turn right onto the red stripe trail as you exit Comuna Râmeţ. After about 250 metres, turn right to cross a meadow to the south, going up into the forest, rising above Râmet Monastery and the serene song of the nuns.

After 1km turn right to cross another meadow to the south. You will have beautiful views of Mănăstirii Gorge and the village of Pleşa on the eastern flank of the northern half of the gorge (the trail runs parallel with the southern half of the gorge). After 1km step over a makeshift fence. After another 300 metres you'll see a small house and possibly cows. Walk past the house and turn left (southwest) and down. There's another house to your right. Before you continue though, walk up to the cross on the hilltop for a beautiful panorama **view**. About 400 metres after the houses you'll pass an old well; then, after you pass another house, continue south on a forest road.

After 600 metres or so you'll see a waymark and arrow on a concrete pole pointing to the right (southwest), towards the cliffs of Piatra Cetii. Follow this. The path soon gets overgrown with very tall flowers. Waymarks are very sparse and there isn't much of a path – but keep heading south-southwest and listen for water. Mind the wires over the path (twice)! You'll ultimately see a marked tree and arrow and the stream, after about 150 metres through the jungle.

Keep heading south along the stream for a little bit until you get to a wooden water basin and a marked tree. Turn left (east) onto a well-marked dirt track, which veers south after a while. When you get to a crossroads, turn right (southwest). After about 800 metres, cross another wire – there's a mark plus the number 47 on a concrete electricity pole to the right. Get off the main track and walk down from one pole to the next, down a grassy hill. (You could also stay on the track but that would take longer.)

Turn right onto the track when you get back to it. Step over another wire; a muddy section follows – there are cows around here that trample the ground. When the track forks, keep left and continue down south towards Răicani. Initially the path leads through a meadow, then it goes steadily down through a forest. The forest road is unmarked for about 500 metres. After another 500 metres or so the road forks – keep left (south). When you meet the gravel road, make a sharp right (northwest). After 250 metres you'll see an arrow – cross the stream and continue on the other side, up into the forest again.

When you see a wooden barn with an arrow on it after 1km, walk up to it. Pass through the gate and turn left onto a forest road (southeast). When you arrive at a small farm with a flock of sheep, step over an electric fence twice; you will see a signpost to the right soon. Turn right onto the red triangle trail towards Piatra Cetii and Cabana Întregalde (which no longer seems to exist but it's still on the signpost). Cross two more wires. After you pass a hazel tree, you will see another electric fence. Don't continue down the obvious path; instead, turn right (north) towards Piatra Cetii, staying to the left of the fence.

When you see a barn and an arrow on a tree, turn left (northwest) and go steeply up a path to a meadow at the foot of Piatra Cetii. Look out for another arrow after 350 metres or so; turn right (north) and then left (west-southwest) into the forest – there's an inconspicuous mark on a rock just hidden among the trees. Make your way for 500 metres or so up to the **Piatra Cetii** plateau (1233m); this

Aim for this rock once you're on the Piatra Cetii plateau

involves some easy scrambling. There are fewer waymarks here and some prickly bushes and nettles.

At the (very overgrown) plateau, with its beautiful views, it takes a lot of goodwill to see a trail; the best you can do is head southwest for about 100 metres, aiming for the rock (see photo) until you get back to the marked trail again, which then heads southwest into the valley. When you see an arrow after 500 metres or so, follow it west across a meadow. Halfway, at the info panel, turn left (southwest) onto a narrow grassy trail down into the forest. After some 800 metres you'll see the back of a sign; turn left through a gate onto the yellow cross trail. (Alternatively, you could walk over the Întregalde Gorge plateau. To do this, continue on the red triangle trail – this will make your day a bit longer and more challenging. This route joins the main route at the village of Modoleşti, just north of Întregalde.)

Pass some apple trees, then cross a meadow to the south and head into the forest – there are some nettles here. Soon you'll meet a shallow stream; descend alongside it until you meet the **DJ107H road**. Turn right onto the gravel road to make your way to Întregalde via the splendid gorge and the village of **Modoleşti**. The gorge is about 4km from where you meet the road. Traversing it is easy since the road runs all the way through the gorge. After the gorge, walk southwest for two more kilometres until you reach **Întregalde**. If you have time to spare, do explore the wonderful Găldiţa Gorge.

Start	Exit to Poşaga de Jos on the DN75 road
Finish	Ţară Nomadă Hostel and Camping in Runc
Distance	25km
Total ascent	965m
Total descent	920m
Grade	Moderate
Time	6hr
Maximum altitude	1382m (Scăriţa Belioara)
Maps	Munţii Gilăului şi Muntele Mare, 1:50 000, Erfatur-Dimap, or Munţii Trascău, 1:55,000, Munţii Noştri
Access	If you're approaching this route from Sălciua de Jos, either take a bus or hitchhike east to Poşaga de Jos (6km). Buses depart just east of the centre, near the suspension bridge over the Arieş River; they are supposed to leave around 7.30am and 12.15pm. If you're approaching from Cluj, take the 6am or 1pm bus to respectively Abrud or Câmpeni and get off at the junction to Poşaga de Jos. The journey takes 2hr–2hr 30min. At the end of the walk, from Runc it's a 4.5km walk south to the bus stop at the Ocoliş junction on the DN75, from where you can catch a bus to Cluj. See https://autogari.ro.
Accommodation	Ţară Nomadă Hostel and Camping in Runc; Pensiunea Crama or Cabana Oco in Ocoliş; Dupa Gard bio retreat in Poşaga de Jos
Water	Shop in Poşaga de Jos; springs after 7 and 10km; spring water from taps along the road from Runc to Ocoliş

This delightful route to the nature reserve of Scăriţa Belioara first takes you through three villages: Poşaga de Jos, Poşaga de Sus and Belioara, and past Poşaga Monastery – giving you a taste of life in the countryside below this beautiful calcareous nature reserve. Scăriţa Belioara is a paradise for botanists and entomologists; many rare plant and butterfly species can be found here. Scăriţa means 'little ladder'; expect some steep rocky climbs, after which you will be rewarded with beautiful views over the Muntele Mare and Trascău Mountains from the plateau.

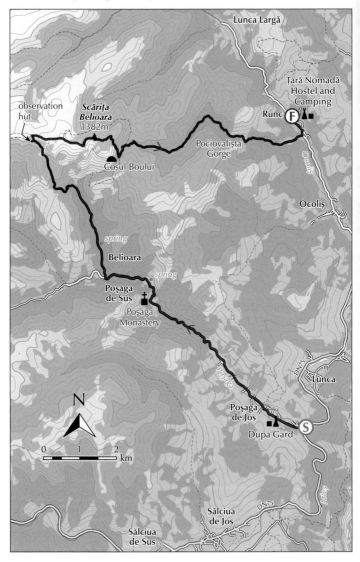

Moți house on the outskirts of Belioara Village

Hitchhike or bus it to the exit to Poşaga de Jos on the DN75 road, then walk 3km to **Poşaga de Jos**. It's unlikely you'll get a ride on this road, but the walk up to the start of the trail is rather enjoyable. About 3km from the junction the asphalt road deteriorates into a dirt road. After a further 3.3km you'll see **Poşaga Monastery** on your left-hand side; the red cross trail starts here. You can enter the monastery but only if dressed appropriately (no shorts or tight/revealing clothes) and you are not allowed to use your mobile phone inside.

Walk along the Poşaga Stream until you enter **Belioara Village** after 1.2km. After a further 900 metres, turn right (north), off the main road, towards the craggy peaks of Scăriţa Belioara. After 2.7km you'll see a signpost to the plateau at the top of Scăriţa Belioara, Şesul Craiului. Turn left to stay on the red cross route towards Scăriţa Belioara. (Alternatively, you can turn right here and follow the circuit route in the other direction. This will take you past the Coşul Boului cave with its 60m-tall portal, and meets the trail described below at the point where the red circle trail changes into the blue triangle trail to Runc.)

349

View from the Scăriţa Belioara plateau

Pass through a wooden gate and turn right (south). After 400 metres you'll see a faded red circle on a wooden fence; turn right here onto a narrow trail that goes up steeply. Soon you'll see waymarks on a large beech tree on the right (red cross and circle). The trail goes briefly through the forest, then winds up a steep rocky slope. Red arrows point you in the right direction. Then, as you approach an altitude of 1000m, the trail delves back into the mercifully shady forest.

When you reach a meadow with some old wooden huts around 1150m, walk up to the signpost at the end of it. The trail swings to the right (northwest), taking you back into the woods. When you come to a large open area with a signpost and an **observation hut**, turn right (east) onto the red circle route to Scăriţa Belioara. After 1km, another signpost marks the start of the blue triangle trail to Runc, which combines with the red circle trail. Here you have the option to descend to Runc via the blue cross trail, but continuing on the blue triangle/red circle trail is highly recommended for its stunning views.

After reaching the highest point on the plateau (1382m – **Scăriţa Belioara**), descend through fields of willow rose. The forest has been affected by wildfire here. When you emerge out of the woods after 1km or so, take a sharp left (north) at the signpost. You'll see a waymark on a tree at the far end of the meadow. (Alternatively, you can continue on the red circle trail from here to complete the Scăriţa Belioara circuit; this will take you back to Poşaga.)

Traverse the meadow, descending northeast until you meet the path again. After 700 metres the trail swings to the right (east); you'll be walking next to a brook. After a further 1km or so the stream flows into a larger one and the trail swings to the left (northeast) and becomes a forest road, which takes you all the way down to Runc through the **Pociovalişta Gorge**. After 5km on the forest road, turn left onto the road to find **Ţară Nomadă** on your right after 400 metres.

ROUTE 35

Runc–Scăriţa Belioara–Lunca Largă–Runc

Start/finish	Ţară Nomadă Hostel and Camping in Runc
Distance	19.5km
Total ascent/descent	960m
Grade	Moderate
Time	5hr
Maximum altitude	1382m (Scăriţa Belioara)
Maps	Munţii Gilăului şi Muntele Mare, 1:50 000, Erfatur-Dimap, or Munţii Trascău, 1:55,000, Munţii Noştri
Access	Take a bus from Autogara Fany, Strada Giordano Bruno 1–3 in Cluj to Ocoliş (2hr) – they depart at 6am and 1pm. If searching for buses on https://autogari.ro make sure you enter Ocoliş, AB as your destination – there are more places with the same name. The bus will drop you off on the DN75 at the exit road to Ocoliş – from there it's a 4.5km walk to Ţară Nomadă Hostel and Camping.
Accommodation	Ţară Nomadă Hostel and Camping in Runc; Pensiunea Crama or Cabana Oco in Ocoliş
Water	There are blue water pumps all along the main road that leads through Ocoliş, Runc and Lunca Largă. You'll be walking alongside water for much of the trail, but there are no springs.
Note	The route involves walking alongside (and at times picking your way through) streams; this hike should therefore be avoided after heavy rain.

This is another approach to Scăriţa Belioara, a gorgeous calcareous nature reserve with steep walls and oddly shaped turrets and pinnacles in the Muntele Mare, and is a circular route starting from the other end of Route 34. It takes you through the Pociovalişta Gorge at the start and Runc Gorge at the end.

Many unmarked trails lead up into the hills east of Runc, where the villagers' cows graze; exploring these would make for a rewarding day out in itself.

From Ţară Nomadă Hostel and Camping in **Runc**, turn left onto the main road. After 400 metres, turn right (southwest) onto the blue triangle trail to Scăriţa Belioara. The forest road winds slowly up past the last houses of Runc, through the

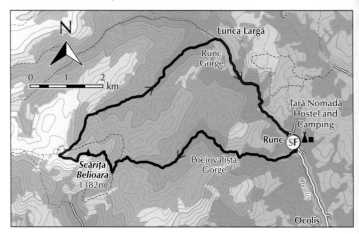

Pociovaliṣta Gorge, where you'll find yourself surrounded by tons of butterflies. Twenty of them per square metre is no exception in spring. The road forks several times; stay on the main road at all times, following the blue triangle waymarks.

After 5km on this road, the path swings to the right (northwest). It essentially goes up a streambed, but there should be plenty of space on either side of the stream to walk (except perhaps after heavy rain). After 1.2km, take a left turn (southwest); there's a very obvious waymark on a tree and one a bit further up on a rock. The trail bends to the left, then immediately right, up into the beech forest. The gradient becomes much steeper here.

After 1km the trail narrows; it veers to the left (south) and leads steeply up to a grassy meadow. Cross it to the southwest to reach a signpost; continue northwest to stay on the blue triangle route, which has now merged with red triangle and red circle. The trail delves back into the woods again here. From here it's about 1hr–1hr 30min to Scăriṭa Belioara. The path zigzags steeply up a largely barren hillside. After less than a kilometre you'll reach another signpost; follow it west to **Scăriṭa Belioara**.

From the highest point of the plateau, follow the circuit trail (red circle and blue triangle) until you get to another signpost. Turn right (northeast) onto the blue cross trail which will take you back to Runc via the Runc Gorge in about 3hr. Descend eastwards – there isn't much of a trail, and the terrain is very uneven, so mind your ankles. There are (at least) two rocks with waymarks; then a tree with an arrow to the left (northeast). Head for the tree with the waymark, then to a small birch with a narrow blue band. Head northeast – there are two more marks on trees. Then cross a meadow to the east – there's a big waymark on a tree.

The sugarloaves of Scărița Belioara

The trail follows a stream; sometimes you can walk next to it, but often you will have to walk through the shallow stream filled with dead wood. The going isn't easy, but the descent is very gentle. After about 2km the stream veers to the left and the trail continues down a forest road alongside it. Follow the trail for 4km to the hamlet of **Lunca Largă**, then turn right towards **Runc Gorge**, along the Ocoliș Stream. After 2.5km you'll arrive at the end of the gorge, which is easy to traverse – a gravel road runs through it. In spring and summer you'll see a lot of butterflies here. Another 500 metres brings you back to Țară Nomadă in **Runc**.

THE PADIŞ REGION

ROUTE 36
Statiunea Vârtop–Cetăţile Ponorului–Padiş–Pietroasa

Start	Statiunea Vârtop
Finish	Pietroasa
Distance	54.2km
Total ascent	2700m
Total descent	3290m
Grade	Easy-moderate
Time	4 days
Maximum altitude	1410m (Pietrele Boghii, Excursion 3)
Maps	Padiş map, 1:30,000, Erfatur-Dimap, covers the central Padiş area; as does Bihorului: Platoul Padiş, 1:55,000/1:25,000, Munţii Noştri. Bihor Mountains, 1:60,000, Erfatur-Dimap covers the wider Apuseni Mountains (not strictly needed for this route).
Note	There are many flocks of sheep in the Padiş area, and therefore guard dogs – bring trekking poles to keep them away if necessary and do not walk right through a flock.

This is one of many possible approaches, and one of the two in this book (the other being Route 37), to the heart of the Apuseni Mountains – the Padiş region. The backbone of this route consists of three stages; all are fairly easy and take you straight through the lush heart of the Padiş region from south to north, exiting to the west. On the way, there are three excursions, all of which (especially the first two) are a bit more challenging than the main stages and explore the spectacular karst scenery this area is renowned for. It is possible to combine this route with stages from Route 37; there are plenty of options from Cabana Padiş.

Access
Take the Ariesul bus from Cluj to Câmpeni (3hr 10min); it leaves at 1pm from Autogara Fany, Strada Giordano Bruno 1–3. From Câmpeni, there's another Ariesul bus to Arieşeni, but it doesn't leave until 6.45pm. However, it does not go all the way to Vârtop which is about 11km further up; you will have to cover this final stretch by

hitchhiking. There should be plenty of traffic on the road during the summer season. There's an earlier bus to Arieșeni at 2.15pm, which you can catch if you take the 6am bus from Cluj (4hr); if you miss this and would rather not wait for the late bus you might want to hitchhike all the way to Vârtop to save time.

At the end of the trek, there's a bus to Oradea from Pietroasa (1hr 40min) at 11.30am (AutoGenn); if you want to go anywhere else (Alba Iulia with its impressive citadel is worth seeing – it's a 3hr ride away), hitchhiking is probably your best bet.

Accommodation and food
There are huts or other accommodation at the start and finish of each stage, except in Pietroasa – so it is possible to do this route without a tent (provided you make your way out of Pietroasa before dusk). Camping is allowed in designated areas only, the Padiş area of the Apuseni being a national park.

In Vârtop: Pensiunea Marieta and Hotel Four Seasons. **Around Cetățile Ponorului:** Cabana Cetățile Ponorului (if you want to stay in the cabana, reserve a bed beforehand – it's a popular place); Poiana Ponor (camping only); the shepherds in Poiana Glăvoi usually have two spare beds. **In Padiş:** Cabana Brădeț; Pensiunea Turistică Padiş; Popaş Turistic Padiş, La 5 Casute. (Cabana Padiş has been under renovation/construction for a long time and it's unclear when it will open again.) There are several other options, all on the DJ763 road. **In Boga:** Pensiunea Cristal and Flóra Pánzio.

There's a small shop at Pensiunea Marieta. Hotel Four Seasons a little further up the road in Vârtop serves good food. Cabana Cetățile Ponorului serves meals and sells drinks and chocolate as well.

STAGE 1
Vârtop–Cabana Cetățile Ponorului

Start	Pensiunea Marieta, Vârtop
Finish	Cabana Cetățile Ponorului
Distance	6.7km
Total ascent	420m
Total descent	480m
Grade	Easy
Time	2hr 30min
Maximum altitude	1280m (shortly after the start in Vârtop)
Water	There's a stream on the trail, but best fill your flasks at the start.

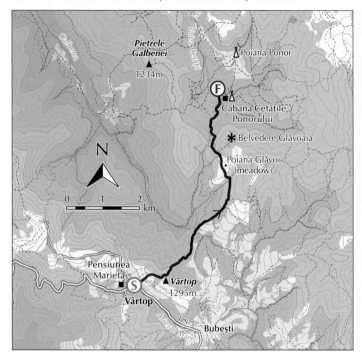

The red stripe trail to Cabana Cetățile Ponorului departs from the DN75 road, right next to Castelul Alpin and **Pensiunea Marieta** – these are among the first houses you meet coming from the direction of Arieşeni. Walk northeast initially to cross a meadow; there are waymarks on sheds and trees. Then head north up a hill covered in blueberry and blackberry bushes. After about 550 metres head east again. This brings you to a wider grassy and level track.

Soon the trail bends to the left, into the forest. When the forest opens up, descend north down a gravel road. There are no waymarks for a while. When a broad trail comes in from the left after perhaps 700 metres, stay on the trail you are on, which veers off to the right; you'll see a large arrow on a tree. There are no waymarks for the next 200 metres. When they reappear, the path forks; keep left. After 700 metres you'll come to a crossroads; go straight ahead, but keep right (there are two trails heading north). This marks the start of the second ascent on this route.

After almost 1km the path forks; keep left to stay on the main trail (northeast). Shortly you'll see the red triangle trail to Arieşeni come in – stay on the red stripe trail and keep heading northeast. After 600 metres cross a stream, then bear left, heading west and up.

The trail soon brings you to a large open area with a small white house and some corrals. This is **Poiana Glăvoi**. Cross it to the north; there's a signpost to Cetăţile Ponorului up a tree on the right. There are shepherds here, herding a flock of 700 sheep – expect guard dogs. You can buy delicious cheese here; they also have two spare beds.

Having crossed the meadow you'll see a red 'dartboard' trail to Belvedere Glăvoaia, signed 20min; either take the detour and retrace your steps back to the red stripe trail or continue straight towards Cabana Cetăţile Ponorului. Very soon, the path forks; keep left (northwest). When the trail meets a dirt road after 700 metres, turn right (north) along a stream. After less than a kilometre on this road you'll arrive at the wonderful **Cabana Cetăţile Ponorului**. They sell maps, postcards and t-shirts here and offer great meals. If you brought a tent, you can pitch it in the adjacent forest and they'll let you use the facilities in the cabana. Alternatively, you can walk half an hour north to Poiana Ponor and pitch your tent there.

EXCURSION 1
Cetăţile Ponorului circuit

Start/finish	Cabana Cetăţile Ponorului
Distance	5km
Total ascent/descent	340m
Grade	Moderate
Time	2hr
Maximum altitude	1110m (near doline three)
Water	At Cabana Cetăţile Ponorului
Note	The areas around the dolines may be slippery underfoot; take care and avoid this hike in bad weather.

This is a delightful walk with plenty of challenges. It's fairly short, so it can be done on the same day as the access route. Cetăţile Ponorului ('Fortress of Ponor') is one of the largest karst formations in Romania, and consists of three large dolines that are over 300m deep. This walk takes you through dolines one and two, to the entrance of some of the caves (access to these is possible only under supervision and with caving equipment – see https://travelguideromania.com for opportunities) and over the edges of the steep walls of dolines two and three, where balconies offer splendid and perhaps vertigo-inducing views down.

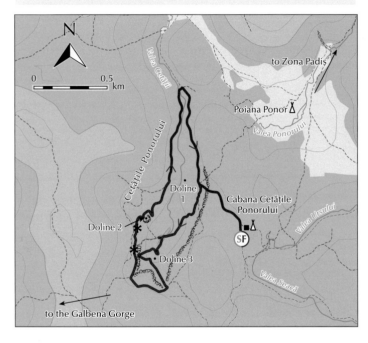

To enter Cetățile Ponorului, continue northeast from the cabana on the red stripe trail for 500 metres, then turn left onto the blue circle trail, combined with yellow circle for a while. When these two part ways after 50 metres or so, keep right to stay on the blue circle trail. This is a pleasant rocky path, which winds down to the entrance of the first doline. There are stairs and cables to assist you on your way down. Be careful – it can be very slippery here because the humidity is high (you will notice a drop in temperature as you descend). Before you continue from the doline, do descend to the huge cave; its entrance is 75m high (the highest in

Europe). A river disappears underground here, to emerge 900 metres further up through the Galbena spring.

Continue to doline three by means of an iron staircase. After you've climbed out of doline three, turn right to a *punct de belvedere* (**viewpoint**); yellow and blue circle merge briefly once more. When they part again after 300 metres, turn right (north) onto the blue circle trail. As you walk along the edge of **Cetățile Ponorului** you'll be rewarded with beautiful and vertigo-inducing views of the dolines – in particular doline two, on the edge of which you are now walking. There are several balconies along the way.

After 1.5km, turn right (north); the path descends again. Turn right when you see a sign back to the cabana. Walk up to the forest road, then turn right (south) and continue to **Cabana Cetățile Ponorului**, which you'll reach after about 1km.

To extend this excursion

This route can be extended in several ways. The full blue circle circuit (5–6hr) leads all the way to Cabana Padiş; however, a shorter extension to Poiana Ponor and the Ponor spring can also be made.

EXCURSION 2
Galbena circuit

Start/finish	Cabana Cetățile Ponorului
Distance	11km
Total ascent/descent	1050m
Grade	The section through the gorge is difficult; the rest of the trail is fairly easy.
Time	6hr
Maximum altitude	1275m (just after Piatra Galbenei)
Water	Fill flasks at Cabana Cetățile Ponorului; plenty of water on the trail but it will need filtering.

This excellent circular route from Cabana Cetățile Ponorului explores the Galbena Gorge (Cheile Galbenei). It is considerably more challenging and longer than the Cetățile Ponorului circuit, and should only be undertaken if you feel confident of your grip – this route involves a lot of hanging from cables and rocks and walking over chains. Don't attempt it on a wet day.

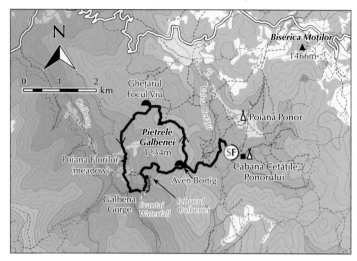

From **Cabana Cetăţile Ponorului**, walk north. After 500 metres turn left onto the combined yellow and blue circle trail. Some 50 metres into the forest the blue and yellow circle part; keep left (southwest) to stay on the yellow circle trail, signed towards the Galbena Gorge, 3hr 30min. Soon, head up a narrow rocky gully for about 100 metres; then follow a beautiful path that takes you deeper into the forest. After about 250 metres on this path the blue circle trail briefly merges with yellow circle again – continue southwest. The blue and yellow circle trails soon part again – turn left. After 600 metres turn right onto the yellow 'dartboard' trail to Pietrele Galbenei ('Galbena Rock') – 1hr according to the signpost, but more like 35min in reality.

Shortcut to the Galbena Gorge
If you want to head straight for the Galbena Gorge you could instead go straight ahead here (just 45min to the gorge) – but then you will have to go exactly the same way back, or do the circuit in the other direction.

Very soon after turning right, you'll come to a 45m-deep pit cave, **Aven Borţig**. There's a gigantic ice block at the bottom – not visible from above though. Stay well away from the edges! Turn right again to stay on the yellow dartboard trail to Pietrele Galbenei. After 1.6km, bear left (southwest) to **Pietrele Galbenei** (1234m), which is 5min away. To get to the viewpoint, head up the rocks to the left (south). The steep and tall limestone feature offers a beautiful panorama over Poiana Florilor ('Flower Valley'). Seen from here, however, it is more forest than flowers.

To continue, get back to the trail and follow the yellow dartboard signs down; after 600 metres turn left to **Ghețarul de le Focul Viu** – it's about 10min from the sign.

> **Peștera Ghețarul de la Focul Viu** ('Ice Cave of the Living Fire'), despite its ambiguous name, really is an ice cave. You can't enter it but you can see the ice block through the grate.

After the ice cave, turn left (southwest) signed towards Poiana Florilor and the Galbena Gorge. Please note there are two trails here; the signpost is slightly misleading. Take the left one, which descends north and is marked yellow circle and red stripe. Cross a meadow; after that, the trail delves back into the forest. A stream crosses the path; then the trail goes through another meadow. Turn right (southwest) to **Poiana Florilor**; this time you will see plenty of flowers.

From Poiana Florilor it's 15min to the entrance of the gorge over a cart track which soon deteriorates into a narrower trail. After about 800 metres you'll reach a road; to enter the **Galbena Gorge**, turn left, cross the Galbena River over a bridge and head up again on the other side (southeast). Shuffle over a (rather flexible) chain. There are cables and grips for your hands. After the chain section, a cable helps you head up the rocks to the right; after that another cable leads you through a natural tunnel, down again. This section can be slippery and very steep; a firm grip is needed!

Continue for 300 metres to arrive at the gorgeous **Evantai Waterfall**. There's a cable attached to the rocks here, but there's no foothold – the safest option is to take your shoes off and wade through the water and climb up the rocks, through a smaller waterfall. (This is less difficult than it may sound.) After the waterfall, the trail bends to the left (northeast) and goes up; there's a waymark right above the waterfall. The path hugs the flank of the massive rock the waterfall flows from; you will soon pass two giant caves which the water flows through. When you reach the second cave, follow an arrow to the right, then immediately up to the left, following another arrow, up the sheer rock wall – there's a chain. Pass a series of glorious smaller waterfalls, and eventually reach the blue eye of **Izbucul Galbenei**.

> This **pool** is one end of a siphon cave at the head of the gorge. Its waters come all the way from Cetățile Ponorului, and here give birth to the Galbena River after flowing underground for almost 4km.

Walk around the pool so that you end up on the other side of the stream, then head southwest for a bit, parallel to the stream. The trail soon swings to the northwest, up into the forest. After perhaps 250 metres there are four signposts on trees. Turn right towards Padiş (northeast). The trail winds up through the forest and brings you back to the point where you turned right to Aven Borţig. Continue east, down the way you came. Follow the yellow circle trail back to the road and turn right to arrive back at **Cabana Cetăţile Ponorului** after 500 metres.

Alternative route
There's an alternative entry to this route; walk all the way to Poiana Ponor (about 30min from the cabana) and then turn left onto the yellow circle trail, and do the circuit in the other direction. This way you'll miss out on the beautiful Galbena Rock section – but you will avoid having to do the first section twice.

STAGE 2
Cabana Cetăţile Ponorului–Zona Padiş

Start	Cabana Cetăţile Ponorului
Finish	Zona Padiş
Distance	5km
Total ascent	310m
Total descent	85m
Grade	Easy
Time	1hr 30min
Maximum altitude	1320m (Cabana Padiş)
Water	Fill flasks at Cabana Cetăţile Ponorului

This is an easy connecting walk that allows plenty of time for another walk from Zona Padiş.

From **Cabana Cetăţile Ponorului**, walk northeast for 100 metres; then turn right (southeast) onto the red triangle trail to Padiş. After about 150 metres turn left, cross a meadow and a stream, and continue northeast, up a narrow trail into the forest. After 200 metres turn left (north). After a further 900 metres you'll arrive at a meadow; turn left to continue north and downhill into a wonderful valley, **Poiana Ponor**, home to sheep and cows, and a temporary lake in spring.

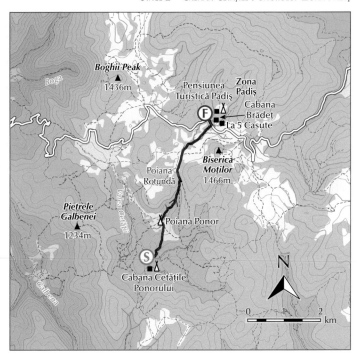

Bear left to walk towards the road. Cross the stream and walk up to the sign-post, then turn right (north) and continue on the blue/yellow circle trail. After 400 metres cross the shallow stream again and continue east-northeast. Red triangle waymarks will reappear again here. After 1km you'll reach another meadow, and descend to another large grassy valley called **Poiana Rotundă**.

Continue until you arrive in an open area with shepherd huts, caravans and corrals – there might be flocks accompanied by guard dogs. Turn right onto the gravel road and continue until you reach an asphalt road. **Cabana Brădeţ**, Cabana Padiş and **La 5 Casute** are on the right. If you prefer to stay at **Pensiunea Turistică Padiş**, turn left instead. You can pitch your tent here for a small fee. The showers aren't great, but the food and the welcome you will get are. There's plenty of other accommodation around. You can easily take in the next walk on this day, or make a short excursion to the Moţi church on the peak to the south-east of the cabanas (1466m).

EXCURSION 3
Pietrele Boghii circuit

Start/finish	Zona Padiş
Distance	9km
Total ascent/descent	460m
Grade	Moderate
Time	3hr
Maximum altitude	1410m (Pietrele Boghii)
Water	Fill flasks in Zona Padiş
Note	Take a torch if you want to explore Boghii Cave

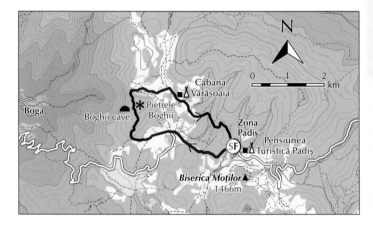

From **Pensiunea Turistică Padiş**, turn left onto the asphalt road to Pietroasa. It's marked blue cross, yellow stripe and red circle. Follow it for just over 2km until you get to a signpost. Follow the red circle trail west towards Pietrele Boghii ('Rocks of Boga'). After almost 1km, after you've passed another signpost, the trail delves into the forest and begins to ascend.

> The **forests** of the Padiş region are famous for their vegetation inversion: the beech forest grows above the coniferous forest (mainly spruce here). This forest is home to chamois, deer and wild boar.

View over the Boga amphitheatre from Pietrele Boghii

After another kilometre you'll reach **Pietrele Boghii**, from where you have splendid views over the so-called Boga amphitheatre and the western part of the Bihor Mountains. To continue, turn right (north), back into the forest, then left; the path winds steeply down around the face of the rock and leads to **Boghii Cave**. It's quite deep, so use a headlight if you want to explore it.

From here, retrace your steps all the way back up and past Pietrele Boghii until you see a tree on your left marked with a red dartboard waymark plus the words 'Varasoaia 45min'. Follow these down to the north. The path gradually swings to the northwest as it follows the edge of the amphitheatre.

As you exit the forest, head down to the right into a grassy valley; waymarks disappear for a while here. Cross the meadow to the east and head for the bus stop-type sign on the gravel road, over the remains of a cart track, then turn right (south-southeast) onto the road towards **Cabana Vărăşoaia** (blue/red stripe) and follow it for 1.7km until it splits into three. There's a blue stripe signpost to Padiş on a shed; follow this, continuing southeast down a dirt road. After another 2km you're back on the road you started from. A 100-metre walk up the road brings you back to **Pensiunea Turistică Padiş**.

STAGE 3
Zona Padiș–Pietroasa

Start	Zona Padiș
Finish	Boga or Pietroasa
Distance	9km to Boga; another 8.5km to Pietroasa
Total ascent	120m to Boga; another 230m to Pietroasa
Total descent	870m to Boga; another 440m to Pietroasa
Grade	Easy
Time	3hr; plus 2hr to Pietroasa
Maximum altitude	1280m (2km from the start)
Water	Fill flasks in Zona Padiș

This walk takes you out of the Apuseni, towards the west. You can either head straight for Pietroasa and take a bus, or, perhaps more likely, hitchhike to your next destination (Oradea or Alba Iulia for instance) – or stay in the village of Boga overnight and do the busing or hitchhiking on the next day.

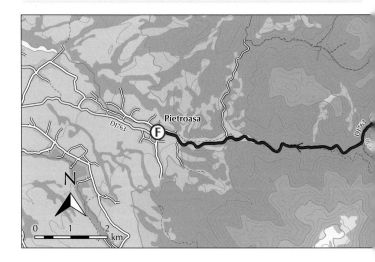

From **Zona Padiş**, follow the DJ763 road to Pietroasa for just over 2km, then continue on a track that veers off the road to the west. It's marked red stripe, red circle and blue cross. After 1km on this track, head up into the forest. When you see an info panel about the coniferous forest after 300 metres, stay with the trail as it inconspicuously veers to the left (southwest); there's a faded blue cross on the first tree on the left. After 400 metres the track swings to the right – west, then southwest; when you see the road, descend to it (southeast) and turn right onto it.

After 600 metres or so on the road you'll see a signpost to Glăvoi and Cabana Cetăţile Ponorului to the left. Ignore this and continue down the asphalt road; there's a waymark on an electricity pole on the left. About 100 metres after the signpost you'll see a wooden house with a bright red roof; this is **Cantonul Silvic Scariţa**, a forester's lodge. Turn right off the road just before the house and follow an unmarked cart track that leads north-northwest past the beehives.

A kilometre on this path brings you back to the road again. Walk down the hairpin in the road; after about 250 metres, cut off another corner via a forest track. Walk down the road for perhaps 20 metres, then cross it; cut another corner and cross again. You should see a faded blue waymark here; there's a blue arrow on a tree across the road.

Follow the waymarks northwest. When the path forks, keep right (northwest), then left onto a dirt road for about 50 metres until you see a signpost to Boga and Piatra Ciunghilor. Make your way up towards the latter, following the blue triangle

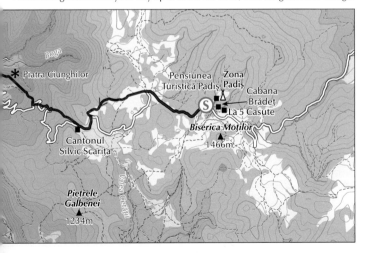

Looking down onto Boga from Piatra Ciunghilor

waymarks. **Piatra Ciunghilor** offers fine views over Boga and back to the Boga amphitheatre to the right. From here it's a 40min descent to Boga Village.

When you meet the DJ763 road again you can either follow it down to **Pietroasa** (another 8.5km) or stay overnight in one of the pensions in Boga.

ROUTE 37

Gârda de Sus–Scărişoara ice cave–Padiş–
Cabana Vărăşoaia–Stâna de Vale

Start	Gârda de Sus
Finish	Stâna de Vale
Distance	48km
Total ascent	2455m
Total descent	2060m
Grade	Easy-moderate
Time	4 days
Maximum altitude	1670m (below Cârligatele Peak, Stage 3)
Maps	Padiş map, 1:30,000, Erfatur-Dimap, covers the central Padiş area; as does Bihorului: Platoul Padiş, 1:55,000/1:25,000, Munţii Noştri. Bihor Mountains, 1:60,000, Erfatur-Dimap covers the wider Apuseni Mountains (not strictly needed for this route).
Note	There are many flocks of sheep in the Padiş area, and therefore guard dogs – bring trekking poles to keep them away if necessary and do not walk right through a flock.

This route traverses the heart of the Apuseni from southeast to northwest, allowing you to visit the famous Scărişoara ice cave, home to the world's second largest ice block and many intriguing ice formations. It is best visited in May or June. The route consists of three fairly long main stages supplemented with an excursion to one of the Apuseni's karstic areas, the Someşul Cald circuit with its many caves and tunnels. It crosses Route 36 in Zona Padiş, so you can combine stages from this route with stages or excursions from the previous route.

Access
Take the Ariesul bus from Cluj to Câmpeni (3hr 10min); it leaves at 1pm from Autogara Fany, Strada Giordano Bruno 1–3. From Câmpeni there's another Ariesul bus to Arieşeni, but it doesn't leave until 6.45pm. There's an earlier one at 2.15pm, which you can catch if you take the 6am bus from Cluj. Get off the Arieşeni-bound bus in the centre of Gârda de Sus (about 1hr).

Stâna de Vale is at the end of a road so it can be hard to find a ride down to Beiuş; however, there's a bus on Friday, Saturday and Sunday during the summer and winter months (June–August and December–February). It leaves from

Hotel Iadolina at 11am and 3pm, journey time 45min – though check locally. From Beiuş, you can take a bus back to Câmpeni (and onwards to Cluj) or head to Oradea.

Accommodation and food
In Gârda de Sus: Pensiunea Danciu, Pensiunea Marinarul, Pensiunea de Sub Munte Dobra; **at Ghețari:** Pensiunea Scărişoara (this is a wonderful traditional Moți farm; you can pitch your tent here or rent a room. Meals are excellent and there's wi-fi), Pensiunea Rustic, Cabana Ghețari; **at Casa de Piatră:** Casa de Piatră (pension), Stone House Village (wooden huts/retreat); a**t or near Zona Padiş:** Cabana Brădeț, Pensiunea Turistică Padiş, Popaş Turistic Padiş, La 5 Casute (Cabana Padiş has been under renovation/construction for a long time and it's unclear when it will open again), Cabana Vărăşoaia; **in Stâna de Vale:** camping spot, and Hotel Iadolina. Please be aware that the Padiş area of the Apuseni Mountains is a national park and that camping is only permitted in designated areas.

There are several small shops in Gârda de Sus, and there are plenty of tourist stalls selling drinks and snacks around the Scărişoara ice cave. Hotel Iadolina in Stâna de Vale has a decent restaurant. There's a bar en route in Casa de Piatră Village (Stage 2).

STAGE 1
Gârda de Sus–Ghețari and Scărişoara ice cave

Start	Pensiunea Danciu, Gârda de Sus
Finish	Pensiunea Scărişoara, Ghețari
Distance	5km to Ghețari; another 1.5km to Scărişoara ice cave (and back)
Total ascent	400m
Total descent	40m
Grade	Easy
Time	1hr 30min to Ghețari; another 20min to Scărişoara ice cave (and back)
Maximum altitude	1175m (at the DC260 road)
Water	Buy water in Gârda de Sus

Head north onto the DJ750 road from the signpost in the centre of **Gârda de Sus**, next to Pensiunea Danciu. The road is marked blue circle, blue stripe and

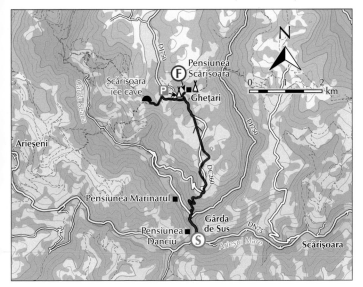

red cross. After just over 500 metres, turn left (Pensiunea Marinarul is on this road), then immediately right (east), up onto a narrow trail into the woods marked red cross.

Cross a meadow, initially to the southeast, then northeast. When you meet the **DC260 road**, turn right onto it. There's a shortcut to cut off a few hairpins. After almost 3km on and off the road, just after the red cross has been joined by the blue stripe, you'll see **Pensiunea Scărișoara** on your right – one of the first houses of Ghețari. There are several other pensions along the road.

To make your way to the Scărișoara ice cave, leave your luggage at Pensiunea Scărișoara (or wherever you're staying) and continue up the DC260 road. Turn left after you've passed a parking lot and a camping area. From here it's 10min to the **ice cave**.

> **Scărișoara ice cave** is home to the world's second largest ice block, and the oldest one at that: it's around 10,000 years old. It has a volume of about 120,000m3. At its thickest, it is 22.5m. Do put something warm on before entering the cave since there is quite a drop in temperature.

After visiting the cave, simply retrace your steps to return to Ghețari.

Haystack-dotted meadow near Gheţari

STAGE 2

Gheţari–Padiş–Cabana Vărăşoaia

Start	Pensiunea Scărişoara, Gheţari
Finish	Cabana Vărăşoaia
Distance	20km
Total ascent	830m
Total descent	650m
Grade	Moderate
Time	6hr 15min
Maximum altitude	1375m (below Gudapu Peak)
Water	At start and finish, and several springs on the gravel road, plus the stall in Casa de Piatră.

From **Pensiunea Scărişoara**, walk back up to the **ice cave**. Pass the entrance of the cave and continue north on the blue triangle trail. After 200 metres or so the trail veers to the left, off the main path, to the west; look for an arrow and follow it. When you see another arrow on a tree turn left (west) through a fence, crossing a meadow. Cross another meadow to the north, then follow an arrow to the west, down.

After 800 metres, after you've descended down a meadow with a barn, cross the road and head northwest, uphill, back into the forest. After about 400 metres the trail heads northwest, over some fallen trees; don't continue on the obvious path! After one more kilometre you'll see a small wooden house; pass to the left

Casa de Piatra village

of it and head south, downhill. When you come down to a gravel road, cross the stream over the bridge and turn right onto it.

After almost 1.5km you can make a small detour to Izbucul Tauzului: an 87m-deep spring (in which a diver drowned, according to a plaque on the rock wall). It's the deepest water-filled cave in Romania and has a total length of 424 metres.

There are several springs along this road. After some 3km you'll reach **Casa de Piatră Village** – a great place for a break. You can even order a placintă (somewhat like a thick pancake, often served with cheese) at the little bar. There's a pension here, as well as a retreat with wooden cabins.

About 1km after Casa de Piatră you can turn right to explore **Vârtop Cave** (30min off the trail). Around 3km later the road deteriorates into a rocky path and swings to the left. After another 1km turn left (west) off the trail; there's a waymark on a rock. With Gudapu Peak (1476m) to your left, head up a grassy hill to the right (northeast), then down again to the northwest, down a rocky section into another valley. Walk north along a sheep trail (unmarked), then walk down to the dirt road until you reach the asphalt road; from here it's 1km to **Zona Padiş**.

You can either stay at Zona Padiş or continue to Cabana Vărăşoaia, which is less than 1hr further up and situated in a much more pastoral area. To get there, walk down the road until you get to a bend, then turn right (north) off the road onto the blue stripe route and follow it all the way to **Cabana Vărăşoaia**. Camping is not allowed here, but you can rent a nice little wooden hut (casuţă).

EXCURSION
Someşul Cald Gorge circuit

Start/finish	Cabana Vărăşoaia
Distance	8km
Total ascent/descent	640m
Grade	Moderate
Time	4hr
Maximum altitude	1360m (beyond Cuptorul Cave)
Water	At Cabana Vărăşoaia
Note	Take a torch if you want to explore the caves

This is a fun circuit from Cabana Vărăşoaia. It will take you past spectacular caves and dazzling drops. It's a short route, but it comes with plenty of surprises and challenges.

From **Cabana Vărăşoaia**, turn left onto the gravel road. After 1.5km, leave the road and follow the red circle marks to the northeast. After about 500 metres you'll reach **Cetăţile Rădesei**, which is essentially a 212m-long karst tunnel. You can either enter it now or at the end of the circuit, because you'll return to this point. Whatever you do, to continue on the red circle trail, walk up the narrow trail that leads up into the forest to the left of the cave, until you come to an info panel and a signpost after another 500 metres or so. It's best to follow the trail clockwise, so turn left (northeast) and cross a shallow stream to follow it in the recommended direction.

> It's possible to visit **Tunelul Mic** ('Small Tunnel') here, but it's a bit hard to find; essentially, when you have to cross the stream a second time, you have to follow it to the left and climb over some boulders. The tunnel really is small, but if you want to have some fun on the trail you can try to crawl through it. Be careful not to fall into the 'bathtub' at the end of the tunnel though. Retrace your steps to return to the main trail.

Continuing northeast, around 2km from the start of the red circle trail you'll reach the northernmost corner of the circuit.

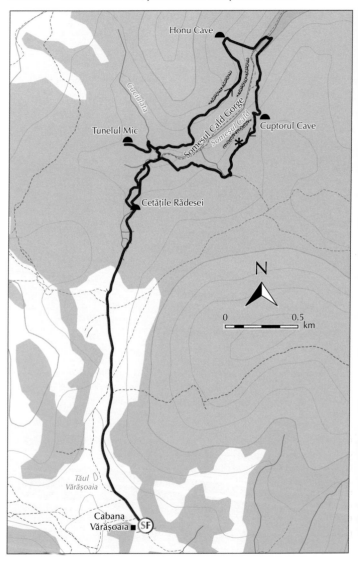

Here you can visit **Honu Cave**. It's rather deep, and since there are no holes in the 'ceiling' as in Cetăţile Rădesei, it's pitch-dark (so you'll need a good torch). The drops hanging from the ceiling look like diamonds, and the water dripping from the rocks has created intriguing shapes.

After a short descent you'll reach the Rădeasa Stream; cross the stream and climb to the highest point of the circuit, past **Cuptorul Cave** (which you could enter but it requires scrambling up to the entrance over very loose and fine scree – and back down again). The ascent is steep and tricky. At the highest point, around 1350m, there's a beautiful **viewpoint** from where you can look down into the Someşul Cald Gorge – although this can be a bit daunting if you have a fear of heights. Some 3km from the start of the circuit, you will have completed it; make your way back to **Cabana Vărăşoaia** the way you came.

STAGE 3
Cabana Vărăşoaia–Stâna de Vale

Start	Cabana Vărăşoaia
Finish	Camping spot, Stâna de Vale
Distance	15km
Total ascent	585m
Total descent	730m
Grade	Easy
Time	4hr 30min
Maximum altitude	1670m (below Cârligatele Peak)
Water	At Cabana Vărăşoaia, at Izvorul Minunilor and the camping spot at the end

From **Cabana Vărăşoaia** turn left onto the gravel road again; where the red circle trail departs right, follow the gravel road to the left. Stay on the gravel road, marked red and blue stripe, at all times. Ascend to about 1660m. After about 5km you'll see a signpost; go straight ahead to stay on the blue/red stripe route to Stâna de Vale, signed 2hr–2hr 30min. Another blue stripe trail departs right to Cabana Vlădeasa – ignore this. After about 5.5km from here you'll reach **Poiana Poienii**. Poienii Peak (1625m) is to your right and a path goes up it, but ignore this too.

Make a sharp right turn (there's no obvious trail) and head north to reach a signpost, then descend northeast to find a gravel road that takes you down to another signpost. Turn left onto the yellow triangle gravel road for 50 metres, then turn right (northwest) off the road onto a narrow trail marked red stripe, yellow triangle and yellow circle. When you reach another gravel road after the best part of a kilometre, either head straight ahead onto a grassy trail for a shortcut or turn right onto the road until you reach an asphalt road and **Izvorul Minunilor**, a spring of some fame and a well-known Romanian mineral water brand.

To find the camping spot, turn left onto the road into **Stâna de Vale**; when the road forks, keep left. You'll see the (very rudimentary) camping spot on your left when the monastery is on your right.

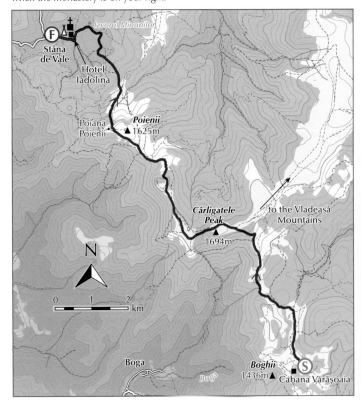

APPENDIX A
Route summary table

This table is based on main stages only. Alternative entry and exit routes are not included.

No	Route title	Duration	Distance	Grade	Ascent/descent	Maximum altitude	Page No.
The Mountains of Maramureş							
1	Şetref Pass to Rotunda Pass	4 days	60km	Moderate-difficult	4220/3770m	2303m	56
2	Breb–Creasta Cocoşului–Neteda Pass	6hr	16km	Moderate	1000/500m	1450m	70
3	Groşii Ţibleşului to Arcer, Ţibleş and Bran Peaks	7hr	23.5km	Difficult	1690/750m	1840m	75
4	Repedea to Prislop Pass	4–5 days	88.5km	Moderate-difficult	5270/4600m	1961m	78
The Eastern Carpathians							
5	The Suhard	2–3 days	49km	Moderate	2110/1610m	1932m	94
6	The Rarău–Giumalău	3 days	46.5km	Easy-moderate	1885/1975m	1857m	101
7	The Călimani	3 days	51.5km	Easy-moderate	2350/2365m	2100m	109
8	Izvorul Muntelui to Durău	3 days	22.4km	Moderate	1575/1615m	1900m	118
9	Bălan to Lacu Roşu	3 days	34km	Easy-moderate	1680/1530m	1792m	124

No	Route title	Duration	Distance	Grade	Ascent/descent	Maximum altitude	Page No.
The Mountains around Braşov							
10	Braşov to Râşnov	2 days	24km	Easy-moderate	1400/1330m	1604m	135
11	Şapte Scări Gorge and Piatra Mare Peak from Dâmbu Morii	4hr 40min	17.5km	Moderate	1100m	1844m	140
12	Timişu de Sus to Dâmbu Morii via Tamina Gorge	5hr	17km	Moderate	1100/1245m	1787m	143
13	A north-south traverse of the Baiului	6hr 30min	28km	Moderate	1360/1680m	1895m	146
14	Across the Baiului and Grohotiş	2 days	42km	Easy-moderate	2165/1990m	1840m	150
15	Cheia to Bratocea Pass	1–2 days	22km	Moderate	1685/1435m	1954m	157
16	Poiana Braşov to Bran	5 days	64.5km	Moderate	4480/4775m	2507m	163
17	Into the Bucegi from the Prahova Valley	4 days	51.5km	Moderate	3750/2620m	2507m	176
18	The northern ridge	4–5 days	42.5km	Moderate-difficult	3720m	2238m	186
19	The southern ridge	7hr 45min	17km	Difficult	1555/1435m	2195m	201

No	Route title	Duration	Distance	Grade	Ascent/descent	Maximum altitude	Page No.
The Făgăraş Mountains							
20	Iezer-Păpuşa circuit	2 days	29km	Moderate	2130m	2470m	209
21	From the Iezer-Păpuşa to the Făgăraş	3 days	48.5km	Moderate	2890/3110m	2470m	216
22	Traversing the Făgăraş from east to west	5–6 days	97.8km	Moderate-difficult	6205/6380m	2544m	223
From the Olt to the Jiu							
23	From Păltiniş to Petroşani	4–5 days	67.5km	Easy-moderate	3225/3965m	2519m	241
24	Cozia circuit	1–2 days	12.5km	Moderate	1400m	1667m	254
25	Cheia Village–Buila-Vânturariţa ridge–Băile Olăneşti	3 days	53.7km	Moderate-difficult	2770/2795m	1885m	259
The Retezat Mountains							
26	Cârnic to Cabana Gura Zlata via Bucura Lake	3–4 days	33km	Moderate-difficult	2880/3140m	2509m	272
27	Poiana Pelegii to Cârnic via Bucura Lake	3 days	23km	Moderate-difficult	1960/2535m	2509m	284
28	From the Vâlcan to the Retezat	2–3 days	42km	Moderate	2660/2500m	2081m	292
29	Jigora Saddle to Cabana Buta	4 days	57km	Moderate	3545/3350m	2229m	301

No	Route title	Duration	Distance	Grade	Ascent/descent	Maximum altitude	Page No.
The Banat Mountains							
30	Domogled Peak circuit from Băile Herculane	4hr 40min	11km	Moderate	1040m	1105m	313
31	Poiana cu Peri circuit from Băile Herculane	5hr 30min	14.5km	Easy	740m	779m	315
32	The gorges of the Semenic	3 days	80km	Easy-moderate	2055/1580m	709m	318
The Apuseni Mountains							
33	The gorges of the Trascău	4 days	84km	Moderate	3945/3870m	1233m	332
34	Poşaga de Jos–Scăriţa Belioara–Runc	6hr	25km	Moderate	965/920m	1382m	347
35	Runc–Scăriţa Belioara–Lunca Largă–Runc	5hr	19.5km	Moderate	960m	1382m	351
36	Statiunea Vârtop–Cetăţile Ponorului–Padiş– Pietroasa	4 days	54.2km	Easy-moderate	2700/3290m	1410m	354
37	Gârda de Sus–Scărişoara ice cave–Padiş– Cabana Vărăşoaia–Stâna de Vale	4 days	48km	Easy-moderate	2455/2060m	1670m	369

There are many more cabanas than those mentioned below; only the cabanas en route have been listed. Others can be found on the relevant maps. There are two websites that may also help you find cabanas and refuges, although they are in Romanian: to find accommodation info on www.carpati.org, navigate to 'Ghid', then 'Ghid montan' and click on the mountain range of your choice. You'll find the relevant cabanas and refuges listed under 'Cazare' in the right-hand menu. On www.exploregis.ro, choose a mountain range under 'Trasee Turistice'; after clicking on the name an interactive map will appear. Red house symbols denote cabanas; red shelter symbols represent refuges.

For an overview of campsites, see www.takethelongwayhome.eu. www.welcometoromania.eu lists pensions for many (popular) towns in Romania. www.turistinfo.ro (in Romanian) lists accommodation per county and has a search engine. Many but not all of those will also have made their appearance on www.booking.com. Airbnb (www.airbnb.com) works well in larger cities as well. If you want to search for accommodation in Romanian, use 'cazare' and the name of the place where you want to stay. This might well yield more results than searching in English.

Romania's international dialling code is 0040; all phone numbers below should be preceded by this (omitting the first zero of the number) when calling from outside the country. Reception in the mountains often isn't great, so you may have to try several times or text instead.

While some of the websites listed below are in English or have an English-language option, others are in Romanian only. Certain web browsers (such as Chrome) can be adjusted to translate foreign-language sites into English; the translation may be fairly rudimentary but it could help you find the information you need if you're struggling.

The Mountains of Maramureş

The Rodna Mountains
Hanul Tentea
Şetref Pass
tel 0374 930 933 or 0741 400 287
hanul_tentea@yahoo.com

Borşa Turism
Str Pietroasei 9
Borşa
www.borsa-turism.com
tel 0745 271 576

Cabana Croitor
Rotunda Pass
tel 0786 579 645 (Mr Liviu Croitor) or 0755 578 556 (Alex, speaks English)
https://rotundapas.webs.com

Cabana Rotunda
Rotunda Pass
tel 0727 372794 or 0762 084 485

The Gutâi and Ţibleş
Babou Maramures campsite and hostel
Breb 149
http://baboumaramures.com
tel 026 237 4717 or 076 839 7339

Pensiunea Mărioara
Breb 346
Breb
www.facebook.com/
pensiuneamarioarabreb
tel 074 4145 349 or 0262 374 593

Pensiunea Maramu'
Breb 290
Breb
https://pensiuneamaramu.weebly.com
tel 076 0149 552 or 073 4587 905

The Village Hotel
Breb 349
Breb
www.villagehotelmaramures.com
tel 072 3223 059

Pensiunea Adina
Str. Independenței 11
Cavnic
Reservations through www.booking.com
tel 0740 703 449

Casa Olarului
Strada Luncii 1
Baia Sprie
www.casaolarului.ro
tel 0729 047 429

Cabana Mogoşa
Bodi Lake near Baia Sprie
tel 0262 260 800

Pensiunea Schilacy
Strada Țibleşului 439
Groşii Țibleşului
tel 0762 203 874

Munţii Maramureşului
Laver
Repedea 322
Repedea
tel 0723 931 554

SC Longa Prod Com SRL
Repedea (next door to Laver)
tel 0262 366 283 or 0723 730 194

Cabana Alpina
Prislop Pass
tel 0262 342 425; 0745 523 605 or 0741 521 265

Cabana Dacilor
Prislop Pass
tel 0756 496 353 or 0731 852 494

The Eastern Carpathians

Vatra Dornei
Serban Cottage
tel 0742 321 050
Reservations through www.booking.com

Camping Autoturist
Strada Runc 6
Vatra Dornei
tel 0230 371 892 or 0729 308 192

The Suhard
See 'The Rodna Mountains', above

The Rarău–Giumalău
Cabana Giumalău
tel 0748 359121 or 0749 575471

Cabana Rarău
tel 0758 852 959
reservari@hotel-alpin-rarau.ro
https://hotel-alpin-rarau.ro

Salvamont Rarău
tel 0745 313 052

The Călimani
Pensiunea Poarta Călimanilor
Gura Haitiitel 0788 870 463
daniela.tarca@yahoo.com

Pensiunea Perla Călimanilor
Gura Haitiitel 0230 574 491 or 0788 874 794

Cabana Roza Vânturilor
tel 0747 755 488, 0737 836 452 or 0784 064 487

Rețițiș meteo station
tel 0723 625 447

The Hășmaș
Cabana Piatra Singuratică
tel 0744 156 566

The Ceahlău
Cabana Izvorul Muntelui
tel 0233 274 039 or 0746 906 522

Pensiunea CrușituIzvorul Muntelui
tel 0723 589 661

Cabana Dochiatel 0730 603 801
http://cabana-dochia.ro

Pensiunea StefaniaLacu Roșu
tel 0758 877 399

The Mountains around Brașov

Brașov
Some good options in the old city centre:

Casa Terezia
Str. Nicolae Balcescu 25
Brașov
tel 0742 488 739
www.casa-terezia.ro

Casa Corona
Str. Castelului 21
Brașov
tel 0727 106 500, 0771 429 199 or 0727 106 504
www.casacorona.ro

Hotel ARO Sport (budget hotel)
Strada Sf. Ioan 3
Brașov
tel 0752 212 168
Reservations through www.booking.com

In the Astra district, near Piatra Mare:

Coronensis Apartment
Strada Cărpaților 66
Atel 0728 175 072 (Mr Sorin Rusu)
sorin10000@gmail.com
See www.airbnb.com

Hotel Astra
Strada Panselelor 2
Brașov
tel 0721 272 768 or 0268 272 768
www.hotelastra.ro

Twins Apartments
Strada Calcarului 9
Brașov
tel 0368 410 710 or 0723 044 224
rezervari@twins-apartments.ro
Reservations through www.booking.com

Postăvaru
Cabana Postăvaru
tel 0368 101 036
https://cabanaPostăvaru.ro

Club Rossignol
Poiana Brașov
tel 0722 794 162 or 0722 222 314
www.clubrossignol.ro

Cabana Poiana Secuilor
tel 0727 692 763
www.booking.com

Cabana Trei Brazi
tel 0268 892 057 or 0747 027 929
www.cabanatreibrazi.com

Piatra Mare
Vila 7 Scari
Strada Piatra Mare 15
Timişu de Jos
tel 0745 700 593

Vila Canionul 7 Scari
Strada Canionului 21
Timişu de Jos
tel 0744 494 978

Cabana Rustic House
Strada Piatra Mare 4
Timişu de Jos
tel 0799 099 350

Cabana Piatra Mare
tel 0744 322632 (Mr Attila Kovacs)

Baiului–Grohotiş
Vila Veveriţa
Strada Mihai Eminescu 41
Predeal
tel 0749 047 789

Cabana Susai
Predeal
tel 0268 457 204

Florei Refuge
tel 0729 170 973
www.ompemunte.ro
Search for 'Refugiul Florei' on Facebook

Ciucaş
Cabana Vârful Ciucaş
tel 0725 431 318 or 0727 149 800
contact@cabana-varful-ciucas.ro
www.cabana-varful-ciucas.ro

Complex Cabana Ciucaş
Strada Principală 435
Cheia
tel 0733 908 411
https://complex-cabana-ciucas-cheia.
business.site

The Bucegi
Cabana Diham
tel 0726 20 32 62
www.diham.ro

Cabana Omu
tel 0744 567 290 or 0744 221 582
www.cabana-omu.ro

Camping Aviator
Bulevard Independenţei 64
Buşteni
tel 0745 102 596
http://ecamping.ro

Cabana Babele
tel 0744 772 710
www.babele.ro

Cabana Padina
tel 0788 207 553, 0729 079 757 or
0729 469 697
www.cabana-padina.ro

Cabana Bolboci
tel 0722 829 367 or 0723 682 940

Cabana Zănoaga
tel 0741 588 724, 0786 781 672 or
0786 781 673
www.facebook.com/CabanaZanoaga.ro

Camping Zănoaga
tel 0735 506 111 or 0725 721 187
https://carpatmontana-serv.ro

Cabana Valea Dorului
tel 0244 313 531, 0722 477 086 or
0720 821 511

Hotel-Cabana Piatra Arsă
tel 0742 101 216
www.facebook.com/
HotelCabanaPiatraArsa

The Piatra Craiului
Cabana Gura Râului
tel 0722 592 375 or 0744 307 978
www.cabanaguraraului.ro

Cabana Curmatura
tel 0745 454 184

Cabana Plaiul Foii
tel 0726 380 323
www.cabanaplaiulfoii.ro

Cabana Căprioara
on the DN22 towards Dâmbovicioara
tel 0770 410 059

In Măgura:
Pensiunea Dobre, Strada Principală 188
tel 0744 885 941
www.pensiuneacasadobre.ro

Villa Hermani, Sat Măgura 130
tel 0740 022 384
www.cntours.eu

Pensiunea Moșorel
tel 0766 226 444
www.cazarepensiunemagura.ro

The Făgăraș Mountains

The Iezer-Păpușa
Cabana Voina
tel 0744 313 145

Cabana Cuca
tel 0348 820 101, 0774 698 211 or
0733 885566

Cabana Valea Sâmbătei
tel 0757 401 346 or 0755 612 918
razvan_zraila@yahoo.com
www.simbata.ro

Floarea Reginei Pension
Complex Turistic Sâmbăta
tel 0745 234 884

Popaș Sâmbăta
Complex Turistic Sâmbăta
tel 0744 573 694
www.popas-sambata.ro

The Făgăraș Chain
Cabana Plaiul Foii
tel 0726 380 323
www.cabanaplaiulfoii.ro

Cabana Bâlea Lac
tel 0745 072 602
cabana_balealac@yahoo.com
http://balealac.ro

Cabana Podragu
tel 0745 319 766
www.podragu.ro

Pensiunea IoanaTurnu Roșu
tel 0269 527 822

Not en route but an excellent base
before and/or after a hike into the
Făgăraș:

Camping De Oude Wilg
Strada Prundului 311
Cârța
tel 0269 521 347 or 0723 186 343
de_oude_wilg@yahoo.com
www.campingdeoudewilg.nl (in Dutch)

From the Olt to the Jiu

The Cindrel
Cabana NoraVârful Bătrâna 1
Păltiniș
tel 075 38 01 284

Cânaia Refuge
tel 076 56 59 218 (Mr Doru Podia)

Cabana Oașa
on the DN67C (Transalpina)
tel 0258 738 001 or 076 11 05 072
voisanioana@yahoo.com
http://cabana-oasa.ro

The Parâng
Cabana Obârșia Lotrului
tel 074 47 00 180
www.cabanaobarsialotrului.ro

Vila Iulian
Stațiunea Parâng
tel 078 78 28 945 or 072 72 13 408

Hotel Rușu
tel 074 20 87 221/222
info@hotelrusu.ro
www.hotelrusu.ro

The Cozia
Mănăstirea Turnu
tel 0250 750851 or 0746 345 826
(Father Damian)

The Buila-Vânturarița
Buila Basecamp
Cheia Village
tel 0721 223 358 (Mr Mihai Sandu)

Cabana Cheia
tel 0723 279 899 (Mr Ion
Dumbrăvescu)

The Retezat
Cabana Codrin
Cârnic
tel 0721 411 309, 0742 793 620 or
0723 215 301
carnic_retezat@yahoo.com
www.codrin.ro

Cabana Lolaia
Cârnic
contact@cabana-lolaia.ro
www.cabana-lolaia.ro

Cabana Pietrele
tel 072 271 5595 or 037 497 5188
cabanapietrele@gmail.com
www.pietrele.ro

Cabana Gențiana
tel 073 396 3292, 072 133 1125,
072 802 8409 or 073 767 1778

Cabana Gura Zlata
on the DJ685 road at the end of the red
triangle route
tel 0744 648 599

Cabana Buta
tel 0725 337 748

Cabana Cheile Butii
tel 0741 063 365 or 0758 233 787
cheile_butii@yahoo.com
www.cheile-butii.ro

The Vâlcan
Stațiunea Straja (various options)
https://cazarestraja.info

Pensiunea Retezat
tel 0722 538 551
office@pensiunearetezat.com
www.pensiunearetezat.com

The Țarcu
Țarcu meteo station
tel 072 362 53 40

The Banat Mountains

Băile Herculane
Hotel Trandafirul Galben
Strada Trandafirilor 76
Băile Herculane
tel 0255 560 516
trandafirul_galben_cs@yahoo.com
www.trandafirul-galben.ro

Pensiunea Soimul
Strada Zavoiului 104
Băile Herculane
tel 0740 668 457
www.pensiuneasoimul.ro

See www.cazare.baileherculane.ro for
an overview of hotels and pensions in
Băile Herculane.

Sasca Română and Sasca Montană
Pensiunea Cheile Nerei
Sasca Română 55
tel 0721 095 591
www.cheilenerei.ro

Casa cu Roți
Sasca Română 74
tel 0721 108 777
www.casacuroti-cheilenerei.ro

Cabana Agathos
Strada Principală
Sasca Montană
tel 0727 210 623 (Mrs Livia Buciuman)

Cazare Iedera
Strada Principală 535
Sasca Montană
tel 0720 573 965

La Vechea Moara Pension & Restaurant
Strada Principală 530
Sasca Montană
tel 0726 307 762 or 0729 521 482
www.vechea-moara.ro

Anina
Pensiunea Anina
Strada Minis 4
Anina
tel 0745 152 770

Carașova
Pensiunea Perla Carașului
Carașovaon the DN58 road
tel 0751 752 783

Reșița
Casa Bănățeană
Strada Minda 30
Reșița
tel 0745 419 767

Hotel Dusan și Fiul
Strada 24 Ianuarie 150
Reșița
tel 0255 224 722
www.dusansifiul.ro

The Apuseni Mountains

The Trascău and Muntele Mare
Cabana Cheile Turzii
at the end of the DJ103I road, 15km
from Turda
tel 0748 759 063

Pensiunea Torockó
Strada Tohely 175a
517610 Rimetea
tel 0258 768 240
zcsonka@t-online.hu

Camping Gyopár
Strada Tohely 157a
517610 Rimetea
tel 0744 542 563
www.gyoparpanzio.hu

See www.erdelyiturizmus.hu for more
pensions in Rimetea.

Pensiunea Codru
Strada Valea Sălciuței 223
Sălciua de Jos
tel 0762 588 977 or 0769 642 623

Raven's Nest
Sub Piatrătel 0721 492 451
http://ravensnest.eu

Țară Nomadă Hostel and Camping
Strada Principală 31517527 Runc
Ocoliș
tel 0732 858 045 or 0358 824 124
https://taranomada.com

Pensiunea Crama
Ocoliș
tel 0358 505 150

Dupa Gard Poşga de Jos
tel 0 722 910 724
www.dupa-gard.com (in German)

Cabana Râmeţ
tel 0729 034 370

Mănăstirea Râmeţ
tel 0258 880111

Citadel Hostel
Strada Vasile Alecsandri 64
Alba Iulia
tel 0740 026 205

The Padiş Region
Pensiunea MarietaVârtop
tel 0740 692 358

Hotel Four Seasons
Vârtop
tel 0729 989 515
www.4seasons.ro

Cabana Cetăţile Ponorului
tel 0740 007 814
zonapadis@yahoo.com
www.padis.ro

Cabana Brădeţ
tel 0743 048 266
ade_tere@yahoo.com

Pensiunea Turistică Padiş
tel 0788 335 050

Popaş Turistic Padiş
tel 0720 099 590

La 5 Casute
tel 0732 833 783

Pensiunea CristalBoga
tel 0757 181 877 or 0756 653 265

Flóra PánzioBoga
tel +36 30 556 8880

Pensiunea Danciu
Gârda de Sus 51
tel 0763 131 329 or 0358 402 201

Pensiunea de Sub Munte Dobra
Gârda de Sus 50
tel 0748 215 689

Pensiunea Marinarul
Gârda de Sus 148B
tel 0358 402 727 or 0763 792 977 (Mr
Ioan Burcuta)
jb.ioaneill@gmail.com

Pensiunea Scărişoara
Satul Ghetari 242
tel 0744 902 621 or 0744 528 363
pascanicodim@yahoo.com

Pensiunea Rustic
Satul Ghetari (on the road to the ice
cave)
tel 0743 475 645 or 0757 147 547

Cabana Vărăşoaia
tel 0372 763 409, 0788 601 815 or
0788 297 015

Hotel Iadolina
Stâna de Vale
tel 0744 599 334
www.hoteliadolina.ro

Casa de Piatră
tel 0767 970 979 (Mrs Ioana Gligor)

Stone House Village (wooden huts/
retreat)
tel 0774 632 214
www.facebook.com/stonehousevillage

The Vlădeasa Mountains
Cabana VlădeasaRogojel
tel 0743 062 378
iocabanavladeasa@yahoo.com

Casa Careel
Tranişu 172B
tel 0364 737328
tranisu172@gmail.com
http://careel.eu

APPENDIX C
Useful contacts

While some of the websites listed below are in English or have an English-language option, others are in Romanian only. Certain web browsers (such as Chrome) can be adjusted to translate foreign-language sites into English; the translation may be fairly rudimentary but it could help you find the information you need if you're struggling.

Transport

Airlines and airports

International airports
Bucharest Henri Coandă (also known as Otopeni)
www.otp-airport.ro

Bacău
http://bacauairport.ro

Cluj-Napoca
http://airportcluj.ro

Constanța
www.mk-airport.ro

Craiova
www.aeroportcraiova.ro

Iași
www.aeroport-iasi.ro

Satu Mare
www.aeroportulsatumare.ro

Sibiu
www.sibiuairport.ro

Suceava
www.aeroportsuceava.ro

Târgu Mureș
www.targumuresairport.ro

Timișoara
http://aerotim.ro

Airlines
Tarom
www.tarom.ro

Blue Air
www.blueairweb.com

Wizz Air
https://wizzair.com

Ryan Air
www.ryanair.com

KLM
www.klm.com

Air France
www.airfrance.com

Lufthansa
www.lufthansa.com

Trains
CFR
www.cfrcalatori.ro

Regio Călători
https://regiocalatori.ro

TFC
https://transferoviarcalatori.ro

Interregional Călători
www.viaterraspedition.ro

Buses
For long-distance bus travel, see https://autogari.ro. The search engine is excellent, but please be aware that not all information may be up to date; this depends on the bus companies and some are more lax than others in updating their information. It's always worth double-checking by making a phone call. You might want to ask a Romanian to help you do this

since many operators will not speak English. Some companies let you make reservations online through the Autogari website; in most cases you will have to phone – or just turn up in time if they don't accept reservations. Relevant local public transport companies are listed below.

The Mountains of Maramureș
Buses in and around Baia Mare
www.urbisbaiamare.ro

From Baia Mare to Groșii Țibleșului
Versav Trans
0740 030 097

The Eastern Carpathians
Buses in and around Vatra Dornei
www.sincarom.ro

The Mountains around Brașov
In Brașov and to Poiana Brașov
www.ratbv.ro

From the Olt to the Jiu
In Sibiu, and from Sibiu to Păltiniș
https://online.tursib.ro

The Retezat
In the Jiu Valley between Petroșani and Uricani
www.zmk.ro

The Apuseni Mountains
In Cluj
www.ctpcj.ro

Car
BlaBlaCar (carpooling app)
www.blablacar.com

Shops

Outdoor stores
Bucharest: Decathlon, Nootka Sport, Himalaya, Sport Virus

Cluj: Decathlon, Nootka Sport, Altisport

Brașov: Decathlon, ProAlpin, Himalaya, Sport Virus

Sibiu: ProAlpin, Sport Virus, Explorer Sport

Bookshops
The most well-supplied national book chain is Cărturești; https://carturesti.ro. You'll find it in Bucharest, Brașov, Cluj, Sibiu, Timișoara and many other cities. In Brașov you'll also find Humanitas and St Iosif; in Sibiu, Humanitas, Erasmus and Schiller. All of these sell maps and travel guides.

Online resources

If you have any queries to which you cannot find the answers in this book (changed phone numbers, etc), you might want to ask around in the 35,000-strong 'Nu sunt singur pe munte' Facebook group. It's in Romanian but there will be plenty of people who will be able to answer your questions in English.

General information
http://romaniatourism.com

www.welcometoromania.eu

www.uncover-romania.com

Weather forecasts

www.meteoblue.com
(website and app)

www.accuweather.com
(website and app)

www.yr.no
(website and app)

Mountain info

Except for the first three, these websites are all in Romanian, but with some effort you will be able to glean very useful information from them if you want to explore trails/areas that are beyond the scope of this book. A list of certified tourist guides and mountain guides can be downloaded from http://ghizimontani.org/ghizi-montani-atestati (Romanian website).

www.summitpost.org

http://amazingromania.net
(app available)

www.roamaniac.com
(the author's blog)

www.carpati.org

www.carteamuntilor.ro

www.exploregis.ro

www.montaniarzi.ro

Maps and apps

Stanfords
www.stanfords.co.uk

ManyMaps
www.manymaps.com

https://muntii-nostri.ro
(app available; highly recommended)

www.eco-romania.ro
(app available)

https://dimap.hu

Websites of national parks

This is not an exhaustive list; it only covers the parks dealt with in this book. Most websites are in Romanian but some have an English version.

Apuseni
www.parcapuseni.ro

Bucegi
www.bucegipark.ro

Buila-Vânturarița
www.buila.ro

Călimani
www.calimani.ro

Ceahlău
www.ceahlaupark.ro

Cheile Bicazului-Hășmaș
www.cheilebicazului-hasmas.ro

Cheile Nerei-Beușnița
www.cheilenereibeusnita.ro

Cozia
https://cozia.ro

Domogled-Valea Cernei
www.domogled-cerna.ro

Munții Maramureșului
www.muntiimaramuresului.ro

Munții Rodnei
www.parcrodna.ro

Piatra Craiului
www.pcrai.ro

Retezat
www.retezat.ro

Semenic-Cheile Carașului
http://pnscc.ro

APPENDIX D
Language notes and glossary

Romanian may be a Romance language, but it is an isolated one and comes with its own peculiarities. Over time, it has been influenced by the surrounding Slavic languages, Hungarian, French and other languages. In terms of vocabulary, you will recognise much if you know one or more other Romance languages; its grammar heavily leans on Latin, having borrowed three of its cases. This guide and glossary should help you to get by in day-to-day situations, but delving a little deeper into the language won't do any harm, especially since many if not most people in the countryside and in the mountains won't speak any English. A good introduction course to the language can be found at www.learnro.com and www.duolingo. com offers a Romanian course as well. See https://dexonline.ro if you want to consult a Romanian to English (and vice versa) dictionary.

Pronunciation
Romanian spelling is largely phonetic, meaning letters are usually used consistently to represent a particular sound. However, there are a few sounds that will be very foreign to the non-Romanian ear and take some practice to pronounce, as well as some letter combinations that result in different sounds to when they appear individually. Below is a key to the most important pronunciation issues.

â/î: This is probably the most challenging sound for a non-native speaker to pronounce. It is somewhat similar to the German ü, but not quite the same. To produce it, shape your mouth as you would for the 'ee' as in 'feet', but say 'oo' as in 'foot'. Since a spelling reform in 1993 the official spelling is â, but you will still often see it spelled î. Examples: *vârf* (peak), *pâine* (bread), *în* (in) – if occurring at the beginning or end of a word it is always spelled î.

ă: An unstressed syllable, as in the 'e' in the second syllable of 'present'. Examples: *măr* (apple), *casă* (house).

e: It is important to note that e is never pronounced as a schwa, not even at the end of a word. It is pronounced as 'e' as in 'bed'. Examples: *bine* (good), *puternic* (strong). If it's positioned at the beginning of a word it's pronounced 'ye', as in 'yet'. Examples: *este* (he/she/ it is), *eu* (I).

i: At the end of a word, the letter i is pronounced as a 'j', but very subtly. Examples: *frați* (brothers), *turiști* (tourists). An exception is made for words ending in -tri, such as *kilometri* (kilometres), in which it does get pronounced as 'ee' as in 'cheese'.

c: Before e and i, the letter c is pronounced as 'tch' as in 'chocolate', but as 'k' elsewhere. Examples of the former: *cine* (who), *facem* (we make). Examples of the latter: *casă* (house), *carte* (book). Example with both: *concert* (concert).

g: Much the same principle as for c – before e and i, g is pronounced 'j' as in jam, and as a hard 'g' elsewhere. Examples of the former: *gem* (jam), *geam* (window). Examples of the latter: *gară* (station), *drag* (dear).

j: Pronounced as in the 's' in 'pleasure'. Examples: *joi* (Thursday), *joc* (game).

ş: Pronounced 'sh' as in 'shirt'. Examples: *şi* (and), *ştiu* (I know).

ţ: Pronounced 'ts' as in 'tsunami'. Examples: *ţară* (land), *aveţi* (you have).

Grammar

Although it won't be necessary to master the whole of Romanian grammar when heading to Romania for a couple of weeks, it will be useful to know about a few principles. Perhaps the first thing to remember is that in Romanian the definite article is attached to the end of the noun. Hence, neuter *izvor* (spring) becomes *izvorul* (the spring) and masculine *băiat* (boy) becomes *băiatul* (the boy). The definite article is a little harder to spot with feminine nouns that end in ă, because it simply changes to a, as in *apă* (water) to *apa* (the water). Definite articles are also used if the noun is followed by a name; *vârf* (peak) becomes Vârful Moldoveanu, *lac* (lake) becomes Lacul Capra, *vale* (valley) becomes Valea Tătarului, *chei* (gorge) becomes Cheile Turzii. In the plural feminine nouns either end in -e or -i; masculine nouns always in -i; neuter nouns get -uri, -e or -i. It would go too far to explain the particulars of this!

Adjectives are inflected according to the gender of nouns they accompany. On the trail this may be especially relevant when asking for directions. Yellow is *galben*, but yellow stripe is *banda galbenă*, blue stripe *banda albastră*. Red circle is *punct roşu*, but red stripe *banda roşie*. *Punct* (circle/point) and *triunghi* (triangle) are both neuter and do not influence the ending of the adjective.

Personal pronouns (in the nominative case, ie when used as a subject) are usually omitted in Romanian, but they can be used if it is necessary to disambiguate the meaning of a sentence or if one wants to stress the pronoun. Thus, 'I am' is simply *sunt*, as is 'they are'; if you'd want to distinguish between the two you'd say *eu sunt* and *ei/ele sunt* (m/f) respectively. In any case, it is not wrong to use the personal pronoun.

Greetings and introductions

English	Romanian
Hello (formal)	Bună ziua
Hi	Bună
Hello (informal)	Salut, Servus
What's your name?	Cum vă/te cheamă?
My name is...	Numele meu este.../Mă cheamă.../Sunt...
Goodbye	La revedere
Bye	Pa
See you later	Pe curând/Pe mai târziu
Good morning	Bună dimineața
Good evening	Bună seara/O seară bună
Goodnight	Noapte buna
How are you?	Ce faceți? (formal)/Ce faci? (informal)
How have you been?	Ce mai faceți? (formal)/Ce mai faci? (informal)
Fine, thank you	Bine, mulțumesc
I am, he is, she is, we are, you are, they are	Eu sunt, el este, ea este, noi suntem, voi sunteți, ei/ele sunt (in practice 'este' is often replaced by 'e')
I'm English/Dutch/French	Sunt englez(ă)/olandez(ă)/francez(ă) (m/f)

English	Romanian
I am from England/The Netherlands/France	Sunt din Anglia/Olanda/Franța
Mr, Mrs, Miss Smith	Domnul, Doamna, Domnişoara Smith
Sir	Domnule
Madam	Doamna
Miss	Domnişoară

Essential words/phrases

English	Romanian
Yes	Da
No	Nu
Please	Vă rog (formal)/Te rog (informal)
Thank you	Mulțumesc
Thank you very much	Mulțumesc frumos
You're welcome	Cu placere
Sorry (Excuse me)	Mă scuzați (formal)/Scuze (informal)/Scuză-mă (informal)
I beg your pardon?	Poftim?
I don't understand	Nu înțeleg
I understand	Am înțeles
I don't speak Romanian	Nu vorbesc românește
I (only) speak a little Romanian	Vorbesc (doar) puțin românește

English	Romanian
Could you repeat that more slowly please?	Puteți să repetați mai rar vă rog?
How do you say ... in Romanian?	Cum se spune în română ...?
Do you speak English?	Vorbiți engleza?

Basic phrases

English	Romanian
Excuse me (when you are about to request something)	Nu vă supărați
Excuse me (when you are trying to get past someone)	Mă scuzați/Scuze/Pardon
I'm sorry	Îmi pare rău
Just a minute!/Right away!	Imediat!/O secundă/Un moment!
Here you are	Poftiți (formal/plural)/Poftim (informal)
Please come in	Poftiți înauntru
Cheers!	Noroc!/Sănătate!
I don't know	Nu știu
I like/I don't like...	Îmi place/Nu-mi place...
Great!	Genial!
Let's go	Să mergem
Come on!	Haideți! (formal)/Hai! (informal)

English	Romanian
Please could I have...	Vă rog.../Îmi puteți da...
I'd like...	Aș dori...
Do you have...?	Aveți...? (formal)/Ai...? (informal)
I/we need...	Am nevoie de...
How much does it cost?	Cât costă?/Ce preț are?
How can I help you?	Cu ce vă pot ajuta?
I am looking for...	Caut...
Have a nice trip!	Drum bun!

Numerals

English	Romanian
0	zero
1	un, o
2	doi, două
3	trei
4	patru
5	cinci
6	șase
7	șapte
8	opt
9	nouă
10	zece
11	unsprezece
12	doisprezece, douăsprezece
13	treisprezece
14	paisprezece

English	Romanian
15	cincisprezece
16	şaisprezece
17	şaptesprezece
18	optsprezece
19	nouăsprezece
20	douăzeci
21	douăzeci şi unu
30	treizeci
40	patruzeci
50	cincizeci
60	şaizeci
70	şaptezeci
80	optzeci
90	nouăzeci
100	o sută
101	o sută unu
200	două sute
1000	o mie
first	primul/prima
second	al doilea/a două
third	al treilea/a treia

Time, days, months and seasons

English	Romanian
What time is it?	Cât este ceasul?
It's nine o'clock	Este ora nouă
It's a quarter past nine	Este ora nouă şi un sfert
It's a quarter to nine	Este ora nouă fără un sfert
It's half past nine	Este ora nouă şi jumătate
morning	dimineaţă
noon	prânz
evening	seară
night	noapte
day	zi
today	astăzi
tomorrow	mâine
the day after tomorrow	poimâine
yesterday	ieri
week	săptămână
month	lună
year	an
Sunday	duminică
Monday	luni
Tuesday	marţi
Wednesday	miercuri
Thursday	joi
Friday	vineri
Saturday	sâmbătă
January	ianuarie
February	februarie
March	martie
April	aprilie
May	mai
June	iunie
July	iulie
August	august

English	Romanian
September	septembrie
October	octombrie
November	noiembrie
December	decembrie
spring	primăvară
summer	vară
autumn	toamnă
winter	iarnă

General vocabulary

English	Romanian
what?	ce?
when?	când?
where?	unde?
who?	cine?
which?	care?
how?	cum?
why?	de ce?
on	pe
in	în
to	spre, la
of	de
from	din/de la
from… to…	de la… până la…
under	sub/dedesubt
above	sus/pe
with	cu
without	fără
and	şi

English	Romanian
or	sau
before	înainte de
after	după
now	acum
later	mai târziu
late	târziu
delayed	întârziat
cancelled	anulat
here	aici
there	acolo
this	acest (before a noun); acesta (m.sg.), această (f.sg.) (after a noun); asta (after a noun or on its own; informal, commonly used)
that	acela (m.sg.), aceea (f.sg.) (after a noun)
because	pentru că
beautiful	frumos, frumoasă
big	mare
small	mic, mică
open	deschis
closed	închis
opening times	orar/program de lucru
difficult/more difficult	greu/mai greu (also heavy/heavier); dificil/mai dificil

399

English	Romanian
easy/easier	uşor/mai uşor (also light/lighter); facil/mai facil
far	departe
fast	repede
slow	încet
warm	cald
cold	rece
much/many	mult/mulţi
near	aproape
far away	departe
very	foarte

Asking for directions and transport

English	Romanian
left/to the left	stânga/la stânga
right/to the right	dreapta/la dreapta
straight ahead	drept înainte
turn around	întoarceţi-vă
via	prin
Excuse me, can I ask you something?	Nu vă supăraţi, pot să vă întreb ceva?
Excuse me, do you happen to know...?	Nu vă supăraţi, ştiţi cumva...?
Where is...?	Unde este...?
Where is it?	Unde este?
How do I get there?	Cum ajung acolo?

English	Romanian
I've lost my way	M-am rătăcit
Do you know where ... is?	Stiţi unde este...?
Is this the road to...?	Acesta este drumul spre...?
Could you show me on the map (where we are right now)?	Îmi puteţi arăta pe hartă (unde ne aflăm acum)?
Is this the bus/train to...	Ăsta e autobuzul/trenul spre...
station	gară
bus station	autogară
hitchhiking	autostop
car	maşină
taxi	taxi
train	tren
bus	autobuz
minibus	maxitaxi
plane	avion
airport	aeroport
One ticket/two tickets to..., please	Un bilet/două bilete pentru..., vă rog
arrivals	sosiri
departures	plecari
entrance	intrare
exit	ieşire
platform	peron

Accommodation

English	Romanian
pension, guest-house, B&B	pensiune
room	cameră
single room	cameră single
double room	cameră dublă
Do you have a single/double room?	Aveţi o cameră single/dublă liberă?
I'd like to make a reservation	Doresc să fac o reservare
passport	paşaport
identity card	buletin
I have/we have made a reservation	Am rezervat
I/we haven't made a reservation	N-am rezervat
one night	o noapte
two nights	două nopţi
toilet	toaletă
bathroom	baie
kitchen	bucătărie
camping spot	loc de campare
campsite	camping
tent	cort
wooden cabin	casuţă

On the trails

English	Romanian
road	drum
forest road	drum forestier

English	Romanian
path	potecă
trail	traseu
summer trail	traseu de vară
winter trail	traseu de iarnă
waymarking	marcaj
yellow	galben
blue	albastru
red	roşu
stripe	bandă
triangle	triunghi
circle	punct
signpost	indicator
waterfall	cascadă
spring	izvor
water	apă
drinking water	apă potabilă
lake	lac
tarn	tău
river	râu
stream	pârâu
rock, rocks	piatră, pietre
falling rocks	cadere de pietre
danger	pericol
dangerous	periculos
Careful! Attention!	Atenţie!
Watch out!	Aveţi/ai grijă!
No trespassing	Accesul interzis/ Trecerea interzisă
detour	ocolire

English	Romanian
cliffs	stâncării, stânci
meadow	poiană
saddle	şaua, curmătură
pass	pas
peak	vârf
cave	peşteră
forest	pădure
tree	copac
pine	pin
spruce	molid
fir	brad
beech	fag
blueberries	afine
cranberries	merişoare
mushrooms	ciuperci
mountain, mountains	munte, munţi
massif	masiv
crevice	crăpătură
gorge	chei
mountain hut	cabana
refuge	refugiu
shelter	adăpost
building	clădire
monastery	mănăstire
hermitage	schit
sheepfold	stână
hill	deal, colină

English	Romanian
valley	vale
ridge	creastă
spur	culme
chasm	prăpastie
ascent, ascending	urcare
descent, descending	coborâre
bear, bears	urs, ursi
dog, dogs	câine, câini
shepherd	cioban
sheepdog	câine ciobanesc
Does it bite?	Muşcă?
It bites/It doesn't bite	Muşcă/Nu muşcă
sheep	oaie, oi
cow, cows	vacă, vaci
horse, horses	cal, cai
wolf, wolves	lup, lupi
snake	şarpe, şerpi
viper, vipers	viperă, vipere
lynx, lynxes	râs, râşi
eagle, eagles	acvilă, acvile
marmot, marmots	marmotă, marmote
map	hartă
hiking map	hartă de drumeţie
hiking	drumeţie
walking	plimbare

English	Romanian
climbing	alpinism, escaladare
hiking boots	bocanci
crampons	colțari
ice axe	piolet
gas canister	butelie de gaz
stove	arzător

The weather

English	Romanian
weather	vreme
sun	soare
sunny	însorit
cloud, clouds	nor, nori
clear	senin
overcast	acoperit
sky	cer
rain	ploaie
hail	grindină
frost	brumă
ice	gheață
wind	vânt
strong wind	vânt puternic
(thunder)storm	furtună
lightning	fulger
fog	ceață
snow	zăpadă
sunrise	răsărit
sunset	apus de soare

English	Romanian
What's the weather going to be like?	Cum va fi vremea?
It's going to rain	Va ploua
It's going to snow	Va ninge
It's snowed a lot	A nins foarte mult
It's going to be very stormy	Vor fi furtuni puternice
There are strong winds	Bate un vânt puternic
It's minus/plus 10 degrees	Sunt minus/plus zece grade
It's cold/warm outside	E frig/cald afară

Emergencies

English	Romanian
Help!	Ajutor!
Stop!	Stop!
Let go of me!	Lăsați!
Don't touch me!	Nu mă atinge!
What happened?	Ce s-a întâmplat?
I fell / he/she fell	Am căzut/Are căzut
My head/arm/foot/leg/chest/stomach hurts	Mă doare cap/brat/picior/picior/piept/burtă
I've been bitten by a dog/viper	M-a mușcat un caine/o viperă
I'm not feeling well	Îmi este rău/Mă simt rău

403

English	Romanian
I'm sick	Sunt bolnav(ă) (m/f)
hospital	spital
A&E	urgență
Please call the emergency number!	Vă rog sunați numarul de urgență!

Food and eating out

English	Romanian
menu	meniu
food	mâncare
drinks	băuturi
starters	antreuri
main course	felul principal
dessert	desert
pastry	prăjitură
pie	plăcintă
pancakes/crêpes	clătite
breakfast	mic dejun
beer	bere
wine	vin
red wine	vin roșu
white wine	vin alb
a glass of...	un pahar de...
brandy (often plum/ apple)	țuică/horincă/ pălincă/rachiu (depending on the region)
blueberry liqueur	afinată
cherry liqueur	vișinată

English	Romanian
sparkling water	apă mineral
still water	apă plată
coffee	cafea
tea	ceai
milk	lapte
sugar	zahăr
oatmeal	fulgi de ovăz
powdered milk	lapte praf
salt	sare
bread	pâine
butter	unt
sour cream	smântână
fresh cheese	brânză
yellow cheese	cașcaval
Could I see the menu please?	Aș putea să văd meniul vă rog? (or simply, 'Meniul vă rog?')
May I take your order?	Aș putea să iau comanda acum?
Have you made your choice?	Ați ales?
We haven't decided yet	N-am ales încă
I would like...	Doresc.../ Aș dori.../Aș vrea...
Would you like...?	Doriți...?
Two beers, please	Două beri, vă rog

English	Romanian
Can I pay, please?	Nota de plată, vă rog?
I'm a vegetarian	Sunt vegetarian(ă) (m/f)
I don't drink alcohol	Nu beau băuturi alcoolice
fasting food (vegan)	mâncare de post
Enjoy your meal!	Poftă bună!/ Poftă mare!
Cheers!	Noroc!

English	Romanian
cabbage rolls with rice and minced meat	sarmale
grilled minced meat rolls	mititei (mici)
smoked pork fat	slănină
meat stew	tocăniță
fried breaded cheese	cașcaval pane
aubergine salad/ spread	salată de vinete
roasted pepper and aubergine spread	zacuscă
jam and sour cream doughnuts	papanași

Traditional Romanian dishes

English	Romanian
sour soup	ciorbă
soup	supă
tripe soup	ciorbă de burtă
meatball soup	ciorbă de perișoare
vegetable soup	ciorbă de legume
chicken soup	ciorbă de pui
beef soup	ciorbă de vacuță
bean soup with smoked ham	ciorbă de fasole cu afumătură
polenta	mămăligă
polenta with fresh cheese and sour cream (a staple in mountain huts)	mămăligă cu brânză și smântână (MBS)

APPENDIX E
Further reading

A Brief Illustrated History of Romanians, Neagu Djuvara. Humanitas, 2014
A Concise History of Romania, Keith Hitchins. Cambridge University Press, 2014
Athene Palace: Hitler's 'New Order' Comes to Rumania, R.G. Waldeck. University of Chicago Press, 2013
Romania: Borderland of Europe, Lucian Boia. Reaktion Books, 2001
Warum ist Rumänien anders? (in German), Lucian Boia. Schiller Verlag, 2016

Travelogue
Along the Enchanted Way: A Romanian Story, William Blacker. John Murray Publishers, 2009
In Europe's Shadow: Two Cold Wars and a Thirty-Year Journey Through Romania and Beyond, Robert Kaplan. Random House, 2016
Never Mind the Balkans: Here's Romania, Mike Ormsby. Compania, 2008

Novels
Bengal Nights, Mircea Eliade. University of Chicago Press, 1995
Life Begins on Friday, Ioana Pârvulescu. Istros Books, 2018
Recollections from Childhood, Ion Creangă. Tiberian Press, 2019
The Land of Green Plums, Herta Müller. Granta Books, 1999
Why We Love Women, Mircea Cărtărescu. University of Plymouth Press, 2011

Poetry
Testament: An Anthology of Modern Romanian Verse (bilingual), ed. Daniel Ioniță. Editura Minerva, 2015

Vegetation and wildlife
Atlas Flora României (in Romanian), Aurel Ardelean. Editura All, 2011
Romania: A Birdwatching and Wildlife Guide, James Roberts. Burton Expeditions, 2000

Climbing
Dimension Vertical: Climbing Guidebook Romania, Gerald Krug. Geoquest, 2010
Rock Climbing Atlas: South Eastern Europe, Marloes van den Berg. Rocks Unlimited Publications, 2006
Rock Climbing in Romania: A Climbing Guide of Braşov Crags, Ciprian Drăghici. Ciprian Drăghici, 2010

NOTES

NOTES

NOTES

NOTES

DOWNLOAD THE ROUTES
IN GPX FORMAT

All the routes in this guide are available for download from:

www.cicerone.co.uk/948/GPX

as GPX files. You should be able to load them into most formats of mobile device, whether GPS or smartphone.

When you go to this link, you will be asked for your email address and where you purchased the guide, and have the option to subscribe to the Cicerone e-newsletter.

www.cicerone.co.uk

LISTING OF CICERONE GUIDES

Walking in Sardinia
Walking in Sicily
Walking in the Dolomites
Walking in Tuscany
Walking in Umbria
Walking Lake Como and Maggiore
Walking Lake Garda and Iseo
Walking on the Amalfi Coast
Walks and Treks in the Maritime Alps

BELGIUM AND LUXEMBOURG
The GR5 Trail – Benelux and Lorraine
Walking in the Ardennes

SCANDINAVIA:
NORWAY, SWEDEN, FINLAND
Trekking the Kungsleden
Walking in Norway

POLAND, SLOVAKIA,
ROMANIA, HUNGARY
AND BULGARIA
The Danube Cycleway Vol 2
The High Tatras
The Mountains of Romania
Walking in Bulgaria's National Parks
Walking in Hungary

SLOVENIA, CROATIA, SERBIA,
MONTENEGRO, ALBANIA
AND KOSOVO
Mountain Biking in Slovenia
The Islands of Croatia
The Julian Alps of Slovenia
The Mountains of Montenegro
The Peaks of the Balkans Trail
The Slovene Mountain Trail
Walking in Slovenia: The Karavanke
Walks and Treks in Croatia

SPAIN
Camino de Santiago – Camino Frances
Coastal Walks in Andalucia
Cycle Touring in Spain
Cycling the Camino de Santiago
Mountain Walking in Mallorca
Mountain Walking in
    Southern Catalunya
Spain's Sendero Historico: The GR1
The Andalucian Coast to Coast Walk
The Camino del Norte and
    Camino Primitivo
The Camino Ingles and Ruta do Mar
The Mountains of Nerja
The Mountains of Ronda
    and Grazalema
The Northern Caminos
The Sierras of Extremadura
Trekking in Mallorca
Trekking in the Canary Islands
Walking and Trekking in the
    Sierra Nevada
Walking in Andalucia

Walking in Menorca
Walking in the Cordillera Cantabrica
Walking on Gran Canaria
Walking on La Gomera and El Hierro
Walking on La Palma
Walking on Lanzarote and
    Fuerteventura
Walking on Tenerife
Walking on the Costa Blanca
Walking the Camino dos Faros

PORTUGAL
Portugal's Rota Vicentina
The Camino Portugues
Walking in Portugal
Walking in the Algarve
Walking on Madeira
Walking on the Azores

GREECE
The High Mountains of Crete
Trekking in Greece
Walking and Trekking in Zagori
Walking and Trekking on Corfu

CYPRUS
Walking in Cyprus

MALTA
Walking on Malta

INTERNATIONAL CHALLENGES,
COLLECTIONS AND ACTIVITIES
Canyoning in the Alps
Europe's High Points
The Via Francigena Canterbury to
    Rome – Part 2

MOROCCO
Mountaineering in the Moroccan
    High Atlas
The High Atlas
Walks and Scrambles in the Moroccan
    Anti-Atlas

TANZANIA
Kilimanjaro

SOUTH AFRICA
Walking in the Drakensberg

TAJIKISTAN
Trekking in Tajikistan

JAPAN
Hiking and Trekking in the Japan Alps
    and Mount Fuji
Japan's Kumano Kodo Pilgrimage

JORDAN
Jordan – Walks, Treks, Caves, Climbs
    and Canyons
Treks and Climbs in Wadi Rum,
    Jordan

NEPAL
Annapurna
Everest: A Trekker's Guide
Trekking in the Himalaya

BHUTAN
Trekking in Bhutan

INDIA
Trekking in Ladakh

CHINA
The Mount Kailash Trek

NORTH AMERICA:
USA AND CANADA
The John Muir Trail
The Pacific Crest Trail

SOUTH AMERICA:
ARGENTINA, CHILE AND PERU
Aconcagua and the Southern Andes
Hiking and Biking Peru's Inca Trails
Torres del Paine

TECHNIQUES
Fastpacking
Geocaching in the UK
Lightweight Camping
Map and Compass
Outdoor Photography
Polar Exploration
Rock Climbing
Sport Climbing
The Mountain Hut Book

MINI GUIDES
Alpine Flowers
Avalanche!
Navigation
Pocket First Aid and Wilderness
    Medicine
Snow

MOUNTAIN LITERATURE
8000 metres
A Walk in the Clouds
Abode of the Gods
Fifty Years of Adventure
The Pennine Way – the Path,
    the People, the Journey
Unjustifiable Risk?

For full information on all our guides,
books and eBooks, visit our website:
www.cicerone.co.uk

Explore the world with Cicerone

**walking • trekking • mountaineering • climbing • mountain biking •
cycling • via ferratas • scrambling • trail running • skills and techniques**

For over 50 years, Cicerone have built up an outstanding collection of
nearly 400 guides, inspiring all sorts of amazing experiences.

www.cicerone.co.uk – where adventures begin

- Our **website** is a treasure-trove for every outdoor adventurer. You
can buy books or read inspiring articles and trip reports, get technical
advice, check for updates, and view videos, photographs and mapping
for routes and treks.

- **Register this book** or any other Cicerone guide in your member's
library on our website and you can choose to automatically access
updates and GPX files for your books, if available.

- Our **fortnightly newsletters** will update you on new publications and
articles and keep you informed of other news and events. You can also
follow us on Facebook, Twitter and Instagram.

We hope you have enjoyed using this guidebook. If you have any
comments you would like to share, please contact us using the form on
our website or via email, so that we can provide the best experience for
future customers.

CICERONE

Juniper House, Murley Moss Business Village, Oxenholme Road, Kendal LA9 7RL

✉ info@cicerone.co.uk   cicerone.co.uk